MATILDE DE LA TORRE
SEX, SOCIALISM AND SUFFRAGE IN REPUBLICAN SPAIN

LEGENDA

LEGENDA is the Modern Humanities Research Association's book imprint for new research in the Humanities. Founded in 1995 by Malcolm Bowie and others within the University of Oxford, Legenda has always been a collaborative publishing enterprise, directly governed by scholars. The Modern Humanities Research Association (MHRA) joined this collaboration in 1998, became half-owner in 2004, in partnership with Maney Publishing and then Routledge, and has since 2016 been sole owner. Titles range from medieval texts to contemporary cinema and form a widely comparative view of the modern humanities, including works on Arabic, Catalan, English, French, German, Greek, Italian, Portuguese, Russian, Spanish, and Yiddish literature. Editorial boards and committees of more than 60 leading academic specialists work in collaboration with bodies such as the Society for French Studies, the British Comparative Literature Association and the Association of Hispanists of Great Britain & Ireland.

The MHRA encourages and promotes advanced study and research in the field of the modern humanities, especially modern European languages and literature, including English, and also cinema. It aims to break down the barriers between scholars working in different disciplines and to maintain the unity of humanistic scholarship. The Association fulfils this purpose through the publication of journals, bibliographies, monographs, critical editions, and the MHRA Style Guide, and by making grants in support of research. Membership is open to all who work in the Humanities, whether independent or in a University post, and the participation of younger colleagues entering the field is especially welcomed.

STUDIES IN HISPANIC AND LUSOPHONE CULTURES

Studies in Hispanic and Lusophone Cultures are selected and edited by the Association of Hispanists of Great Britain & Ireland. The series seeks to publish the best new research in all areas of the literature, thought, history, culture, film, and languages of Spain, Spanish America, and the Portuguese-speaking world.

The Association of Hispanists of Great Britain & Ireland is a professional association which represents a very diverse discipline, in terms of both geographical coverage and objects of study. Its website showcases new work by members, and publicises jobs, conferences and grants in the field.

STUDIES IN HISPANIC AND LUSOPHONE CULTURES

Matilde de la Torre

Sex, Socialism and Suffrage in Republican Spain

❖

Deborah Madden

l

LEGENDA
Studies in Hispanic and Lusophone Cultures 56
Modern Humanities Research Association
2022

Published by Legenda
an imprint of the Modern Humanities Research Association
Salisbury House, Station Road, Cambridge CB1 2LA

ISBN 978-1-83954-085-1 (HB)
ISBN 978-1-839540-86-8 (PB)

First published 2022

Copy-Editor: Dr Ellen Jones

CONTENTS

❖

Para mi madre, Patricia,
una mujer indomable

ACKNOWLEDGEMENTS

❖

My academic interest in Matilde de la Torre dates back to my doctoral research at the University of Sheffield, where I was awarded a White Rose College of the Arts & Humanities AHRC studentship to research Iberian women writers. The 2019-2020 AHGBI-WISPS Dorothy Sherman-Severin Research Fellowship then allowed me to pursue a focused study of De la Torre and funded invaluable research trips to Spain and Mexico. A postdoctoral scholarship from the Leverhulme Trust facilitated the final stages of the research process and completion of the manuscript. More recently, I have been fortunate to make contact with two scholars who share my enthusiasm for investigating the life and works of De la Torre, Dr Luis Pascual Cordero Sánchez and Dr Francisco Layna Ranz, both of whom have kindly shared copies of their work to augment my understanding of this exceptional woman.

Thanks is due to colleagues, supervisors and friends at the Universities of Sheffield and Manchester for their support and guidance. Library and archival staff at the Biblioteca Nacional de España and local and state archives throughout Madrid, Asturias, Salamanca and Mexico City were helpful and knowledgeable. Particular gratitude is owed to staff at the Archivo de la Fundación Pablo Iglesias, who utilised their unparalleled knowledge of the PSOE to guide and support my research. I am also grateful to Dr Anja Louis, Dr Caragh Wells and Professor Catherine Davies, who all provided insight and feedback on earlier versions of this project. Input from anonymous reviewers and editors at the *Journal of Spanish Cultural Studies*, where I published an article based on Chapter Three of this book, pushed me to develop and nuance my arguments, which, I hope, has allowed me to do De la Torre's multifaceted texts justice and illuminate her brilliant political mind.

To *mi gente*, for their unwavering support. Particularly my Dad, Brian Madden, who instilled in me the meaning of Nil Satis Nisi Optimum, the motto of our beloved Everton Football Club that inspired the grit and determination needed to complete this book. (Dad: there are references to buses in Chapter Three, pp. 93–94.) *Abrazos* and *besos* are owed to my *tío* Ged Rogan, Sophie Byrne, Carlos van Tongeren, Steph Wright, Kirsty Hemsworth and Cyd Sturguss, all of whom are great sources of wisdom and world-class drinking buddies. Above all, special, heartfelt thanks is owed to Tom Jackson, who not only provided love, guidance and encouragement, but also acted as a soundboard as I worked through ideas and, later, forensically copyedited this manuscript. I am exceptionally lucky and grateful to have such a compassionate, intelligent teammate; *te quiero, cariño*.

Finally, special mention to two family members, who, though they will never read this book, are critical to its genesis. Firstly, my uncle John Madden, who lived in Madrid in 1973 as part of his Spanish degree. A lifelong socialist, he returned to Liverpool with anecdotes about the bleakness and brutality of Francoist Spain. I am privileged to now own many of his books on Spain and leftist politics. Secondly, my mother, Patricia Madden, who, despite insurmountable odds, read English at the University of Liverpool. My mother's improbable trajectory through life laid the foundations for my own appreciation for literature and the feminist and socialist politics that underpin this research. Mum: this book is for you, I only wish my literary analysis was as distinguished as yours.

D.M., Madrid, August 2022

INTRODUCTION

❖

> No he conocido nunca espíritu más indomable unido
> a la más atrayente suavidad femenina, mayor eficacia con más dulzura.
> — María Lejárraga (Martínez Sierra 1989: 220–21)

> [Una] criatura extraordinaria, de carácter indómito, superior y alegre,
> libre como un pájaro, de ideas muy suyas
> que acabaron derivándose hacia la política extrema.
> — María Blanchard (quoted in Saiz Viadero 2007: 28)

Women's political emancipation was amongst the most revolutionary of the feminist reforms enacted by Spain's Second Republic (1931–39), with the right to vote and hold political office transforming Spanish women's relationship with the state. Matilde de la Torre (1884–1946) was one of Spain's first female politicians, winning a seat for the Partido Socialista Obrero Español (PSOE) in Oviedo in the 1933 and 1936 elections. A vocal advocate of women's and workers' rights, De la Torre played an active role in seminal moments and debates in Republican Spain, including the struggle for women's suffrage, the 1934 Asturian revolution and the Civil War (1936–39). Despite her remarkable career and contribution to many of the decisive debates and demonstrations at this critical juncture in Spanish history, there is a lacuna of scholarship on De la Torre's political life and emphatically politicised written output. Building on scholarship dedicated to women erased from critical and cultural history in post-Civil War Spain, this book offers the first comprehensive account of De la Torre's politically motivated texts. A close analysis of her eclectic output will chart the evolution of her ideological convictions, from her early activism in Restoration Spain to her exile in Mexico after the Civil War, augmenting critical understanding of women's relationship with revolutionary politics in early twentieth-century Spain.

The ubiquity of dialogue in De la Torre's writings means that her work can be understood as manifestations of female-voiced political discourse, as the texts encapsulate her ideological introspection and engagement with the hegemonic, oft-patriarchal, political establishment. Accordingly, Bakhtinian theories of dialogism and heteroglossia inform the critical analysis, a theoretical perspective that has been embraced by several feminist literary critics and which bears strong identifications with liberal and democratic politics. The nexus of socialist ideation, feminist thought and Spanish political history that De la Torre interrogates in her writing was expedited and shaped by Republican politics, both as a metaphysical construct and through the inauguration of the Second Republic that made her political career possible. Republican Spain, for De la Torre, is therefore both an abstract conceptualisation of a liberated, democratic political system and the radical administration that engendered many of her fundamental political ideals. With this in mind, this book interrogates De la Torre's output and politics in conjunction with the discourses and political philosophies that impacted women, focusing on how De la Torre delineates women's precarious, often paradoxical, relationship with leftist politics. To this end, this Introduction first provides an overview of De la Torre's life and works, before summarising the central political and cultural contexts that underpin this study: Spanish women's political emancipation and women's writing in early twentieth-century Spain. An outline of critical approaches to the texts is then discussed, including a summary of Bakhtinian theories of dialogism, which is followed by an overview of the chapter analyses.

Matilde de la Torre (1884–1946)

Born in Cabezón de la Sal, Cantabria, on 14 March 1884, De la Torre was raised in a liberal, middle class family that included several prominent cultural and political figures. Her grandfather, Cástor Gutiérrez de la Torre, founded the newspaper *La Abeja Montañesa* in 1856 and her uncle, Enrique Gutiérrez-Cueto, was the founder and director of the Santander-based *El Atlántico* (1886–). The writer Concha Espina was related by marriage and the two shared a close bond, with De la Torre credited with awakening Espina's social consciousness (Sierra Álvarez 2004: 64). Conflict between De la Torre and Espina, José María de Juana notes, was limited to their profound disagreement on religion; though Espina was a devout Catholic, De la Torre, 'por el contrario, se mostraba muy crítica con la Iglesia' (2019: 944). The writer and translator Consuelo Bergés, who authored *Explicación de octubre: Historia comprimida de cuatro años de República en España* (1935), was also a close family friend (Trallero Cordero 2004: 54), while De la Torre's niece, Ángela de la Torre, was a politically active teacher based in Cantabria. Likely inspired by her aunt's legacy, Ángela would become a vocal critic of the Francoist dictatorship (López Sobrado 2012: 29). Perhaps the most illustrious of De la Torre's relatives is her cousin, the painter María Blanchard. The two lived together during their adolescence and, as indicated by the epigraph at the beginning of this Introduction, Blanchard revered De la Torre's character and political conviction. Other than a brief marriage to a cousin in Peru in 1917, which was annulled within fifteen days, De la Torre would never marry or have children, dedicating her personal life to caring for her disabled brother, Carlos. Though details are sparse, it seems that De la Torre was unsatisfied by the reality of married life; 'la vida no era como le había planteado su enamorado desde la distancia' (Saiz Viadero 2010: 325–26).

Before entering politics, De la Torre focused her professional life on her other great passions: music and education. She founded *Voces cántabras* in 1924, a folk singing troop that promoted the culture of the Cantabrian region (Olarte Martínez 2010: 23–24). From 1930, advertisements for the choir were publicised in the Spanish press[1] and, in 1932, they performed at London's Albert Hall. For her efforts to promote the Cantabrian musical tradition, De la Torre was deemed a 'savior' of the genre by a contemporary American music aficionada (Alford 1934: 445). In 1925, she founded the 'Academia Torre', a co-educational establishment that implemented the ideas of the Institución Libre de Enseñanza; an educational project inspired by Krausism that advocates academic and ideological freedom and tolerance (see Chapter Two). Echoing De la Torre's liberal politics, the academy implemented a secular, holistic educational model that prioritised intellectual development and philosophical reflection over dogma and test taking. Critics of De la Torre and her school would sardonically dub her 'Platón con faldas' for this revolutionary educational initiative (Tavera 2005: 214), which is just one example of how abuse levied at De la Torre by her political adversaries was often laced with misogynistic undertones.

In 1931, De la Torre formally joined the PSOE, the Party that she would represent in the 1933 and 1936 elections. As detailed throughout this book, she dedicated her political career to workers' causes, defending the right to strike, supporting unions and championing the working classes in Spain. A vocal critic of fascism and war, she frequently condemned politically sanctioned violence and oppression, and would continue to defend freedom, individual liberty and the socialist cause during the Spanish Civil War (1936–1939). In 1933, the year she was elected to the Cortes, De la Torre spoke at a series of events organised by the Juventudes Socialistas to encourage women to vote (Calderón Gutiérrez 1984: 77) and began co-directing the PSOE's women's section, along with Matilde Cantos (1898–1987) and Matilde Huici (1890–1965), a group known collectively as the 'Three Matildes' (Tavera 2005: 214). As her work with her Party's women's section would suggest, a defining characteristic of De la Torre's political career was her collaboration with female colleagues. She shared a close personal and professional relationship with María Lejárraga (1874–1974),[2] a fellow Socialist, and took part in a series of shared initiatives with the communist Dolores Ibárruri (commonly known as 'la Pasionaria'). From July 1934, De la Torre co-directed the Comité de Mujeres contra la Guerra y el Fascismo with Ibárruri, Lejárraga and Isabel Oyarzábal (García 2015: 21–22) and, from 1937, she presided over the Asociación de Mujeres Antifascistas along with Ibárruri, Cantos and Huici (Tavera 2005: 212; also see: Ibárruri 1979: 191; Zambrana Moral 2009).

Throughout her career, De la Torre was a well-respected, loyal member of the PSOE, which Antonio Martínez Cerezo describes as 'su querido Partido Socialista' (2000a: 2). She participated in numerous commissions, including Marina, Hacienda y Economía, and was a *suplente* in the committees dedicated to Defensa Nacional, Instrucción Pública and Justicia (Juana 2019: 947). In 1937, she became the Minister of Comercio y Política Arancelaria under the Francisco Largo Caballero government. In spite of her successful political career, De la Torre is often overlooked in analyses of leading female figures in early twentieth-century Spain, routinely overshadowed by her more famous colleagues.[3] Her written output has received even less critical attention. De la Torre's writing career is mostly limited to her prolific output in the press, notably *El Socialista*, the paper of the PSOE, *La Libertad* and *Avance*.[4] From 1925 to 1937 she published roughly four hundred articles in Santander based publications, including *El diario montañés*, *La Atalaya*, *El pueblo cántabro* and *La Voz de Cantabria*. In 1976, a collection of her articles from *La Voz de Cantabria*, *La montaña en Inglaterra* (1976), was published posthumously by José Ramón Saiz Viadero. Writing in March 1930, José del Río Sainz, De la Torre's colleague at *La Voz de Cantabria*, was effusive in his praise of her journalistic articles:

> Ha revolucionado la literatura regional y ha empezado a imprimir su huella vigorosa en la literatura periodística de España. Puede decirse que los escritos de Matilde de la Torre, por lo varonil de su concepción, por lo humano de su pensamiento y por los temas universales que aborda, aun en aquellos que se refieren exclusivamente a conflictos y a pleitos de su pueblo constituyen el tipo de periodismo más moderno que ha aparecido en nuestra Prensa. (Quoted in Juana 2019: 945)

Such exuberance, however, should not detract from the covert implication that, according to Sainz, a fundamental quality of De la Torre's writing is its masculinist tone ('por lo varonil de su concepción'). Not only does this speak to a critical shrewdness that characterises her written output, given it suggests that De la Torre effectively modelled her press articles for their predominantly male readership, it also serves as a reminder that De la Torre's sex was a factor in how her work was produced and received. Accordingly, tensions between De la Torre's feminist convictions and her aim of engaging with Spain's androcentric cultural and political debates are tangible throughout her book length publications, which defy categorisation given she produced an eclectic mix of genres, subject matter and media.

In this study, the analysis focuses on De la Torre's five politically motivated texts: the epistolary feminist novel *Jardín de damas curiosas* (1917); *Don Quijote, rey de España* (1928), a political and cultural history of Spain; *El ágora* (1930), a critical commentary about the Spanish Restoration; the political satire *El banquete de Saturno: Novela social* (1931); and *Mares en la sombra* (1940), a quasi-autobiography of De la Torre's experiences during the Asturian revolution and Civil War. De la Torre's other output is either related to her interest in culture, such as *Soles y brumas de España* (1948), an anthology about Spanish music and folklore, or are short vignettes like 'La ciudad nueva' (1930), which is a two page short story about a boatload of passengers excitedly reaching their destination (as discussed in Chapter Two, this could be interpreted in relation to De la Torre's optimism about the burgeoning republican movement). The texts examined in the book are therefore the only extended writings about politics in De la Torre's oeuvre. The salient characteristic shared by all the works selected for analysis is a sustained interest in the political and legal structures of Spain, a subject matter that is tackled in various forms in all of De la Torre's literary output. The Spanish literary critics familiar with her writings also make this association in relation to her non-fiction[5] and fiction[6] and, as will be evidenced throughout this book, De la Torre's publications can be understood as direct responses to shifts in Spain's political climate. Republican Spain, indeed, would prove a felicitous context for her ideological development.

The rebels' victory that concluded the Spanish Civil War brought about the fall of the Second Republic and, with it, the end of De la Torre's political career. Her personal library in Santander was burnt down, either during the conflict or after the Nationalists' victory (Lloréns and Aznar Soler 2006: 341), which is one possible reason many of her writings were lost. The War and Francoist regime that followed capsized De la Torre's life, as she was forced to abandon her beloved homeland and important personal relationships became strained; as José Ramón Saiz Viadero notes, her allegiance to the Republican government infuriated her long-time friend Concha Espina, whose support for Francoism resulted in 'ácidas y malévolas alusiones sobre Matilde en su diario de guerra' (2007: 55). After first fleeing to France, she sought exile in Mexico in 1940, along with her brother, Carlos, and other leading Republicans, including Margarita Nelken and her PSOE colleague Venerada García Manzano (Alted Vigil 2008: 70; Capdevila-Argüelles 2011: 15; Domínguez Prats 2012: 802). There, De la Torre continued her interest in folklore and singing, becoming a member of the Sociedad Folklórica de México (Meierovich 1989: 190) and collating *Soles y brumas de España*, which would be published in 1948, two years after her death.

Tragically, the final years of De la Torre's life were marred by ill health and professional frustrations. As she writes in a letter dated 26 June 1943:

> Salimos al exilio en edad en la que, aun disponiendo de salud, es difícil eso que llamamos 'reconstruir la vida.' Quisiéramos haber aportado al acervo de la Patria Mexicana nuestro trabajo y excelsa voluntad. No pudo ser. Mi hermano Carlos venía ya paralítico y no ha logrado mejoría en su terrible y dolorosa enfermedad. Yo procuré trabajar. Escribí libros que, por lo que fuera, no hallaron editor, busqué colaboraciones de Prensa; pero mis gestiones, sin fuerzas físicas ni apoyos de influencias fueron perdidas. Mis fuerzas dieron fin y llevo dos años entre la vida y la muerte. (Quoted in Saiz Viadero 2007: 20)

For her loyalty to Juan Negrín, who became *persona non grata* within the PSOE as he was deemed responsible for the fall of the Second Republic, De la Torre was expelled from the Party in April 1946, along with thirty-six of her colleagues. Poignantly, her expulsion was formalised posthumously, just days after her death from tuberculosis on 16 March. The Francoist purge of left-wing thinkers meant that she was effectively erased from the collective consciousness for almost forty years. After the dictator's death, there have been some efforts to memorialise De la Torre's contribution to Spanish politics: to commemorate fifty years since the election of Spain's first *diputadas*, the Centro Cultural Matilde de la Torre was founded in Santander in 1981; and, to celebrate the centenary of her birth (in 1984), *El País* published a short piece in homage of her life (Gijón 1984). Though De la Torre was formally readmitted to the PSOE at the 2008 Party conference, her legacy as one of Spain's trailblazing female socialists remains obscure, as Spanish women's role in the Second Republic was limited to an auspicious, yet short-lived, epoch.

Women's Political Emancipation in Spain

As touched on at the beginning of the Introduction, Spanish women's relationship with formal political structures has historically been tense. With women's social, legal and political subordination to men codified in law under the 1870 Penal Code and 1889 Civil Code,[7] political parity was a low priority for first wave feminists. Accordingly, first wave feminism in Spain is often characterised by its focus on social, rather than political, emancipation. Critics therefore tend to ascribe a conservative image to Spanish feminism (see, for example: Enders 1999: 389; Labanyi 2002: 76; Johnson 2003: 26), and there is broad consensus that the early Spanish women's movement was inherently weak and achieved little (see, for example: Bieder 2018: 158; Franco Rubio 1982; García Méndez 1979; Koonz 1998; Roig 1981; Scanlon 1986). As Monserrat Roig posits, '[e]l feminismo llegó tarde y mal' (1981: 13). When considering 'los posibles motivos del retraso del movimiento feminista en España', Geraldine Scanlon identifies religion and socio-economic climate as critical: 'Por lo general, los países en los que floreció el feminismo eran protestantes y estaban industrializados (Inglaterra, Alemania, Estados Unidos)' (1986: 5). Indeed, the early feminist movement was impeded and stunted by the insidious influence of Catholicism, with the oppressive role of the Church so powerful that Catherine Davies deems it the 'greatest obstacle to women's emancipation in Spain' (1998: 7).

Another critical obstacle to the development and spread of feminist thought were extreme illiteracy rates amongst women, as debate was mostly limited to the pages of female authored and directed press.[8] The pioneers of the women's movement would therefore focus their efforts on improving women's educational opportunities; Concepción Arenal, (in)famous for her ironic commentary on hegemonic gender norms in La mujer del porvenir (1884), would focus explicitly on women's education in La mujer en la educación (1892), while Emília Pardo Bazán condemns Spain's educational systems for keeping women 'en perpetua infancia' in La mujer española (1976 [1890]). Reforming marriage legislation — specifically the introduction of a divorce law — was another core objective for Spain's early feminists. A salient example is Carmen de Burgos's El divorcio en España (1904), which utilised findings from a survey published in the press to argue that public perception supported a liberalisation of the law. The objectives of many women's organisations, which would prove crucial in affording women an empowered public role in early twentieth-century Spain, reflect this emphasis on education and marriage reform; fundamental feminist objectives that surpassed ideological demarcation. Both the relatively traditionalist Asociación Nacional de Mujeres Españolas (ANME)[9] and the more radical Cruzada de Mujeres Españolas,[10] for instance, would centre much of their efforts on improving women's education and amending marriage laws.

Whereas marriage and educational reform were aims shared by revolutionary and conservative feminists alike, suffrage was a polemical source of contention. The lack of any clear consensus on women's voting rights is illustrated by Burgos's views. While she would argue in La mujer en España, published in 1906, that 'ahora darle el derecho de voto es poner un arma peligrosa en manos de un niño' (1906: 46) because, like many feminists, she believed women were not sufficiently educated to vote, Burgos would become a staunch advocate of women's suffrage in the later years of her career. In 1921, Burgos would present a signed manifesto to the Cortes, demanding the vote for women (Bieder 2018: 178; Guallart 2011: 139; Nash 2004: 243). In *La mujer moderna en sus derechos*, Burgos elaborates on her ideological shift: 'Las mujeres que interesan por cuestiones de moralidad, de higiene, de educación y pacifismo, saben bien que necesitan reclamar el sufragio, no por vano orgullo, sino para tener medios de trabajar en mejorar el porvenir' (2007: 264–65).

Unexpectedly, it would be during the authoritarian dictatorship of Miguel Primo de Rivera (1923–1930) that (some) Spanish women would be granted political parity when, in 1924, the regime afforded single women over twenty-three years old the right to vote in local elections (Davies 1998: 102). Rather than indicate the government's belief in women's rationality, however, these limited voting rights were passed as women were assumed to be the 'instinctive allies of the right and the Church' (Brooksbank Jones 1997: 1). Other civil liberties under the Primo de Rivera regime therefore remained severely limited: the 1928 Penal Code,[11] for instance, enacted severe sanctions for abortion (Art. 525; Art. 527) and gave women harsher penalties for adultery than men (Art. 620). It would not be until the inauguration of Spain's Second Republic in 1931 that women became the legal equals of men. In the words of Roberta Johnson, the Republican government was a 'dream' for the feminist movement (2002: 42) as it facilitated and expedited a range of reforms that benefitted women. The 1931 Constitution legalised divorce and afforded married women equal rights to their husbands (Art. 43), protected the rights of female workers (Art. 40), particularly mothers (Art. 46), and, crucially, outlined voting equality for both sexes (Arts. 9, 36, 52, 68) and legislated women's right to hold political office (Art. 53).

In the first elections in which women were eligible to run for office, held in 1931, the first *diputadas* in Spanish political history were elected: Clara Campoamor for the Partido Radical Republicano, Victoria Kent for the Partido Republicano Radical Socialista and Margarita Nelken, who stood for the PSOE. Although female suffrage was technically granted by the 1931 Constitution, women would not vote until 1933 when additional legislation was passed in the Cortes. There was, therefore, a period when Spanish women could stand for election but not vote; a paradox that is borne out in De la Torre's political writings. Ironically, women's suffrage would ultimately pass thanks to male Republican politicians, as there was no consensus amongst female politicians — or feminists — that female suffrage would be beneficial for women or the left. When the Cortes debated the matter, the only three female *diputadas* in the chamber were divided on the issue: Campoamor voted in favour, Kent voted against and Nelken abstained (Davies 1998: 106). Kent, in line with her party's position, believed that Spanish women were not yet 'politically sophisticated enough to support the socialist cause' (Tolliver 2011: 247), while Nelken defended her stance by reasoning that Spanish women were not sufficiently prepared or experienced to vote at all.

As she argued in 1919, it would only be when 'una cultura femenina tan alta como la masculina' was realized that women should vote: 'Este será el mejor feminismo, y él conducirá naturalmente, *racionalmente*, al voto de las mujeres' (Nelken 1975: 192; original emphasis).

As the foregoing evinces, socialist women, particularly those who, like De la Torre, supported female suffrage, faced hostility from within their own circles, marginalised by both leftists and feminists. The debates and policies of the PSOE, De la Torre's party, at this juncture in Spanish history reflect these tensions; as Frances Lannon notes, although a secretariat for 'women's issues' was established in 1918, 'there was always a debate about whether a preoccupation about women was a distraction from the primary concern with class' (2011: 277). The intersection of emancipation for women and the working class, particularly friction between the two, is also tangible in left-wing political theory and rhetoric, an ideological tension that is explored in detail in Chapter Three. Across Spain's political spectrum, moreover, the subservience and subordination imposed on women led many on the left to assume that women would be more likely to vote for conservative parties, susceptible to coercion by their husbands and Catholic priests. The potency of this supposition was such that the victory of the right-wing coalition Confederación Española de Derechas Autónomas (CEDA) in the 1933 elections — the first in which women could vote and when De la Torre first won her seat — was unduly blamed on female voters.[12]

While women were gaining ground in state politics, women's groups imbued with expressly political — that is, socioeconomic or ideological — concerns were also becoming increasingly popular. In February 1936, just five months before the outbreak of the Spanish Civil War, the anarchist women's group Mujeres Libres was founded by Lucía Sánchez Saornil, Amparo Poch and Mercedes Comaposada (Nash 1975: 12). In response to the sexism that pervaded anarchist circles,[13] the organisation 'focused on psychological independence for women, the advocacy of female identity, personal autonomy, and self esteem' (Bieder and Johnson 2017: 2), proliferating its teachings through the anarchist press, specifically *Mujeres Libres* and *Tierra Libre*.[14] Though De la Torre was not actively involved with Mujeres Libres, the group's double militancy — combining revolutionary and feminist politics[15] — resonates with her politics. Another group formed during the Second Republic, on the other hand, epitomised the antithesis of De la Torre's beliefs: the Sección Femenina (SF), the women's branch of the Falange that was headed by Pilar Primo de Rivera, the daughter of the dictator Miguel and sister of José Antonio, who founded the Falange Española. Despite providing a political outlet for its high-ranking women, specifically Pilar Primo de Rivera, the SF conditioned Spanish women to dedicate themselves to domesticity and childrearing. There was, in this sense, an inherent paradox to this organisation as, though the SF maintained a 'vision of woman as an active participant in the economic and spiritual reconstruction of the nation' (Richmond 2003: 9; also see: Ofer 2009: 16; Stucki 2019), its core political philosophy centred on a fascist conceptualisation of womanhood that negated political agency.

As detailed in Chapter Four, the Spanish Civil War afforded women further access to the public sphere via combat and in industry jobs that had previously been filled by men. Membership of women's groups of all ideological extractions boomed, with women orchestrating humanitarian initiatives and, in some instances, fighting alongside men on the front (see Chapter Four). Female politicians on the left, including De la Torre, were heroic in their efforts to defend the Second Republic; a salient example of women's passion and cultural impact is Dolores Ibárruri's anti-fascist 'No pasarán' speech, which continues to form part of communist folklore. After the Nationalist victory, the SF were tasked with inculcating women to fulfil the role of the 'ángel del hogar', a model of female behaviour that encompassed domesticity, chastity, patience and subservience (see, for example: Aldaraca 1991; Fuentes Peris 2003; Kirkpatrick 2003: 30–36; Nash 1999; Urruela 2005). Women's rightful place, in accordance with this belief, was in the private sphere of the home, and any attempt to contest, subvert or disrupt traditional gender norms was considered not only harmful to society, but wholly unnatural. Accordingly, women's 'political participation was discouraged as unfeminine' (Brooksbank Jones 1997: 2), meaning Spain's politically emancipated women would be effectively silenced until 1977, when the first democratic elections after the dictator's death were held. Socialist women would play a critical role in Spain's restoration of an electoral democracy and the post-Francoist restructure of the PSOE,[16] continuing the legacy of Republican women like De la Torre.

The Politics of Women's Writing in Spain

Against a backdrop of women's emancipation, political reform and increased literacy rates in Spain, the scene was set for a boom in women's writing. Catherine Davies deems the 1920s and 1930s particularly 'fertile ground' for Spanish women writers (1998: 108) and critics have noted how seismic shifts in the social and political climate inspired a surge of politically motivated writings by women (Johnson 2003: 276; Kirkpatrick 2003: 28). Increased educational and professional opportunities meant that women were able to produce, read and purchase literature as never before. An upsurge in pamphlet-style novellas paved the way for female authors to make a living from writing, while literary salons afforded wealthy, well-connected women a means of engaging with the cultural sphere, as the development of women's ideological and creative autonomy became interconnected. Nonetheless, feminist scholars observe how relatively few female authors from this period are well known today (Johnson 2002: 42; Leggott 2008b: 13–14), as Spain's predominantly male literary canon impeded the extent to which women's writing could form part of the collective cultural consciousness (Arkinstall 2009: 13; Bellver 2001: 11; Brown 1991: 14; Hart 1993: 3). Accordingly, as Emilie Bergmann and Richard Herr observe, the lack of critical attention to Spanish women's writing has created the 'erroneous impression that women have been literary outsiders throughout the century' (2007: 2).

Critical analyses have been conducted and bio-bibliographical resources have been compiled, therefore, with the aim of reclaiming the 'forgotten' women writers of Spain.[17] The anti-feminist legislation and literary censorship enforced by the authoritarian, patriarchal Francoist regime makes the 'recovery' of these female authors all the more necessary and, indeed, difficult. Censorship during the Franco dictatorship in Spain effectively 'weeded out prewar feminist writing' (Bieder and Johnson 2017: 2), as strict controls and the influence of the Church impacted what type of literature could be published (Davies 1998: 186). Patricia O'Byrne's analysis of post-War writings notes how censorship was particularly detrimental for women's writing, leaving many 'in danger of being forgotten' (2014: 22). A concerted effort to promote Spain's women writers is not just a concern for present-day feminist literary scholars. Pioneering efforts to collate, catalogue and disseminate female-authored fiction from the early decades of the twentieth century include Margarita Nelken's *Las escritoras españolas* (1930a) and *La novela femenina* (1930b), an edited collection of short stories and extracts by contemporary women writers. As well as offering a medium for the promotion and development of feminist discourses, women's magazines and newspapers proved another important outlet for female-authored creative writing. The Spanish publications *Acción* and the women's supplement of *Las Noticias*, for instance, include serialised copies of female-authored fiction, while articles that centre on female authors, readers and feminist fiction were published in 'Escritores y libros feministas' (1923) in the 'Suplemento Femenino' of *Las Noticias*.

In 1935, the communist María Teresa León, who, like De la Torre, wrote politicised fiction, was interviewed about her understanding of 'women's writing'. When asked whether '[l]a literatura femenina' can be distinguished from 'la literatura masculina', she insists not, but, nevertheless, proposes that, as the majority of canonical writers are male, 'la literatura española escribe con tendencias masculinas' (quoted in Marrast 1984: 60–61). For León, thanks to the great strides made in relation to women's emancipation in early twentieth-century Spain, '[n]uestra literatura es una literatura sin sexo' (quoted in Marrast 1984: 60–61). Though León's argument is overly idealised in relation to the extent (and permanence) of women's emancipation in Spain, her argument points to how women's socio-political and creative emancipation are interrelated and, perhaps unconsciously, reflects how male-dominated literary canons shape women's writing. The concept of a literature 'sin sexo' is intriguing, as it evokes what, for some feminists, could be considered an ideal; a form of literary expression liberated from gendered norms and expectations. León's ambiguous description of 'tendencias masculinas', in this sense, signifies an aesthetic and form that is utilised by writers of both sexes and, conceivably, appealing to a mixed-sex readership. As we shall see throughout this book, there is ample evidence to suggest that De la Torre is not only conscious of her status as a woman writer, but, critically, plays on cultural images of both female authored texts and sexed language to reinforce and elucidate her political critiques. The emphasis on dialogue in De la Torre's texts, moreover, means that the author's voice — even when spoken through male characters — is tangible, which makes her status as a *female* author critical.

Thus, while it is not my intention to interpret De la Torre's work through the prism of 'feminine writing' (or *écriture féminine*),[18] which was popularised with the advent of second-wave feminism, the analysis benefits at points from situating her work within a literary tradition of left-wing women's writing. Indeed, as evidenced by the work of Spain's left-wing women writers, such as Lejárraga, León and Nelken, many of the women writing in the early decades of the twentieth century were politically active, as the rise of the revolutionary left would also open avenues for writing and publishing. (Parallels between De la Torre's texts and those of her contemporaries are discussed where necessary in the chapter analyses.) Communist propaganda, for instance, provided Spanish radicals — of either sex — with models and paradigms for writing their life stories and producing didactic texts, while the Spanish anarchist movement proliferated its ideas through the *La Novela Libre* and *La Novela Ideal* series printed by *La Revista Blanca* throughout the 1920s and 1930s.

On one level, then, the cultural and political landscapes were felicitous for De la Torre's written experimentation; as publishers were becoming more accommodating to women writers, political and legal advances were inspiring women to explore avenues for women's liberation. While fiction proved a useful medium for propagating feminist ideals through empowered female protagonists, non-fiction works foregrounded theoretical and didactic arguments. As illustrated by the oeuvres of Burgos, Lejárraga, Montseny and Nelken, many women writers, like De la Torre, utilised a range of genres to defend and articulate their politics. At the same time, however, women writers were still impeded by patriarchal understandings of both literary output and political ideation. Female-authored texts were typically marketed for female readerships, with women writers often limited to traditionally 'female' genres such as *la novela rosa* romance narratives (touched on in Chapter Three) and epistolary novels (as discussed in Chapter One). Even within left-wing circles, women were deemed incapable of interpreting and theorising androcentric political ideologies.

Accordingly, politically motivated women writers typically delineated their ideas through a gendered lens, by focusing on the female perspective. Two fictionalised accounts of October revolutions are salient examples: León's vignette 'Liberación de octubre' (1979 [1933–1936]), which centres on a communist uprising, and Montseny's novella *Heroínas* (2003 [1935/1936]), which is a semi-autobiographical retelling of the 1934 uprising in Asturias. (As discussed in Chapter Three, De la Torre's *El banquete de Saturno* bears some resemblance to these works as it is about a socialist revolution that takes place in October.) León's 'Liberación de octubre' is told from the perspective of Rosa, a non-religious, working-class woman who is tormented by her inability to bear her husband's children. Against the backdrop of a looming revolution, Rosa questions her marriage and is frustrated by the limitations imposed on her by society: 'Rosa no podía salir a la calle porque estaba catalogada entre las mujeres honradas' (León 1979: 29). Though Ramón is apprehensive about the revolt, Rosa sees it as an opportunity for liberation; 'Rosa se precipitó en la Revolución' (1979: 32). An anarchist take is found in Montseny's *Heroínas*, in which the protagonist, María Luisa, is presented with two love interests: Alejandro Pereda, a socialist with political aspirations; and the anarchist, Luis Salcedo, who is a local union leader. Her romantic crossroads functions as a political allegory as, though sorely tempted by the socialist, it is the anarchist — and, therefore, anarchism —

that her heart truly desires: 'A Salcedo podía amársele con el alma y con el cuerpo' (Montseny 2003: 202). It is only after rejecting the prospect of marriage that the revolutionary female protagonist is free to become one of the eponymous 'heroínas' by leading a band of guerrilla rebels. As María Luisa notes, '[s]on días de acción, que no pueden perderse en juegos amorosos' (2003: 207).

Both texts outlined above exemplify how Spain's revolutionary women writers typically focalised political fiction through female protagonists and drew on literary paradigms traditionally identified with women as a means of attracting a female readership. De la Torre, however, did not follow this trend. Perhaps the most intriguing quality of De la Torre's written output is the breadth of genres utilised in her eclectic oeuvre, including examples of the epistolary paradigm (*Jardín de damas curiosas*); a cultural and political commentary (*Don Quijote, rey de España*); a socio-political biography (*El ágora*); a (satirised appropriation of a) socialist narrative (*El banquete de Saturno: Novela social*); and a quasi-autobiographical memoir (*Mares en la sombra*). On one level, such variety illustrates how De la Torre capitalises on generic conventions to reinforce her political perspective, linking the aesthetic with the ideological in such a way as to unpack the significance of both cultural and political convention. Indeed, though opportunities for women writers greatly expanded in the early decades of the twentieth century, social, cultural and aesthetic paradigms inflected by patriarchal logic continued to dictate how women's written output was marketed and received. At many points, as detailed in the chapter analyses, De la Torre plays on sex (both hers and that of her fictional characters) when subverting established paradigms as a means of critiquing social and cultural norms. Thus, not only does drawing on a range of genres exemplify her critical awareness, but it also speaks to De la Torre's efforts to resist hegemonic convention.

At the same time, such diversity and eclecticism also suggest that De la Torre was working out how to characterise herself as a writer. Rather than establishing herself within a particular genre, she tried her hand at several as a means of testing out ideas and different cultural paradigms. In doing so, she experimented with styles traditionally identified with both women (such as the epistolary novel) and men (like socio-political biographies) in what could be considered a concerted — and strategic — effort to eschew categorisation. A salient drawback of this is that it could explain one reason for De la Torre's relative obscurity; given she does not fit cleanly within demarcated literary traditions, she was excluded. Indeed, not only did De la Torre reject traditionally female literary paradigms, such as *la novela rosa* romance narratives, but she also pushed back against the unquestioning propaganda produced by left-wing writers, as examined in detail in Chapter Three's discussion of *El banquete de Saturno*. In this sense, De la Torre's political astuteness and stylistic eclecticism problematised how her work would be reviewed and characterised, as thinking beyond established ideological and literary parameters made her something of a maverick. One core objective of this book, then, is not just to 'recover' De la Torre's forgotten texts, but also to examine how her work relates to and dialogues with that of her contemporaries. By situating De la Torre's ideas within the cultural zeitgeist, the analyses that follow aim to illustrate both how her output has been shaped by her lived experience as a female writer and political commentator, and, critically, how she writes in such a way as to resist the reductive interpretations that this entails.

Critical Approaches to the Texts

As outlined at the beginning of this Introduction, a central component of this analysis is to scrutinise how De la Torre engages with, appropriates and reworks political discourses. Not only does her oeuvre self-evidence a vast knowledge of socialist and feminist theories, it also demonstrates De la Torre's tangible desire to participate in debates from which she was often excluded. The majority of the political writings examined in this book, indeed, were published before her career as a *diputada* began, as fictional and non-fictional texts afforded her a public voice that was otherwise silenced. Accordingly, a major resource for this critical analysis is the vast body of left-wing and feminist writings that inspired and informed De la Torre's political ideation. From the canonical doctrines of Marx and Engels to the lesser well-known feminist-socialist Flora Tristan, there are ample examples of how international socialist discourses have shaped De la Torre's views and writings. Spanish political philosophers inspired by leftist traditions, such as José Ortega y Gasset and his pupil María Zambrano, are also tangible in her texts, with key overlaps detailed in Chapters One and Two. Even though explicit or direct reference to individuals' writings or doctrine is rare (that is, quoted references to specific political philosophers), there is, nevertheless, a palpable sense of retort in De la Torre's writings as she uses her texts to dialogue with the heterogenous political landscape. At the same time, debates and fissures within Spanish socialism inform and shape her output, specifically tensions between Soviet-inspired leftists and those who, like De la Torre, were wary of such an authoritarian reification of socialist doctrine, as discussed in Chapter Three. Different theorisations and perspectives of socialism and revolutionary politics are therefore critical to the textual analyses.

In addition to the wide-ranging left-wing discourses that are in inflected in De la Torre's writings, two other bodies of political debates permeate her work: first-wave feminist thought; and socio-political and cultural analyses of Spanish history. As detailed in Chapter One, a focused interrogation of feminist positions is the driving force of De la Torre's first publication, *Jardín de damas curiosas* (1917). Echoes of the ideas promulgated by the likes of Burgos, Lejárraga and Nelken are tangible throughout, with De la Torre engaging with the arguments of her contemporaries as a means of reinforcing, reworking and developing objectives central to her own theorisations of feminism. De la Torre's international outlook is also evidenced, most notably through references to women's rights in other geographical contexts and well-known feminist leaders such as Emmeline Pankhurst. While one central characteristic of De la Torre's oeuvre is the way she shifts ideological focus in each of her major publications, a common theme throughout her works is a focus on defining and reifying democratic political agency. Political and critical examinations of Spain's political structures, specifically the *caciquismo* and *turno pacífico* systems, have therefore been essential to this study, underpinning how De la Torre conceptualises political liberty and advocates for a functioning democracy.

As noted at the beginning of this Introduction, the emphasis on dialogue and political discourses in De la Torre's writings speaks to Bakhtinian theories of dialogism, which resonate strongly with liberal and democratic politics and are consonant with a feminist critical approach. Thus, though the principal approach here is a close reading of the selected texts, drawing on appropriate socio-political histories and political theories, the Bakhtinian conceptualisation of heteroglossia proves useful for this analysis. Before outlining the core pillars of this critical approach, it is worth acknowledging that Mikhail Bakhtin's primary focus was, indeed, the novel; a literary paradigm that De la Torre does not utilise in all the works examined in this study. Her two fictional texts, *Jardín de damas curiosas* and *El banquete de Saturno*, nonetheless, broadly follow novelistic conventions and, critically, the polyphonic quality of the novel central to Bakhtin's theories is tangible throughout De la Torre's writings. The mutability of language and the heterogenous political perspectives it can encapsulate, in other words, is capitalised on in all the texts selected for analysis in this book. Accordingly, a theoretical grounding in how heteroglossia manifests not only illuminates our understanding of De la Torre's writings, but also speaks to her intentions for the impact of her work. By foregrounding dialogue and discourse, De la Torre invites a critical reader for whom the text(s) will serve as a soundboard that will facilitate ideological introspection.

It is in his seminal *The Dialogic Imagination* that Bakhtin lays out his theory of heteroglossia and the novel. More multifaceted than other genres, this literary genre, Bakhtin reasons, can be defined as follows:

> (1) Its stylistic three-dimensionality, which is linked with the multi-languaged consciousness realized in the novel; (2) the radical change it effects in the temporal coordinates of the literary image; (3) the new zone opened by the novel for structuring literary images, namely, the zone of maximal contact with the present (with contemporary reality) in all its openendedness. (1981: 11)

Firstly, it is worth underlining how the emphasis on temporality is consonant with De la Torre's works: as explicated in all the chapter analyses, De la Torre's publications correspond with key moments in Spain's political history. While the subject matter she tackles in the texts may be focused on other temporal or geographical contexts, the ideas and arguments she interrogates are imbued with a tangible contemporary relevance. Salient examples to illustrate this point include: her reflections on the undemocratic nature of the Restoration *caciquismo* system in *Don Quijote, rey de España* and *El ágora*, both of which were published during the authoritarian Primo de Rivera regime, when political liberty was supressed; and *El banquete de Saturno*, in which she wrote about the corrupt, repressive nature of the Soviet Union at a time when many PSOE leaders were looking to Russia for a revolutionary model. What Bakhtin describes as 'maximal contact with the present (with contemporary reality)' (1981: 11), in this sense, aptly characterises all of De la Torre's politically motivated written output.

Another defining characteristic of De la Torre's texts is the polyvalent quality of their dialogue, which resonates with Bakhtin's conceptualisation of 'multi-languaged consciousness' (1981: 11). Passages and quotations are invested with multiple, often conflicting, ideological perspectives as a means of illuminating the source and implications of the political discourses that De la Torre (re)iterates. As will be discussed in Chapter One, for instance, the speech of De la Torre's protagonist in *Jardín de damas curiosas* is inflected by both revolutionary and reactionary politics, as the character — and, accordingly, the author — navigate antagonistic attitudes in order to actualise a coherent argument. Combined with the tangible contemporaneousness of her work, such mutability and dynamism connote an ongoing, unfinished political position that De la Torre is trying to work through and cultivate in her writings. For Bakhtin, this fluidity links to the novel as, unlike the monotonic epic, the genre depicts 'a realistic reflection of the socially varied and heteroglot world of contemporary life' (1981: 27). It is, Bakhtin explicates, by coming 'into contact with the spontaneity of the inconclusive present' (1981: 27) that prevents the novel from 'congealing' (1981: 27). Authors are therefore 'drawn toward everything that is not yet completed' (1981: 27) and may be inclined to 'openly polemicize with [their] literary enemies' (1981: 27); both qualities that can be applied to De la Torre's output, as she engages with current debates and has a flair for biting wit, often at the expense of her political opponents.

The broadly feminist outlook that informs the analysis of De la Torre's texts is also congruent with a Bakhtinian approach to heteroglossia and dialogism. Indeed, as evidenced throughout this book, Bakhtin's emphasis on providing space for alternative and dissenting viewpoints lends itself well to De la Torre's feminist critique of patriarchal and androcentric political structures and discourses. Throughout the 1980s and 1990s, during which time *écriture féminine* was embraced by many feminist critics (as touched on above), a wealth of feminist takes on theories of dialogism emerged.[19] As Denise Heikinen summarises:

> Bakhtin's theory of dialogism has been embraced by several feminist critics for its ability to provide a platform for marginalized feminine voices to be heard above the din of the monologic, authoritative, and hegemonic voice. (1994: 114)

Similarly, Suzanne Rosenthal Shumway notes how 'feminist literary theory can appropriate Bakhtin's work to produce a powerful analytic tool' (1994: 153) given 'feminism and Bakhtinian theory share a concern for the oppressed and margin-alized others' (1994: 153). Thus, though critics such as Wayne Booth (1982) and Diane Price Herndl (1991) have lamented that Bakhtin himself did not recognise feminist or female-voiced perspectives, his theories of heteroglossia and dialogism seem 'tailor-made for feminist criticism' (Heikinen 1994: 114). In *Feminist Dialogics: A Theory of Failed Community* (1988), for example, Dale Bauer utilises the Bakhtinian model to explore four novels, arguing that the overt silencing of the female voice constitutes a critical commentary on the authoritative, patriarchal ideals that dominate, pointedly making the reader conscious of alternatives. (As detailed in Chapter Three, Bauer's argumentation broadly fits with my analysis of De la Torre's novel *El banquete de Saturno*.)

While a feminist application of Bakhtin's theories is not unproblematic, this theoretical interface is useful for this analysis as a focus on the tensions between the hegemonic 'male' culture and a feminist other permeates De la Torre's written output. One key drawback that Rosenthal Shumway notes, however, is indeed significant, as it is suggestive of De la Torre's intentions as a writer. As Shumway explains, Bakhtin's conceptualisation of dialogue as a 'war without victory' or 'open-ended ideological skirmish' (1994: 155) is a somewhat lacking given 'it is concerned only with detecting the weaker voices in a text, and not with creating and implementing plans for strengthening such voices' (1994: 155). With this in mind, the extent to which De la Torre intends for her texts to inspire a real-world impact — that is, that readers' political actions (participation in debates; voting; party membership) would be shaped by her work — is brought to the fore. One logical interpretation relates to how a critical focus on dialogue is fundamental to another of De la Torre's ideological priorities: political liberty. As Peter Womack details, 'dialogue is historically aligned with political liberty' (2011: 6) as it constitutes 'the discursive form of democracy' (2011: 6). Womack's understanding of a back and forth between speaker and addressee (or, in this case, author and reader) not only suggests that De la Torre is indeed producing her texts in order to elicit a response from her readers, but also that her texts manifest a form of political dialogue. The chapter analyses that follow take this reciprocity into account, focusing on how De la Torre indexes ideological introspection in the works and, consequently, inspires political critique in her readers.

Overview of Chapters

Divided into four chapters, this study analyses De la Torre's political texts chronologically in order to chart the evolution of her political ideation. Chapter One focuses on the epistolary feminist novel *Jardín de damas curiosas* (1917), her first publication, interrogating the genesis of De la Torre's feminist politics by examining four core elements of the text: voice, culture and power; women and the law; suffrage; and women in politics. Published in 1917, the same year a nationwide strike was organised by the socialist Unión General de Trabajadores (UGT) and the PSOE, the narrative constitutes a series of letters from an aunt, *tía* Pulquería, to her niece and nephew. As a means of working through intergenerational feminist debates and negotiating distinct approaches to Spanish feminisms, including radical individualism and a conservative, difference perspective, the protagonist dialogues with her niece and nephew and, accordingly, the progressive feminism and patriarchal tradition that they respectively represent. Theories of feminist dialogics are drawn on to illustrate how De la Torre utilises her female narrator's voice to reflect the pluralism of feminist thought and to contribute self-consciously to contemporary feminist debates. Capitalising on the gendered subtext of the epistolary paradigm, which is traditionally associated with women, De la Torre utilises the text to scrutinise the political capital of the sexed voice; a theme that underpins all the texts examined here.

In Chapter Two, the analysis examines two of De la Torre's non-fictional works, both of which centre on Spain's political and cultural histories: *Don Quijote, rey de España* (1928) and *El ágora* (1930). A close analysis of how De la Torre interrogates Spanish political structures illustrates how she disrupts the dominant cultural narrative by underscoring the political capital of female-voiced discourse and commentary. Core themes that run throughout the texts centre on the political illiteracy and indifference of the Spanish population, or *pueblo*, with *caciquismo* and the *turno pacífico* that characterised the Restoration landscape frequently criticised and condemned as undemocratic. Written and published during the Primo de Rivera regime (1923–1930), both texts engage with the collective melancholy that inflected the Spanish consciousness in the aftermath of the 1898 *desastre* and the political failings of the Restoration system. Explicit and direct references to the question of sex pervade both works, with De la Torre using 'hombre(s)' as a comprehensive term for Spain's politicians and citizens. The use of 'hombre', moreover, indexes a gendered conflict between the 'masculine' political world and the 'feminine' natural environment, which is described in relation to the inherently-female 'Madre Tierra' that De la Torre identifies with regeneration and, accordingly, reformative politics.

Chapter Three interrogates *El banquete de Saturno: Novela social* (1931), a satirical account of Soviet Russia that critiques androcentric socialist discourses. By drawing on Russian travelogues, examples of socialist realism and Marxist doctrine, the analysis illustrates how De la Torre uses the work to dialogue with contemporary socialist debates and theorise a feminist socialism. Published just a month before the seminal vote that passed female suffrage, discussed above, the novel alludes to the anxieties and debates surrounding women's political parity, particularly within socialist circles. With women's capacity for supporting the political left under scrutiny, socialist women such as De la Torre were marginalised by both leftists and feminists. Through the male characters' dialogue, specifically the protagonist Julio, De la Torre works through the implicit patriarchy and misogyny that underpins socialist discourses and condemns the authoritarianism and dogma of the Soviet model. It is through the enigmatic character María — known as 'la Minerva' of the local union — and the echoes of the feminist-socialist theories of Flora Tristan that De la Torre presents an alternative to the androcentric leftist ideations that foment war and authoritarianism.

The final chapter focalizes on De la Torre's memoir, *Mares en la sombra: Estampas de Asturias* (2007 [1940]), which centres on her experiences of the Asturian revolution and the Civil War. Drawing on trauma memory theories, the analysis explores how the fall of the Republic impacted her views on liberal democracy and examines how violence, trauma and memory shape De la Torre's political ideation. *Mares* can be seen to manifest the socialist voices erased by the conflict, as the act of narrating the experiences of De la Torre and her comrades facilitates a cathartic memorialisation that is inflected by leftist and feminist politics. The dialogic quality that characterises all of De la Torre's written output, thus indexes a sense of collective bereavement and suggests a concerted effort to record details that would otherwise be forgotten. Accounts of trauma and violence are gendered in such a way as to legitimise the female experience and commemorate women's contribution to defending the Republic. By focusing on the ways in which De la Torre constructs a collective socialist history, the analysis argues that De la Torre uses her memoir as a means of voicing the Republican experience in order to oppose the dominant Nationalist narrative of the War. A brief conclusion then follows, which considers the evolution of De la Torre's political trajectory and makes some closing remarks on De la Torre's oeuvre and written style.

Notes to the Introduction

1. See: *La Unión ilustrada* 1930: 36; 'Información general de España' 1931: 12; 'Al ministro de Instrucción Pública' 1931: 10; 'Noticias teatrales' 1932: 7; 'La vida musical: El coro *Voces Cántabras* en el T.L.N.' 1932: 2.

2. Critics have noted the close relationship between De la Torre and María Lejárraga (Blanco 2007: 81; Leggot 2008b: 85; Prat 1994: 12), and evidence of this can be found throughout the 1930s. There were documented incidents of them attending meetings together ('Otro periodo histórico' 1933: 3; 'Las primeras cortes ordinarias de la República' 1933: 1; 'El parlamento' 1933: 8; 'La inauguración de Cortes y el momento político español' 1933: 9; 'El programa parlamentario para mañana' 1935: 9) and meeting socially ('Información política' 1934: 2). Antonina Rodrigo provides a detailed account of correspondence between the two women while in exile following the fall of the Second Republic (1994: 310–13).

3. See, for example: Aguado 2005: 132; Álvarez-Uría 2013: 639, 640; Branciforte 2009–2010: 47; Capel Martínez 2007: 39, 2008a: 46, 47, 2012: 28; Delgado and Jerez 2008: 44; Paz 1993: 74; Domínguez Prats 2009: 76; García Colmenares 2010: 54; González-Allende 2010: 83; González Hoyos 2014: 24; Gutiérrez Bringas 1989: 322; Lafuente 2012; Lines 2012: 26; Luque Muñoz and Solano Fernández 2008: 35; Mangini 1995: 29, 34–35, 77; Monterde García 2010: 276; Nash 1998: 374, 2003: 536; Plaza Agudo 2011: 55; Saiz Viadero 2006: 3; Sánchez Blanco 2013: 120; Suárez 2002: 46; Trueba Mira 2002: 183; Villalaín-García 2012. Alpert (2007) omits De la Torre entirely, while other critics observe how little has been published on her life and works (Domínguez Prats 1998: 1237; Delgado Cruz 2008: 12). Frances Lannon mentions De la Torre in a footnote along with other elected *diputadas* in her study of women during the Civil War but does not provide details of her life or accomplishments (1991: 213–14). Furthermore, in her discussion of leading female figures of early twentieth-century Spain, Neus Samblancat Miranda provides only one reference to Matilde de la Torre and classes her as a musician, based on her folk singing, rather than listing her amongst the group of *diputadas* (2006: 10).

4. In her study *¡Salud, compañeras! Mujeres socialistas en Asturias (1900–1937)*, María Antonia Mateos provides a detailed analysis of De la Torre in the press, particularly *Avance* (2007: see, in particular, 133–48).

5. See: Fernández Segura 2012: 33–34; Taillot 2009: 85–86.

6. See: De la Hoz Regules 2012: 232; García Santos 1980: 24; Núñez 1998: 404. María Francisca Vilches de Frutos names Matilde de la Torre as one of eight authors whose relationship with politics and press writings resulted in *la narrativa social* (1982: 32–33), literature with a social message, although she does not make it clear whether she is referring to De la Torre's fiction or non-fiction, or both.

7. Under the 1889 Civil Code, married women were ordered to obey their husbands (Art. 57–61) and, according to the 1870 Penal Code, received harsher penalties for adultery than men (Art. 428).

8. Christine Arkinstall observes how a feminist press began to emerge in Spain in the mid-nineteenth century, citing two Madrid-based weeklies, *Ellas* and *La Mujer*, both founded in 1851, as two influential publications (2018: 114–16).

9. The ANME is considered to be the first women's organisation in Spain. Formed in 1918, the

group was a relatively moderate association that was dedicated to improving educational and professional opportunities for women and reforming the polemical 1889 Civil Code.

10. A progressive organisation established by Burgos in 1921, the Cruzada de Mujeres Españolas, centred its efforts on legalising divorce and promoted women's suffrage.

11. Cited from a reprint of the 'Código penal de 8 de Septiembre de 1928' that was published in 1929.

12. In his thorough analysis of voting patterns, Gerard Alexander (1999) has convincingly argued against the notion that women disproportionately skewed the vote in these elections.

13. Though Temma Kaplan outlines how anarchists in nineteenth-century Cádiz saw women's emancipation as a key objective (1977a: 158; publication also in Spanish translation, 1977b: 103), Mary Nash notes that anarchism did not prioritise women-specific issues (1995: 86). Martha Ackelsberg, for instance, examines efforts from the anarchist Confederación Nacional del Trabajo (CNT) to unionise women, despite overlooking the issue of equal pay (1991: 55).

14. Antonina Rodrigo notes how the group's founding members published articles on women's emancipation in *Tierra Libre* (2002: 88). Sánchez Saornil would also correspond with the secretary of the CNT, Mariano Vázquez, about women's place in anarchism in a series of open letters (Ackelsberg 1991: 97).

15. It is worth clarifying that anarchists typically rejected the feminist label. Federica Montseny, who is the most well-known Spanish female anarchist from this period, associated feminism with bourgeois women (Montseny 1923: 3–5) and advocated social progress for both women and men, which she summarised in her (in)famous declaration: '¿Feminismo? ¡Jamás! ¡Humanismo siempre!' (Montseny 1924: 13). Montseny explicated her stance as follows: 'Nosotros jamás hemos sido feministas, porque consideramos que la mujer debe tener los mismos derechos que el hombre y que, como el hombre, posee las mismas parecidas cualidades y los mismos semejantes defectos' (quoted in Alcalde 1983: 29). For a thorough discussion of Montseny's views on feminism, see Cruz-Cámara 2015: 13–37.

16. In 1976, the Mujer y Socialismo group, which sought to integrate its objectives into the Party platform, took part in the Party's twenty-seventh Congreso, and, in January 1977, the *Mujer y Opción Socialista* was founded, which fought for 'la liberación de la mujer' as 'no se puede llegar al socialismo sin abolir la discriminación actual de la mujer' (quoted in Quaggio 2017: 229). It would not be until October 1982 that De la Torre's Party, the PSOE, returned to power; an electoral victory that is often considered as an end to the country's transition to democracy (Preston 1986: 227). 6.4% of the Socialist's elected representatives were women, which was the highest proportion of all political parties (Sánchez Medero 2008; Roig i Berenguer 2006: 168–69). After the Party's return to power, 'women's national political fortunes were tied even more closely to a single party' (Brooksbank Jones 1997: 13), as many of the critical feminist victories of the (post-)transition era, such as the legalisation of divorce (1981) and abortion (1985), would be passed by a Socialist majority government.

17. See, for example: Brown 1991; Cole 2000; Conde 1954, 1967, 1971; Fox-Lockert 1979; Galerstein 1986; Pérez 1988.

18. Based on Hélène Cixous's 1975 essay 'The Laugh of the Medusa' (English translation, Cohen and Cohen 1976), *écriture féminine* scrutinised the female form in language and text and feminist literary criticism in the latter half of the twentieth century would approach Spanish women's writing in this way (examples include Ballesteros 1994; Ciplijauskaité 1988; Redondo Goicoechea 2001: 20).

19. See Virginia L. Purvis-Smith (1994) for a discussion of how *écriture féminine* and Bakhtin's work interrelate.

CHAPTER 1

❖

Jardín de damas curiosas: Language, Law and Feminisms

Jardín de damas curiosas (1917; henceforth *Jardín*), De la Torre's first literary text, manifests ideological and literary introspection. Presented as a series of letters from an aunt, *tía* Pulquería, to her niece and nephew, *Jardín* is an epistolary novel that textualises intergenerational feminist debates and interrogates the political capital of the sexed voice. Capitalising on the gendered subtext of a genre traditionally associated with women,[1] De la Torre presupposes a dichotomy between Pulquería's letters and the androcentric political domain. Perhaps of most interest for our purposes is the way in which Pulquería's doubts, hypocrisies and ambiguities at once reflect De la Torre's own inconsistencies and the flaws in contemporary feminist discourses. The title of the text encapsulates female solidarity and cultural heritage, as it alludes to a painting of the same name by De la Torre's cousin, María Blanchard, which portrays two women engaged in conversation. *Jardín* functions as both a sounding board for De la Torre's own evolving ideology and a reification of the competing discourses that make up feminist thought. In the Ediciones Mentora copy of *El banquete de Saturno* (1931), *Jardín* is advertised as an '[e]pistolario sobre feminismo' (De la Torre 1931: 4), a description that would arguably be more fitting in the plural, 'feminismos', given the different angles and approaches unpacked in the text. Written and published during the Spanish Restoration, the political establishment that ruled from the failure of Spain's first short-lived experimentation with a Republic in 1874 to the proclamation of the Second Republic in 1931, *Jardín* distils an embryonic version of De la Torre's feminism.

It is worth briefly outlining here how the terms 'feminismo' and 'feminista' are somewhat polemical and polysemantic. Though Karen Offen notes that the words were used in the Spanish press at some point before the turn of the twentieth century (2000: 19), traditionalists argued that feminism would lead to moral decay, as women would abandon their traditional roles of wives and mothers and begin to exhibit male vices such as cruelty, brutality and aggression. Extreme examples of this anti-feminist discourse suggested that women would become physically masculine as a result of feminism, and caricatures of robust women with facial hair circulated. Not unexpectedly, leading figures who supported women's emancipation sought to counter this hysteria by detailing their own interpretation of feminism; Burgos, for instance, defines feminism as the 'vindicación de los derechos de la mujer'

(2007: 70) in *La mujer moderna y sus derechos*, first published in 1927. As Carol Maier outlines, '"feminism" and "feminist" as words [...] may be less international than some critics and translators acknowledge [...] Rather than a dictionary equivalent, the translation of [the terminology] often requires an explanation or parallel term' (1994: 189). According to María Teresa León, speaking in 1935, the polemics surrounding terminology do not mean that women's emancipation did not exist:

> No se habla más de feminismo porque se practica ya, y cuando algo se practica, se olvida la palabra, se ignora el término [...] la mujer en España, es feminista sin saberlo, sin pensarlo, sin recordar cómo y cuándo se incorporó a él, sino con naturalidad. (Cited in Marrast 1984: 62).

Indeed, even in recent decades, some women writers have continued to reject the label 'feminist' in Spain (Bergmann 2007: 2; Davies 1994: 5–7; Ferrán and Glenn 2002: xvii; Glenn and McNerney 2008: 7–8), despite writing works which invite a feminist critical reading.

Though feminist scholars are understandably wary of unduly imposing auto-biographical readings on female-authored work, there are textual clues that invite us to read the character of Pulquería as a mouthpiece for the author. Not only does the first person narrative imply a sense of identification between author and narrator in such a politically charged text, but so too do Pulquería's musings on music and political ambitions point to De la Torre. Indeed, De la Torre's concerted efforts to debate political philosophies, much like her protagonist, attracted much criticism and ire; as noted in the Introduction, she was sardonically dubbed 'Platón con faldas' (see Tavera 2005: 214). The date of publication, furthermore, coincides with two seminal moments that undoubtedly impacted De la Torre's life. Firstly, the year *Jardín* was published, 1917, saw a nationwide revolutionary strike orchestrated by the socialist Unión General de Trabajadores (UGT) and the PSOE. On a more intimate level, 1917 was also the year that De la Torre was briefly married (as detailed in the Introduction), which may explain Pulquería's frustration at women's limited window for a choice that, 'pese á todos los liberatismos, es la verdadera vocación nuestra...' (285).[2] The patriarchal hangover evident here exemplifies how, for De la Torre, the character of Pulquería facilitates both external and internal debate, allowing her to simultaneously work through her own anxieties and doubts and interrogate conservative strands of feminism.

As is the case with all of De la Torre's written output, *Jardín* is best understood as a political commentary; not only is there little in the way of plot or character development that would keep readers engaged, but the epistolary genre is used in such a way as to centre the narrative on Pulquería's voice. We as readers, consequently, are more invested in Pulquería's ideas than the potential familial conflicts sparked by ideological disagreements. In Diane Price Herndl's feminist critique of Bakhtinian theories of dialogism, she observes that an inherent difficulty of dialogic feminism is the question of power; though the 'polyphony within the discourse of feminism' (1991: 19) is a strength, 'the polyphony of the oppressed, like the carnival voices Bakhtin describes, is not composed of voices with political power, but of voices reacting to institutional oppressive power' (Herndl 1991: 19).

Similarly, Karen Hohne and Helen Wussow recognise how a singular female voice could result in 'a silencing of the many experiences and contexts about which and within which women have spoken through the ages' (1994: ix). In *Jardín*, the 'monologic privileging of the (female) gendered other and her voice' (1994: x) that Hohne and Wussow admonish, is skilfully eschewed, because, rather than use the text as simply a mouthpiece for her own views, De la Torre crafts a protagonist that expresses multiple voices.

The intriguing title — *Jardín de damas curiosas* — encapsulates the plurality of first wave feminisms in Spain. By evoking the Garden of Eden, the eponymous garden alludes to both Christian doctrine and, in a more general sense, notions of creation and creativity; fundamental elements for conceiving and developing feminist thought. There is, therefore, a blending of Catholic feminism, which associated women's emancipation with religion (see Hibbs-Lissorgues 2008: 335), and a more radical feminism that prioritises individual liberty and equality. Such overlap between seemingly antagonistic strands of feminism is not unexpected. As Maryellen Bieder notes, Concepción Arenal — amongst the first to advocate for women's equality in Spain — 'partook in all three forms of Spanish feminism, being at times a radical individualist and always Catholic and moderate' (2018: 159). Margarita Nelken, a contemporary and political ally of De la Torre, recognises in *La condición social de la mujer en España* how such incongruities prevent a coherent movement from forming, with such conflict 'un derivado del problema que agita todo el espíritu del país' (1922: 13). *Jardín* constitutes a textualisation of De la Torre working through these conflicts through her unapologetically blunt protagonist.

The use of the epistolary genre reflects both the dialogic character of the text and De la Torre's literary (and therefore political) influences: from 1916, Alda Blanco notes, María Lejárraga (publishing under her husband's name) 'began to pen epistolary essays' (Blanco 1998: 81) that centre on her 'elaboration of feminism' (1998: 81) and 'feminist political strategy' (1998: 82). The intertextual feminist dialogue that this suggests, connoting an intellectual symbiosis between De la Torre and her contemporaries, is further evidenced by Lejárraga's later work, *Eva curiosa: Libro para mujeres* (Martínez Sierra 1930). As well as echoing the title of De la Torre's work, *Eva curiosa: Libro para mujeres*, which constitutes a collection of plays and skits, also mirrors the dialogism of *Jardín*, as the vignette 'Noche de Verano' (25–32) centres on an elderly grandmother giving advice to her grandson, echoing the relationship between Pulquería and her nephew. With this in mind, the 'damas curiosas' can be understood at multiple textual levels: within the narrative (Pulquería and her niece), intertextually (De la Torre and her fellow feminists) and in an extratextual sense, in relation to her female readers.

Though the subject matter and title of the work may imply that *Jardín* was aimed at solely women, an advertisement published in *Mundo gráfico* in 1918 (1918: 13) — a publication with wide appeal — suggests the publishers conceived of a mixed sex, rather than female only, readership. This is evidenced in the text by Pulquería's two interlocuters: her niece and nephew. Having established in the first letter, addressed to her nephew, that, rather than concern for her own interests, she is driven by 'cuenta de las mujeres en general' (9), Pulquería goes on to explore what she describes to her niece as 'un serio problema social' (162) within 'todo este sistema de emancipación femenina' (162). The way in which the protagonist's tone shifts reflects how the fictional niece and nephew represent both a female and male reader respectively and, at the same time, the feminist and patriarchal discourses that the characters embody. The mutability of Pulquería's dialogue brings to mind Peter Womack's definition of Bakhtin's heteroglossia: rather than simply reflecting how 'different people speak in different ways' (2011: 50), heteroglossia reminds us how 'diversity is always on the move, colliding, mutating, blocking and unblocking, generating little eddies of semantic agitation' (2011: 50).

A curious nexus of De la Torre's interest in workers' rights and contemporary discourses about biological determinism are borne out in Pulquería's criticism. While some of De la Torre's feminist contemporaries, such as Carmen de Burgos and Rosa Chacel, would challenge the theories of Gregorio Marañón, José Ortega y Gasset and Georg Simmel that presupposed 'the relative merits of male and female roles based on biology' (Johnson and Castro 2018: 215), much of Pulquería's ire seems to stem from a belief that feminists overlook this at their peril. Plans for a feminist revolution, she tells her niece, to follow up 'la del año 89' (162) — probably a reference to the polemical 1889 Civil Code (examined later in this chapter) — fail to recognise that 'un hombre es más fuerte físicamente que una mujer y diez hombres más que diez mujeres, y mil hombres más que mil mujeres...' (162). Understanding strength in this context in terms of both physical power and political status, Pulquería promotes a cautious approach in accordance with 'las leyes de la Naturaleza' (162); '[e]l reposo y el despacio nos favorecen en lo físico y en lo moral' (162).

Paradoxically, Pulquería's apparent conservatism will, to her mind, facilitate effective social reform that benefits from female and male input; an emphatically radical position. Indeed, her conclusion that '[l]as mujeres somos el poder moderador de esa fiebre de velocidad que ha invadido el hombre' (163) resonates with the image of the 'ángel del hogar', an ultra-conservative model of female behaviour that encompassed domesticity, chastity, patience and subservience.[3] Projecting this moderating quality onto reform, however, reveals a political astuteness and, consequently, a caution that reflects De la Torre's approach to revolution, as further illustrated by the analysis of *El banquete de Saturno* (1931) in Chapter Three. The dialogic conflict within the novel between, to use Bakhtin's terminology (1981: 262–63), the centripetal forces of language identified with the dominant culture (patriarchy, in this instance) and centrifugal forces of language that introduce multiplicity (various strands of feminism) are therefore made manifest in Pulquería, as the protagonist both mimics and counteracts hegemonic discourses. Such emphasis on trepidation and compromise is not only indicative of the competing dialogues De la Torre tries to reconcile through her characterisation of Pulquería, but so too can it be understood as metaphor for a coherent feminist movement that factors in diverse standpoints.

The glowing review of *Jardín* in the conservative-leaning Santander periodical *La Atalaya*, published in 1918, would suggest that De la Torre's efforts to accommodate a traditional sensibility were successful. *Jardín*, the reviewer writes, is laced with 'nobles y elevados discreteos, de pensamientos sutiles y floridos, todo engarzado en un estilo dúctil, flexible y agradable' ('Una escritora montañesa' 1918: 1), resulting in a text 'que hará muy buen papel en toda biblioteca' (1918: 1). De la Torre's moderating approach, as this contemporaneous commentary suggests, is indexed in the literary style; a link between form and politics that pervades her oeuvre. The contrast between how Pulquería addresses her niece and nephew — who we may understand as personifications of a burgeoning feminism and resolute patriarchy respectively — denotes how arguments are repackaged so as to achieve the desired effect. Dialogue, then, constitutes the means through which Pulquería — and De la Torre — may combat women's subordination given the inherent link between voice and power. As Pulquería writes to her nephew, women are 'muy esclavas, ya que estamos oficialmente reducidas al silencio' (31) and, accordingly, must take any and all opportunities to resist this socially-enforced silence: 'Hablamos subrepticiamente, á cencerros tapados, y tal vez por eso hablamos de prisa, con volubilidad, porque tenemos mucho que decir y poco tiempo para ello' (31).

'La masculina verbosidad': The Sexed Voice

The question of a female and feminist collective voice that has come to define feminist re-evaluations of the Civil War and dictatorship is tangible throughout De la Torre's oeuvre. In *Jardín*, the asymmetric power dynamic between women and men is conveyed through a voice that is literally and metonymically sexed. It is by silencing women, De la Torre's protagonist argues in a letter to her nephew, that men enforce their dominance:

> El uso inmoderado que los hombres habéis hecho siempre y continuáis haciendo de la palabra, no es más que un atropello verdadero de nuestra libertad femenina, una manifestación de tiranía insufrible. (29)

An organic link between power and the male voice is acknowledged by Pulquería, as she muses that empowered language, 'voces de guerra, de mando; gritos, amenazas, órdenes' (26), can be identified as a 'lenguaje varonil' (26). As this implies, Pulquería's worldview is shaped, to a degree, by hegemonic gender norms. Rather than justify female subordinance, however, Pulquería conceives of a form of female empowerment that broadly fits with difference, or relational, feminism, in line with the majority of first wave feminist discourses in Spain.[4] Defined by Karen Offen as a type of feminism that focuses on 'women's rights *as women* (defined principally by their childbearing and/or nurturing capacities) in relation to men' (2000: 22), difference feminism reflects the broadly conservative character of first wave feminism in Spain, as outlined in the Introduction. From revering motherhood (13) and recognising women's role within the home (16) to musing about women's physical inferiority (173), Pulquería repeatedly plays on the gendered binaries of domestic/political spaces. The political domain is identified with the male voice, with Parliament — the arena that 'vosotros [hombres] poseáis' (31) — invested with 'la masculina verbosidad' (32).

The word — 'la palabra', which is occasionally capitalised in the text — becomes synonymous with power and, accordingly, men are determined to monopolise it. The sexed dynamic of achieving and maintaining power is reinforced through war imagery, as Pulquería observes that 'la conquista de la palabra debió de ser algo sublime, revolucionario, magnífico' (25) and, in order to underline the prevalence and power of the male voice, goes so far as to echo it in her own female-voiced critique:

> [A]l verse dueños de esta maravilla, y siendo ya para entonces cosa averiguada que el valor de las cosas se acrecienta con la ajena privación de ellas, se dijeron entre sí: 'Esta cosa divina que hemos descubierto, guardémosla para nosotros solos. ¡Las mujeres, que se callen!' (25)

The thinly veiled irony and derision tangible throughout *Jardín*, reminiscent of Concepción Arenal's style, is discernible here as, by ostensibly citing the men who wish to silence women, Pulquería makes a mockery of the demand. Through the use of quotation marks, which underscore the import of speech in dialogic texts (see Womack, 2011: 39), De la Torre, through her female protagonist, reclaims these words, as the text manifests a female commentary on the social and political structures shaped and upheld by men. For Bakhtin, such appropriation is critical to dialogue, as the 'word in language is half someone else's' (1981: 115), only becoming 'one's own' (1981: 115) when it is populated by the speaker's 'own intentions' (1981: 115), 'adapting it to his [or her] own semantic and expressive intention' (1981: 115). Denise Heikinen recognises how this 'spirit of extension and the appropriation of the dialogic word' (1994: 155) can have a distinctly feminist character, as illustrated by the contrast between Pulquería's words and what she means. While the political space can be understood as both a physical and conceptual entity, that is both the male-dominated Parliament and androcentric debates, the philosophical discourses Pulquería critiques tap into the collective male voice that dominates culture.

From her opening letter (to her nephew), Pulquería interrogates male philosophers, citing Schopenhauer and Nietzsche amongst others, and presents a female perspective that highlights the ambiguities in their writings. Addressing the 'señores filósofos' (11), which also seems to include her nephew, she demarcates philosophy as a male phenomenon: 'Mira: es en la vida una mujer precisamente lo contrario que filósofo' (11). For Pulquería, philosophical thought can be fundamentally understood as '"un hombre" viejo, un hombre infinitamente más viejo que los demás viejos y que los demás hombres' (18) that informs our understanding of life and society. One salient problem of this tunnel vision is that women's lives and achievements are misunderstood or underappreciated. Schopenhauer's view that childrearing contributes, in Pulquería's words, to 'la trivialidad de la mujer' (13), for example, is ignorant to the fact that a child 'es la obra más perfecta que puede producirse' (13) and that, without doubt, 'no puede cuidarse sino como la mujer le cuida' (13). Although this interpretation is in consonance with the pro-motherhood stance of some of Spain's most revolutionary first wave feminists, including Nelken, who, like De la Torre, was a socialist, there is, nevertheless, an unsatisfactory aftertaste to Pulquería's argument. Indeed, her conviction that women philosophers would '[c]ontravendría las leyes fundamentales de la Naturaleza' (11) makes it difficult to understand this position as exemplary of the strand of Spanish feminism that simultaneously celebrated motherhood and female empowerment.

De la Torre's personal life, namely the fact she never bore children, would suggest that Pulquería's objection to women renouncing their natural role is as much a personal conflict as a political stance. Unlike Nelken, whose experiences as a single mother, Shirley Mangini explains, made her 'una feroz defensora de la madre' (2009: 172), De la Torre was one of very few public figures who could have disrupted this social expectation. As she was roughly thirty-three at the time of publication, it is conceivable that, on one level, she had begun to re-evaluate the likelihood she would have children and, consequently, the narrative afforded De la Torre a means of projecting her internalised tensions onto the broader political spectrum. Indeed, the didactic format of *Jardín* at both a diegetic and extra-diegetic level, as Pulquería uses the letters to proselytise much in the same way De la Torre engages with her readership, connotes a maternalistic style, which is further emphasised by Pulquería's repeated references to her age, frequently reminding her niece and nephew (and the reader) that she is a mature woman. In a characteristically tongue-in-cheek exchange, for instance, Pulquería recalls a meeting with a potential suitor in which he mused that she 'debe de haber sido encantadora' (52), a back-handed compliment she takes in good humour. Juxtaposing *Jardín* with Nelken's *En torno a nosotras* (1927), a novel in which two sisters debate feminist issues, illustrates how the character's maturity also functions as metaphor for conservativism. In her illuminating analysis of Nelken's text, Rebecca Bender argues that the slightly older sister, Isabel, is depicted as 'the more mature, experienced and perceptive' (2016: 138), despite the fact that her views appear rather more conservative than those of her younger sister, Elena, particularly with regards to maternity.

Similarly, Pulquería's letters to her niece and nephew connote an authority and worldliness that is underlined by the fact only Pulquería's voice is presented in *Jardín*; while the sisters in Nelken's novel engage in a two-way dialogue, De la Torre's reader is only privy to Pulquería's reactions to her niece and nephew's opinions. From this, we may infer two key points about De la Torre's intended readership: it was mixed sex, with a female and male reader embodied by Pulquería's niece and nephew respectively (as noted earlier in the chapter), and, critically, that De la Torre was conscious to avoid advancing feminist values in such a way as to disengage the majority of Spanish women at this juncture in political and cultural history. Drawing on the maternalism associated with differential feminism, also referred to as maternal feminism, De la Torre conceives of a parallel form of philosophy — or body of knowledge — for women that is better suited to the female condition. While women were traditionally the object of philosophical thought, which, for centuries, centred on 'seriamente la cuestión de si la mujer poseía ó no poseía un alma como el hombre' (7), the nurturing, life-giving qualities that make women predisposed to child-rearing suggest the potential for a greater degree of agency than is typically recognised: 'Él duda y destruye. Ella crea y vivifica. Él representa el papel de la muerte, matando ilusiones. Ella el de la vida, infundiéndolas aliento...'

(11). In this sense, the maternal role that Pulquería, like De la Torre, celebrates can be understood symbolically, with the skill and capability to effectively conceive and nurture both children and ideas a natural quality of the female sex.

In differentiating women from men in terms of creation, De la Torre evokes the most well-known Spanish female philosopher of the twentieth century: María Zambrano. As Roberta Johnson explains, Zambrano believed that 'men create (enter intellectual, objectifying life) from the beginning, while women remain closer to nature and thus never experience the terrible metaphysical solitude of which philosophy is born' (2018: 266). Pulquería's ideas broadly resonate with Zambrano's, albeit from a more patriarchal stance, as she muses on how Schopenhauer's masculinity and maleness contributed to his philosophical career. As a man, she argues, Schopenhauer 'fué algo logrado' (11), '[d]emolió creencias, amarguró ilusiones...' (11), yet the female form would have been unsuitable for such ventures: '¿Acaso no sería monstruoso el torvo espíritu de Schopenhauer encarnado en una mujer?' (11). Whereas a man 'puede hacer todo eso sin pasar por un monstruo' (11), a woman dedicated to this field 'sería algo infernal y pesadillesco' (11). It is, perhaps, worth clarifying here that Zambrano's career would not take off until the 1930s, over a decade after *Jardín* was published. The apparent conservatism of Pulquería's position, moreover, is mitigated somewhat by the tangible irony that colours the dialogue. Indeed, *Jardín* blurs the boundary of fiction and non-fiction in such a way as to convey three competing voices through the figure of Pulquería: De la Torre herself, the collective voice of first wave feminism and the patriarchal discourses that shaped cultural and political structures. The inevitable back and forth allows De la Torre, through her narrator, to simultaneously recognise and critique women's silenced voices in contemporary culture and capitalise on established codes of conduct so as to suggest what may be termed a feminised, and consequently gynocentric, form of thought.

Describing the Indian philosophical schools of Mahabharata and Ramayana, for instance, Pulquería considers a 'carácter femenino' (9) given the emphasis on 'felicidad, premio, belleza, dulzura' (9) that are equated with women and womanhood. An ideal state of 'el Paraíso en la tierra' (9) that this approach allows for — which evokes feminine imagery through the link to earth and nature — provides an alternative to androcentric culture that is literally and metonymically associated with the female form. Whereas Zambrano, as noted above, presupposed a dichotomy between women and nature and men and philosophy, Pulquería appears to reconstruct this binary so as to underline an inherently female quality to philosophical schools of thought. Such a reworking, of course, is at odds with dominant philosophies. Nietzsche is one such example, who, like his male contemporaries, is preoccupied with woman as other: 'lo que parece molestarle á el y á otros filósofos (y no filósofos) es la mujer misma, la inevitable, inmanente, inalienable "fémina", con todas sus características' (18). Accordingly, '[l]a Filosofía es una ciencia viril...' (18) and, as such, there is an unwarranted hatred ('el odio' [18]) towards women that, to Pulquería's mind, 'no es hijo legítimo de la Filosofía, sino grito de la materia' (18). In this sense, women's lives allow for a more organic philosophy that is distinct from, yet equal to, male culture: 'hay en la vida de tu mujer más serena filosofía que derrochada en tinta y papel' (17).

The tensions and ambiguities that characterise Pulquería's take on female-led culture manifest here as a critique of dominant philosophical narratives precisely because they are male-dominated and, consequently, misogynistic. It is by combining opinions that appear contradictory, or at least antagonistic, through one voice that De la Torre interrogates the androcentricity of philosophy from a range of feminist perspectives: while the language used to condemn misogynistic subtexts plays on maternal imagery ('no es hijo legítimo' [18]), her detailed and varied knowledge of philosophical schools exemplifies women's intellectual capacity. On one level, this could be taken as a convenient strategy for reaching a broader female readership. As Marlene LeGates observes (2001: 248–54), focalising feminist initiatives around maternity could enable a mass, collective movement, as it transcended political and class divides, reaching women across the political spectrum. Perhaps the most intriguing quality of *Jardín* is the way in which the figure of Pulquería personifies a nexus of competing discourses that — seemingly unbeknownst to the character — she describes as a monolith. Pulquería, in this sense, is at once an apt embodiment of first wave feminism and a mouthpiece for De la Torre.

As well as manifesting Bakhtin's double-voiced discourse, which Peter Womack describes as '[t]wo distinct speakers [that] are heard in the same words' (2011: 67), this literary strategy also bears strong resemblance with Roberta Johnson's analysis of the 'philosophical novel' in early twentieth-century Spain, defined as a text that 'foregrounds philosophy in a discursive manner' (1993: x). The dialogues, Johnson writes, are 'inconclusive and open-ended' (1993: 7), reflecting 'Plato's attitude towards philosophy, seeing it as a quest and a questioning rather than as a rhetoric and persuasion' (1993: 7). As touched on earlier, however, the dialogue in *Jardín* is one directional (Pulquería to her niece and nephew and, accordingly, De la Torre's readers). The lack of 'back and forth' is further emphasised by the epistolary paradigm, as the absence of an interlocuter is abundantly obvious. By emphatically foregrounding the female voice that Pulquería — and, in this instance, De la Torre — recognises is silenced, De la Torre uses the text as a means of engaging with both the male-dominated culture embodied by her nephew and the less-experienced feminist ideologies represented by her niece. Reading these dynamics metaphorically, Pulquería's one-sided dialogue with her nephew can therefore be understood as a collective female voice reacting against a culture that is literally and metonymically male. Pulquería's slight that her nephew proverbially 'hides behind' the great male philosophers ('no te escudes con Schopenhauer ni te escondas detrás del chinche de Moebius ni del loco de Weiningen...' [1]; 'tú te escudas en el señor Nietzsche' [17]), with this in mind, reflects De la Torre's evident frustration as she challenges this masculinist dominant culture.

It is in Pulquería's defence of her niece (her nephew's wife) that the metanarrative quality of the text comes to light. Symbolic of the silenced female voice, the niece is subject to criticism by her husband for, somewhat ironically, talking too much, and so Pulquería's letters to the pair become as much an unorthodox form of marriage counselling as a political commentary. Though the husband insists his wife is overly chatty (a complaint that brings to mind the 'nagging' wife stereotype), Pulquería's niece is silenced in the diegesis. There are, in other words, no quotations or letters directly attributed to this character. Whereas the absent voice of Pulquería's nephew, nevertheless, is still able to connote authority and pluralism given the male philosophers with whom Pulquería groups him, her niece's lack of voice, and therefore agency, is hinted at in various ways. Not only are the first three of Pulquería's letters addressed to her nephew, meaning her niece is spoken about rather than to for the first fifty pages of the text, but so too is she described in relation to her husband; 'tu mujer' (1, 12, 15), 'tu esposa' (5) and 'tu pobre y bendita mujer' (14). In lambasting her nephew for complaining, Pulquería points out the double standards for women and men:

> Mira que si en la vida de las mujeres puede alguna vez haber exceso de palabras, en la vida vuestra no hay sino palabras exclusivamente. Ninguna mujer vive de hablar, y muchos hombres sólo de hablar viven. (25)

Words, again, function as a metaphor for power, with the ubiquity of male voices underlined. As we have seen, Pulquería links this culture of silencing women to philosophies that exclude women and, accordingly, are of little interest to women; 'Á ella [tu esposa] y á las demás mujeres en general no les importan ni les preocupan las opiniones ni los agravios de ascetas y filósofos' (20). Not only do women tend to not read philosophy but, if they do, they often misunderstand it ('la comprenden imperfectamente' [20]) as, in Pulquería's words, the female spirit 'no está orientado hacia los boscajes analíticos' (20). Rather than understand this as evidence for female inferiority, however, she insists that women are more practically inclined. While women are focused on the reality of quotidian life, men are distracted, something that is of no concern to a typical woman: 'Con su indiferencia parece deciros á los "clarividentes": "Seguid, seguid filosofando vosotros hasta que os canséis[...]"' (20).

There is, however, a glaring contradiction here that invites us to interrogate the tensions between De la Torre's political and literary strategies: Pulquería, and De la Torre, evidently *do* read and understand philosophy. Indeed, not only does Pulquería demonstrate ample, in-depth knowledge of male philosophers, but so too does she refer to her own ideological stances as her 'filosofía' (1) on the opening page of the text; a metanarrative descriptor that underlines that De la Torre intends for her readers to understand *Jardín* as an exemplar of female-voiced theories. On the one hand, this apparent hypocrisy is reflective of the circumstances in which many leading figures of first-wave feminism found themselves, as these women utilised their own education and publicity so as to critique women's subordinate status. To some degree, it is conceivable that De la Torre is self-consciously acknowledging this inconsistency so as recognise the inevitable pitfalls of speaking of women as a homogenous group. When musing to her nephew about the '[l]a mujer (la tuya y la ajena)' (20), for example, Pulquería is clearly not reflecting on her own tastes or interests.

By contrast, when discussing women's exclusion from political office and legal fora, as we shall explore later in the chapter, Pulquería emphatically speaks on behalf of *all* women using the *nosotras* voice. Rather than understand Pulquería's unwillingness to identify with women with no interest in philosophy as a veiled attempt to suggest her own superiority (an interpretation incongruous with both the character's and author's thoughts on women's liberation), the more probable reason for this conflict is that it reflects a dualism of women as silenced and vocal, emblematising how the sexed voice is depicted in *Jardín*. Presenting women as at once excluded from androcentric culture and, through Pulquería, intellectually and critically engaged, De la Torre can be seen to underline how the text manifests a female — and feminist — voice. Nevertheless, Pulquería's sarcastic afterthought to her nephew about the uproar amongst men should women elect 'un Habladero oficial' (31) can be taken as a self-reflexive admission of the prevailing power of the male voice; though speaking for women, ' "nosotras" ' (31), Pulquería cannot conceive of a spokes*woman* (an 'Habladera oficial'), despite seeming to fit the bill herself.

'Un código feminino': Women and the Law

Having interrogated the culture that silences women by foregrounding the male voice, Pulquería turns her attention to the patriarchal subtexts of Spanish law. Female subordination, which manifests as the literal and metonymic silencing of the female voice in Pulquería's critique, was reflected in laws mired in misogyny. Under the 1889 Civil Code (Arts. 57–61), for instance, single women were under the tutelage of their fathers and married women were legally obliged to obey their husbands, while the 1870 Penal Code (Art. 438) decreed harsher penalties for women found guilty of adultery. Accordingly, Spain's early feminists argued for legal parity and legislative reforms in both feminist manifestos, such as Emilia Pardo Bazán's 'La mujer española' (1976 [1890]), and through the medium of fiction, with Carmen de Burgos's *El artículo 438* (1921) perhaps the most salient example, given its eponymous reference to the infamous article from the 1870 Penal Code that allowed men to murder adulterous wives. Although *Jardín* reads more as a non-fiction socio-political commentary, given its dialogic structure, De la Torre does make use of the fictional format to nuance her criticisms. Whereas Pulquería's letters about philosophical thought are directed to her nephew, mirroring the androcentricity she condemns, her thoughts on the law are addressed to both her niece and nephew, reflecting the way in which the law is pertinent to both women and men and yet emphatically gendered in terms of conception and application. Spanish law, that is to say, should be interrogated by both the men by and for whom it was written and the women lacking agency as lawmakers or subjects. Pulquería makes this point unequivocally when corresponding with her nephew about the potency of the word, a form of power dominated by men that meant 'indudablemente fueron los que siempre "dictaron la ley" ' (25).

A female-focused history of Spanish women's relationship with the law is explored through Pulquería's communication with her niece. As noted earlier, the generational link between the two female characters can, on one level, be read as a metaphor for the evolution of feminism: Pulquería embodies the nexus of embryonic and first wave feminist thought that engages with the ideas of her younger, and at times more progressive, niece. Pulquería's receptiveness is hinted at by her positive reflections on her niece's fortitude, believing her to be 'una mujer valerosa' (191). Though the familiar tie between Pulquería and her niece may suggest an organic hierarchy, with the younger feminist prompting her elder aunt to revolutionise her views, the dynamic between the two constitutes a more symbiotic back-and-forth that serves two purposes. Firstly, and crucially, it avoids alienating women with more moderate feminist objectives, as De la Torre does not present feminist progress as one directional, in the sense that the younger generation improves upon their proverbial foremothers. In contrast, Pulquería is frustrated by what she deems the conservative character of the younger generation:

> Con la juventud no puede contarse para el progreso. La juventud es conservadora... ¡qué digo conservadora! La juventud es conservadora... ¡qué digo conservadora! La juventud es arcaica, vetusta, obscurantista y prehistoriófila. Con la juventud no puede darse ningún paso hacia adelante, porque va siempre con la cabeza vuelta para atrás. (57–58)

The evident vitriol here suggests a call to arms, galvanising the youth about whom Pulquería is so critical to re-evaluate their ideological limitations, presupposing that the younger generation have much to learn from their elders. Not only does this demonstrate how all strands of feminism can inform and inflect one another, it also provides a space for that kind of democratic debate.

Whereas traditional, non-fiction feminist manifestos are more direct and didactic, the salient benefit of a fictionalised feminist text is its ability to encapsulate nuances and paradoxes through its multiple interpretative layers, without undermining its message. De la Torre, in other words, can present various stances through a combination of Pulquería's letters and the ideas of her niece and nephew (which are implied by Pulquería's responses), emphasising the importance of interrogation and debate. There is, then, an elasticity to Pulquería's dialogue, as she is navigating between competing ideological positions so as to invite the reader to engage with these discourses. The second (related) point is that Pulquería's mutually beneficial exchanges with her niece can be understood as De la Torre working through her own conflicting ideas, demonstrating how *Jardín* manifests the author's ideological development. We can interpret this as both De la Torre debating with her younger self who, we may infer, she has come to think of as overly conservative, and, at the same time, a women's movement she deems stunted and reactionary.

Women's legal subordination, Pulquería rightly observes, has been the status quo throughout history. Asked by her niece about when women were, in her view, most liberated, her 'ideal femenino' (116), Pulquería pithily replies that such a time did not exist; 'me parece que toda ley escrita hasta la hora presente nos ha de agotar dentro de sus límites, por anchos que los designen' (116). Not only does Pulquería underline the limitations of law here — presenting it as a suffocating, restrictive force — she also suggests it is fundamentally unnatural for women to be subject to legislative structures. Women, she argues, should demand 'leyes especiales, leyes para mujeres, para nuestro uso exclusivo' (122) and, as a collective, request to be exempt: 'Pidamos ser excluídas del Código civil' (122). The law is, in her words, 'una pura maraña, donde nos enredamos las ciudadanas de manera lamentable...' (120). Unlike, for instance, Burgos's *La mujer moderna* (1927), in which Burgos forensically critiques individual laws, observing how they unduly impact women, De la Torre treats the polemical legal codes in more general terms, focusing on the gendered dynamics of legal structures and legislation. The distinction between how Pulquería presents these differences to her niece and nephew is intriguing. While, on the one hand, she advocates for female specific laws when addressing her niece, a notion that she does not explain or justify in any detail, it is in letters to her nephew that the implications of coding legislation in terms of sex are explored. In a characteristically blunt retort, for example, Pulquería admonishes her nephew for his apparent concern that laws should reflect women's interests: 'Lo más que llegaría á suceder sería que las leyes se volviesen hembras. ¡Y no me parece destinado, señor...! Hasta ahora han sido machos' (216).

Personifying the law in terms of sex reinforces both how existing legislation favours men and, critically, laws reflect those who draft them. A woman studying the law, Pulquería argues, would be inclined to draft and interpret legislation 'al modo mujeril' (215), resulting in different laws as, to her mind, 'un hombre y una mujer son bastantes diferentes' (215). Juxtaposing Pulquería's stance here with Burgos's argument for legal parity based on equality feminism — as Anja Louis notes, Burgos's feminism, 'like first wave feminism in general, defined justice as consisting of gender neutrality and equality before the law' (2005: 22) — connotes a conservatism inflected by traditional discourses about sex. Rather than cite inherent differences between women and men as justification for women's legal subordination, however, Pulquería sardonically notes that, as laws drafted by women would be the antithesis of existing androcentric legislation — 'los antípodas de vuestros juicios' (215) — it is conceivable that they would be superior: 'Y siendo vuestros juicios, hasta ahora, bastante regulares, según confesión de parte... ¿no es lógico suponer que los nuestros sean buenos, ó por lo menos mejores?' (215).

She uses this logic to satirise the notion of legal inequalities based on sex and, at the same time, criticise her nephew's take on feminism: though she acknowledges he is a 'partidario del feminismo' (215), she pre-empts his surprise at her suggestions for female-centric laws, commenting that he favours a 'feminismo benéfico, que consiste en que las mujeres se ilustren mucho, se adoren mucho, se enteren de todo lo humano y lo divino...' (215). The notion of acknowledging women as capable of writing laws and establishing legal codes, however, in Pulquería's view, is beyond her nephew's expectations: '¡pero eso de que confeccionen códigos, seguramente no entra en tus planes!' (215). There is an echo of Concepción Arenal here, as De la Torre uses her protagonist as a mouthpiece to unpack the hypocrisies and shortcomings of conservative feminisms and patriarchal discourses that simultaneously sanctify and infantilise women. For example, Arenal's criticism of the double-standard by which women are deemed inferior to men in Spanish law, but are, nevertheless, subject to the same criminal standards, as she outlines in *La mujer del porvenir* (1884), resonates with Pulquería's argument for a female-centric legislature; facetiously proposing an alternative: '¡Ah, un código femenino!' (215).

The proposal for a gynocentric legal system epitomises the essence of difference feminism: women as different from yet equal to men. Demarcating laws in terms of sex is at once fundamentally conservative and tellingly progressive. While, on one level, it can be read as a scathing critique of existing legal codes that disenfranchise and persecute women, it also echoes traditionalist discourses reaching as far back as the eighteenth century that 'presented men and women as essentially different and irreducible, claiming that among them there was no hierarchy but rather a natural complementarity' (Boluffer Peruga 2018: 42). Such arguments, of course, would inform proto-feminisms in Spain, resulting in the seemingly conservative character of first wave feminism. The inconsistencies in Pulquería's approach reflect both the embryonic formulation of De la Torre's own feminism and a self-conscious, concerted effort to underscore the hypocrisies between what Pulquería argues — and to whom — and what she does. It is, for instance, in a letter to her nephew, who can be read in this context as the personification of androcentric legal structures, that Pulquería outlines her proposals for legal reform. Much in the same way she discusses philosophy, she overstates that she, as a woman, is in no position to dictate laws before evidencing her capability. By emphasising the symbiosis of power and speech through imagery that underlines the importance of language, Pulquería acknowledges how her sex has traditionally excluded her from this task: 'A mí no *me llamarán* nunca para "*dictar*" una ley. Lo primero porque siendo, como soy, una infeliz mujer, moriré s*in haber dicho "esta boca es mía"*' (152; emphasis added).

In spite of the ample confidence she evidences throughout *Jardín*, Pulquería is hesitant to offer her opinión — 'es posible que, puesta yo á dictar leyes, resultaran aún más desatinadas que las existentes...' (152) — an insecurity that we may attribute to De la Torre herself. Not only would this correlate with my reading that Pulquería's characterisation manifests De la Torre's own internal thought process, with her female narrator verbalising her own doubts and uncertainties, it also connotes a degree of self-criticism that would, arguably, make for a sound lawmaker. Proposed changes are described as 'prágmaticas' as well as 'leyes', alluding to the Pragmatic Sanction of 1830 that would change the Spanish political landscape by paving the way for the country's first female monarch since the Reconquista, Isabel II. Such sanctions are, therefore, absolute and, critically, invested with a nexus of gender and power. In a veiled critique of *caciquismo*, which forms the basis of De la Torre's analyses examined in Chapter Two, Pulquería's suggested laws focus on establishing an individual's capability to be an active citizen (of either sex) and, accordingly, vote responsibly. As Pulquería outlines, 'el sufragio sería una de las más excelsas prerrogativas que se pudiera aspirar á poseer, y que para adquirirle debieran aquilatarse bien los méritos del individuo' (154). The emphasis on individual liberty is pertinent for two reasons. On the one hand, it illustrates the self-conscious political commentary in *Jardín*, as the rights of the individual underpinned liberal debates about political representation and male suffrage in nineteenth-century Spain (see Theresa Ann Smith 2016). At the same time, as we shall see in the next section, the question of what qualities would merit citizenship, and therefore the right to vote, was key for early Spanish feminists.

'¡¡He sido sufragista!!': Female Suffrage

The paradoxes of first wave feminisms in Spain are clearly evidenced by the apparent contradictions surrounding Spanish women's right to vote. The typically conservative character of first wave feminism in Spain, which, as noted in the first section of this analysis, Pulquería's views often mirror, would mean that in the late nineteenth and early twentieth century, Spanish feminism can be characterised, in Mary Nash's words, 'more by its social than its political orientation. As a movement, it was not singularly suffragist in focus, and the core of Spanish feminist arguments for women's rights was not individual rights based on the idea of gender equality' (1995: 35; also see Nash 1988: 20). Indeed, many of Spain's early feminists were utterly opposed to women's political involvement, be it voting or standing for Parliament, as the political domain was considered a corrupt, male-dominated environment. Concepción Arenal, for example, argued in *La mujer del porvenir* (1868, written in 1861) that women were unsuited for politics as, like judgeships or the military, it was incongruous with women's compassionate nature, a position that Emilia Pardo Bazán would later criticise:

> La exclusión de ciertas profesiones, como la judicatura; la negación de ciertos derechos, los derechos políticos, eran cosas, no pensadas, sino sentidas, lirismos de un corazón que, sin advertirlo, soñaba todavía a la mujer con aureola, nimbo y vara de azucenas en la mano. ([1893] 1981: 185)

Concepción Gimeno de Flaquer, whose conservatism meant 'she attracted a very different following from Arenal and Pardo Bazán' (Bieder 2018: 170), refracted the suffrage question, focusing on her role to inspire 'a los legisladores la reforma de [las leyes]' (Gimeno de Flaquer 1900: np). Not only were leading feminists divided on the issue, many also changed their position as their careers progressed. Carmen de Burgos is one such example: though Burgos would argue in *La mujer en España* (1906) that 'ahora darle el derecho de voto es poner un arma peligrosa en manos de un niño' (1906: 46) as, like many feminists, she believed women were not sufficiently educated to vote, she would present a signed manifesto to the Cortes in 1921, demanding the vote for women (Bieder 2018: 178; Guallart 2011: 139; Nash 2004: 243). Moreover, Burgos publicly defended women's right to vote in 1908, just two years after her initial reservations, when, in response to an ultimately unsuccessful debate in Parliament regarding limited voting rights for women,[5] she declared: 'Encarno espíritu feminista [...]; de esos que defienden el voto de la mujer o lo discuten con razones' (1908: np).

As outlined in the Introduction, De la Torre's own support for female suffrage would become abundantly clear during her political career; in 1933, the year she was elected to the Cortes, she spoke at a series of events organized by the Juventudes Socialistas to encourage women to vote (Calderón Gutiérrez 1984: 77). Her commitment to this matter is intriguing as it puts her at odds not just with leading feminists, but also her female socialist contemporaries. As outlined in the Introduction, in the vote on female suffrage the only three female *diputadas* in the Cortes were divided on the issue: Clara Campoamor, representing the Partido Radical Republicano, voted in favour, Kent, a member of the Partido Republicano Radical Socialista, voted against and Nelken, who, like De la Torre, represented the PSOE, abstained (Davies 1998: 106). Kent, in line with her party's position, believed that Spanish women were not yet 'politically sophisticated enough to support the socialist cause' (Tolliver 2011: 247), while Nelken defended her stance by reasoning that Spanish women were not sufficiently prepared or experienced to vote at all. As she argued, it would only be when 'una cultura femenina tan alta como la masculina' was realised that women should vote: 'Este será el mejor feminismo, y él conducirá naturalmente, *racionalmente*, al voto de las mujeres' (Nelken 1975: 192; emphasis in original).

Nelken's concern for women's capacity to be full, active citizens resonates with De la Torre's approach in *Jardín*, as Pulquería broadly supports female suffrage while acknowledging the failings of Spanish democracy. In a characteristically barbed observation, Pulquería argues, to her nephew, that '[l]as mujeres no pueden ser ciudadanos además de mujeres' (123). To be a woman, she suggests, 'es ya un oficio equivalente á la ciudadanía más activa y transcendental' (123), and it is for this reason that men dominate political power:

> [E]l hombre no tiene ninguna ocupación "natural y física" que le impida cuidarse de la república [...] Y si gobierna mal, como creo que gobierna, él sólo tiene la culpa, y es de creer que algún día de percate de ello y gobierne mejor. (123)

As the reference to a republic implies, Pulquería combines hypothesis — we must remember here De la Torre is writing during the Restoration — with her assessment of the current political climate that, not unexpectedly, she believes men are governing poorly. De la Torre's staunch republicanism is the most probably reason for this slip into an alternate reality, as, as we shall see in Chapter Three's analysis of *El banquete del Saturno* (1931), her fictional realms are typically under a republican government. The use of quotation marks when considering the 'ocupación "natural y física"' (123) that prevents women from occupying political space underlines how she is echoing her nephew's language so as to dismantle his argument from within. As noted earlier, this visual marker of dialogue emphasises the political capital of appropriating another's words. It is by engaging with the patriarchal discourses her nephew regurgitates and personifies that Pulquería is able to propose an argument for women's political emancipation that fits within existing discourses.

The conciliatory approach this implies suggests De la Torre's efforts to navigate antagonistic discourses so as to conceive of a coherent argument for women's suffrage that builds on, rather than contradicts, established norms. In this sense, De la Torre is able to accommodate the pluralistic viewpoints of her readers and her feminist forerunners. There is, for instance, a hint of Concepción Gimeno de Flaquer, arguably the 'best-known representative of conservative or "moderate feminism" at the turn of the century' (Bieder 2018: 168), in Pulquería's nod to women's 'natural' role. By 1907, Gimeno defended female suffrage on the condition that it would not make women become masculinised, praising 'la tradicional feminidad de luchadoras por la causa de la mujer' (Servén 2013: 410). While Pulquería does not explicitly object to the argument that immutable biological realities dictate, to a degree, women's political exclusion, she does, in an earlier letter to her nephew, lament how women are disempowered, 'sin voz ni voto' (33). Paralleling voice with suffrage both reinforces the political capital of the collective female voice and, crucially, delineates Pulquería's — and we can logically assume, De la Torre's — unequivocal support for women's right to vote. Indeed, Pulquería's argument that it stands to reason that single women are 'las más sufragistas de las mujeres' (11) is likely an acknowledgement from De la Torre that her own relationship status liberated her from more conservative feminist initiatives that centred on domesticity and childrearing.

It is in letters to her niece that Pulquería elaborates on her position; a detail that denotes how, when discussing the suffrage question, De la Torre envisages a female reader. Just as the epistolary paradigm facilitates a targeted dialogue with a female or male readership, depending on the subject matter, and the gendered discourses they represent, it also connotes a didacticism, as Pulquería communicates with a younger feminist. Commending her niece for her 'entusiasmos sufragistas' (62) and addressing her as 'sobrina mía muy sufragista' (78), Pulquería confirms that she too defines herself as such:

> ¡¡he sido sufragista!! Sí, sufragista convencida y consciente; más sufragista que nadie, puesto que tú y otras muchas lo sois ahora porque otros os lo han soplado á la oreja, y yo fui... 'auto-sufragista', 'presufragista' y demás palabrotas que malamente se me puedan aplicar. (91)

To ensure that her niece, and, of course, the reader, are left in no doubt, Pulquería reaffirms that she has long identified as a 'sufragista' (92, 95), a conviction informed by her assessment of the political climate and her moral commitment to defending individual autonomy. Labelling herself '"auto-sufragista"' and '"presufragista"' is particularly telling as suggests that De la Torre supported women's right to vote before it was a commonplace and, crucially, that she has monitored how collective views have evolved. Indeed, *Jardín* is as much an amalgamation of diverse feminist discourses as it is De la Torre's personal reflections on her own relationship with feminism. Galvanising her niece to continue fighting for the vote, Pulquería laments how women are excluded despite being 'seres racionales' (62). Even if only *some* women could vote, she believes, presumably those with higher levels of education, female suffrage would revolutionise women's lives:

> Si las mujeres superiores tuvieran derecho al sufragio, sería señal de que lo tenían las demás mujeres en general, una distinción de categorías... morales, porque la libertad es una especie de palo de ciego que no deja cosa sana y... (96)

Curiously, when defending women's right to vote, Pulquería presents herself as speaking for all women — '[h]abía sido sufragista como lo son todas las mujeres' (95) — which is an ostensibly controversial position given the very evident lack of consensus amongst Spanish women on the suffrage question. Rather than deem this an oversight on De la Torre's part, or a provocation, the way Pulquería reasons for women's right to vote would suggest that, for De la Torre, objections to female suffrage are more commonly a reflection of a distrust of suffrage in general.

In a scathing condemnation of *caciquismo*, Pulquería explains that her interest in the vote is not based on 'ambición del hecho del sufragio, sino por indignación hacia el sufragio mismo' (95). Accordingly, Pulquería facetiously muses that allowing women to vote in such circumstances would only serve to further the chaos: 'Es mucho mejor de lo que parece el que voten sólo los bárbaros y se queden en casa las bárbaras. Todos juntos allí sería ya el caos' (95). The current voting system, she argues, is 'una tan grande paradoja en acción' (106) as 'el milagro de la Igualdad social' (106) is corrupted into 'la esclavitud política' (106), a description that alludes to the *cacique* model and De la Torre's socialist politics. Not only do the references to equality and slavery evoke Marxist discourses (a point explored in detail in Chapter Three), De la Torre also uses this source of contention in order to underscore the need for solidarity. 'Nuestro voto' (97), Pulquería explains to her niece, serves little purpose other than to reinforce a sullied political model: '¡¡Nuestros millones de sufragios sólo servirían para aumentar el poder de los caciques...!!' (97). The use of the possessive — '[n]uestro voto'; '[n]uestros millones de sufragios' — is invested with political agency on multiple levels. While, in a broad sense, it connotes socialist politics through implied collectivity and unity, the fact that Pulquería speaks, in this instance, on behalf of the Spanish population supposes a dual feminist political agency, as Pulquería can be seen to represent the people and self-evidences women's political capability. The text, in this sense, can be seen to manifest De la Torre's political voice at a point in history when she — like all Spanish women — lacked such agency.

Through her outspoken narrator, De la Torre wryly condemns Restoration politics, men (seemingly in general) and the democratic failings of suffrage in its current format. Dialoguing with diverse viewpoints in such a way as to simultaneously defend a pro-women's suffrage position and critique the current political establishment, Pulquería situates her arguments within the Spanish socio-political context. Her female-voiced political analysis, of course, only serves to reinforce her case for women's political parity. Like many of her contemporaries, De la Torre looks to progress abroad as a barometer for feminist activity in Spain, as Pulquería discusses female suffrage in the USA, UK and Russia (64, 67–71), along with the achievements of 'la Pankurst' [*sic*], Emmeline Pankhurst (91, 167). The character's rather hubristic claim that her support for female suffrage predates not only her niece, but also Pankhurst (91), would suggest that De la Torre was familiar with debates regarding women's right to vote throughout her childhood.[6] The precociousness this implies can also be understood metaphorically; as Shirley Mangini explains, Spanish feminists did not typically follow the lead of their English counterparts on the question of suffrage: 'La actitud de las españolas no correspondía con el feminismo anglosajón, lo cual ponía énfasis en el voto femenino' (2001: 93). While some Spanish feminists, notably Burgos, had already come out in support of women's right to vote when *Jardín* was published, Pulquería's reflections on Pankhurst could be understood as an indication that De la Torre felt somewhat isolated amongst her countrywomen for advocating for female suffrage, a not unreasonable reaction. Accordingly, Pulquería can be seen to engage with antagonistic arguments regarding female suffrage so as to present democratic reform — for both female and male citizens — as a logical conclusion. As she writes to her niece, 'el derecho del sufragio otorgado á las mujeres en las actuales circunstancias sociales, en las que es indudable que al hombre no le ha servido para nada el tal derecho' (78).

There is, on one hand, an echo of the counter arguments put forth by the likes of Arenal and Gimeno that politics is fundamentally a masculine activity in Pulquería's critique. Rather than square the blame on the democratic process at its core or political structures, however, De la Torre focuses on the men who uphold it. Effective, fair suffrage, according to Pulquería, is an ideal to which society should aspire — 'ese famoso derecho viene á quedar en la categoría de las llamadas ilusiones, de los sueños, de las... utopías' (77) — and the current system, dictated by men, does not reflect the sanctity of the right to vote: 'El sufragio es bueno; los hombres no son tan buenos como el sufragio' (77). At the same time, De la Torre reorientates the argument proposed by the likes of Nelken and Kent — both leftists, like De la Torre — that women lack the capacity to vote, or at least to vote in their best interests, so as to apportion blame to the state, rather than women. As she explains, the democratic process should be reformed so as to make suffrage a worthy feminist cause; 'Si hubiera voto de calidad y fuera condición precisa la de contrastar esa calidad, el voto sería una cosa justa y racional' (95). Comparing Pulquería's emphasis on the 'calidad' of the vote, another allusion to the failings of *caciquismo*, with Nelken's arguments against female suffrage[7] illustrates De la Torre's apparent faith in women. As Nelken explicates in *La mujer ante las cortes constituyentes* (1931), her opposition was founded in women's susceptibility to patriarchal influence (through their fathers, husbands and priests), which, she believed, would coerce them to vote against women's interests (1931: 22). Accordingly, and despite the acknowledged increase in educated, leftist women, Nelken focused on how best to achieve a socialist victory; 'Una votación no es cuestión de calidad, sino de cantidad' (1931: 21, 30).

De la Torre, in stark contrast, affirms women's inherent collectivism for virtue of being women. As Pulquería argues in a letter to her nephew:

> las mujeres son *la encarnación perfecta de la democracia y del igualitarismo*; porque entre nosotras no hay 'categorías' [...] Las mujeres tenemos un 'espíritu de sexo' que aún no os habéis entretenido vosotros en analizar. Una mujer piensa siempre 'en mujer', y tal vez no piensa, siente, y esta es *la razón de su solidaridad moral*, tan maravillosa que escapa á toda ponderación. Las mujeres somos los seres 'libres' por excelencia. (220; emphasis added)

Men, by contrast, Pulquería maintains, fall into categories — 'todos piensan en algo, y creen en algo, y adoran algo, y están dispuestos á morir por algo' (220) — be it socialists, anarchists or conservatives. The ambiguity of women's political agency in Pulquería's reflection, as they are at once politically diverse ('la encarnación perfecta de la democracia') and a homogenous group, illustrates how, to De la Torre's mind, this exchange dialogues with anti-suffrage discourses across the political spectrum: while Pulquería mimics patriarchal ideation ('[u]na mujer piensa siempre "en mujer"'), her description of women's organic 'igualitarismo' and 'solidaridad moral' strongly alludes to De la Torre's socialism. Pulquería's apparent attempt to placate her nephew by tempering her argument is, arguably, strategic on De la Torre's part, as the protagonist self-evidences the fallacy of her suggestion that women are uncritical beings: 'Nosotras no somos nada. No opinamos nada, ni nada no importa de vuestras algarabías palabreras' (221). Thus, although women are ostensibly presented as a moderating force for democracy, complementing patriarchal discourses, Pulquería's conception of solidarity hints at women's natural leftist leanings, in the name of justice and equality. Indeed, taking '[u]na mujer piensa siempre "en mujer"' as an axiom, a reader will understand this in accordance with their own politics: for a conservative, to think 'as a woman' will evoke domesticity and chastity, while a progressive, like De la Torre, will identify the female psyche with social and political emancipation.

As the foregoing illustrates, multiple textual dialogues are at play in Pulquería's letters. Not only is De la Torre utilising her protagonist to engage with diverging feminist discourses, *Jardín* also facilitates a self-reflexive commentary on such debates. In an exchange that functions at a diegetic level as a communication from aunt to niece but should, at the same time, be read as De la Torre's advice to her feminist readership, Pulquería cautions against her niece's naivety. Productive and efficacious political agency, she explains, will be a hard-fought right:

> ¿De veras crees tú, ni ninguna de tus compañeras, futuras mártires 'de libertad', que si el sufragio fuese una verdad y 'un derecho efecto' os le hubieran concedido los hombres de buena gana? Y otra cosa. ¿De veras creéis que si el sufragio fuese 'una verdad' y un derecho 'efectivo, hubiera habido nunca la necesidad de concedéroslo ni de reclamarle por vuestra parte? No. Si ese fuese, hubiera sido ó pudiera ser es mucho tiempo un derecho 'efectivo'... una 'expresión' de la 'voluntad libre' del pueblo, de la masa, de 'lo más'... á estas fechas estarían resueltos definitivamente todos los problemas que han obligado á la sociedad á ampliarle... (78).

Again, Pulquería's pontification on democratic reform is inflected with De la Torre's socialist politics. While her consideration for the 'pueblo', 'la masa' and '"lo más"' evoke Marxism's objective of liberation for the masses, it is by addressing her niece as part of a feminist collective — 'vuestra parte' — that Pulquería can be seen to project socialist principles onto feminism. That is not to say that De la Torre is, in this instance, proposing a form of socialist feminism (a topic explored later in the chapter), but rather that the concept of solidarity is utilised in such a way as to consolidate a coherent feminist movement. Much in the same way drawing on Marxism to defend a functioning democracy implies an oblique criticism of its authoritarian tendencies, in line with De la Torre's own views, emphasising the importance of a feminist collective also connotes criticism of a movement that De la Torre accurately observes as fractured and incoherent. Read retrospectively, furthermore, Pulquería's reflections serve as an ominous foreshadowing of the conflict regarding female suffrage during the early years of the Second Republic. Fierce resistance to women's right to vote was, of course, partly inspired by the fact that the country was, finally, operating under a functioning democracy. Though De la Torre was writing during a Restoration government that she evidently loathed, she was able to foresee a time when political parity — for women and men — would become reality.

Despite her evident concern for male cooperation, however, which is personified in *Jardín* through Pulquería's nephew, De la Torre failed to account for the fact women's right to vote would, eventually, be approved by the men she is so eager to criticise, rather than the women she aims to inspire. Indeed, De la Torre's bitterness for the men whose voices had been prioritised over hers is tangible in Pulquería's observations about women's political parity. With scathing irony, she laments the means ('las redes') 'completamente desacreditadas ya por los varones...' (78), 'los hombres ignorantes' (103) who achieved the vote ahead of women and offers her niece and her fellow feminists advice that is wholly condescending to men: 'no seáis egoístas y tened compasión de esos pobrecitos caballeros que os precedieron en el uso del sacratísimo derecho del sufragio' (112). The tangible resentment in Pulquería's description of 'esos pobrecitos caballeros' is revealing, as it suggests not only De la Torre's frustration with the men who possess the political power she lacks, despite her evident capability, but also foreshadows her commentaries on androcentric political bodies that will be examined in Chapters Two and Three.

Juxtaposing the call to arms Pulquería communicates to her niece with the more conservative stance she presents in her first letter to her nephew — 'no pido el voto, pido la verdad' (11) — indicates a strategic attempt to reorientate her argument in accordance with her interlocuter: when addressing a man, and the patriarchal structures he embodies, Pulquería is more accommodating to the status quo, but when engaging with a younger feminist, De la Torre's narrator is unapologetically militant. On a diegetic level, this shift illustrates an organic evolution of the character's views as she is introduced to a more a progressive outlook; a logical development that self-reflexively reinforces the political capital of possessing the medium and means to express one's opinion. The ability to communicate with her aunt, that is to say, affords Pulquería's niece a form of political agency. The fact that her letters, like those of Pulquería's nephew, can only be inferred by the reader based on Pulquería's responses only serves to further underline the import of engagement and reception. Read metaphorically, moreover, the change in Pulquería's point of view is a telling commentary on how, in De la Torre's opinion, the feminist movement should re-evaluate its objectives at this critical juncture in Spanish history. Indeed, Pulquería's final instruction to her niece would, over a decade later, be realised by De la Torre during her short-lived, yet eventful, political career: 'Salid, salid por ahí pidiendo voto en buena hora, pero no os limitéis á pedirlo sólo para vosotras. Que vuestro grito sea algo parecido á este: ¡Voto para las mujeres...! ¡Y para los hombres!' (112).

'Yo voy al escaño': Women and Politics

De la Torre's early aspirations of holding political office are abundantly clear in *Jardín*. As I have already argued, voice functions as a metaphor for political agency in the text and, in turn, Pulquería's dialogue can be considered a manifestation of De la Torre's politic contributions. Not unexpectedly, it is when communicating with her niece that Pulquería muses with the idea of running for office. Expressing excitement at the notion she could enter 'la pelea electoral' (63) and, possibly, be elected ('¡¡[...] Hasta quién sabe si me elegirán...!!' [63]), Pulquería considers winning a seat ('yo voy al escaño...' [75]) and underscores the link between government and the political capital of speech: 'voy al Congreso... y hablo' (74–75). Somewhat glibly, she adds, in parenthesis, her concern as to whether the seat will be 'comfortable' — '(Esto del escaño me "escama". Debe ser algo incómodo, ¿no? Podremos llevar un taburete)' (75) — which, in a typically wry manner, reveals misgivings as to whether the political forum is a fitting environment for a woman. Whereas a man could opt to be a politician, general, doctor or writer, Pulquería notes, women lack the same freedom; 'La vida para ella no tiene forma ni aspiración concreta' (119).

At the time of writing, De la Torre's aspirations to attend congress would be practically inconceivable, as it would be over a decade before an openly republican, leftist woman, such as De la Torre, would have the right to speak in Parliament. Nevertheless, limited voting rights would be extended to some women in 1924; as Paloma Díaz Fernández notes, as of 8 March, a date probably chosen to coincide with International Women's Day, a new decree allowed female heads of households over twenty-three years old to vote in local elections, while women twenty-five and over to run to be elected as councillors (2005: 176; 180). Women's political emancipation, moreover, was a key component of 'A las mujeres españolas', the feminist manifesto published by the Asociación Nacional de Mujeres Españolas (ANME)[8] in 1918 (see Díaz Fernández 2005: 178), the year after *Jardín* was first published. As well as exemplifying how the text engages with contemporary debates, Pulquería's political ambitions also reflect how political parity was becoming an increasingly pressing issue for feminists at this time. The inevitable tensions that arose, and how De la Torre works through these conflicts, is reflected in *Jardín* through the contrast between Pulquería's stance when addressing her niece and her nephew. While Pulquería is optimistic in her letters to her niece, she reveals to her nephew that she is apprehensive about society's willingness to accept female leadership:

> tengo la aprensión de que si al ajeno estrépito y griterío añadiésemos nosotras el nuestro y amaneciese la era de la femenina beligerancia en parlamentos, calles y púlpitos... es muy probable que la Humanidad se quedara completamente sorda. (39)

At a diegetic level, there is, of course, a somewhat passive aggressive undertone to Pulquería's fear that women would be ignored, as all of her communication with her nephew in *Jardín* is, fundamentally, an attempt to make herself be heard by a man.

At the same time, this confession reveals De la Torre's trepidation at the prospect of how she would be received in political circles. Regrettably, such hesitation likely stemmed from her experiences with men on the political left, which is the focus of my analysis of *El banquete de Saturno* (1931) in Chapter Three. Traces of De la Torre's socialism are discernible in her depiction of political representation in *Jardín*, denoting the interconnectedness of her ideological positions. Commending the dignity of the 'pueblo', described as 'lo más digno de la Humanidad' (102), Pulquería underscores the social benefit of collectivity and solidarity:

> Si *los intereses de los individuos* fuesen comunes, si la "solidaridad" moral fuese lo bastante poderosa para hacer *á los hombres* olvidarse de su interés material... [...] Pero el motivo de que *el hombre no sea libre* está dentro *del hombre mismo*. Los intereses individuales se anteponen instintivamente á todo interés general. (107; emphasis added)

The friction Pulquería observes between the collective good and individual interests is not only central to critical analyses of socialist discourses, but, as well shall see throughout this book, a core element of De la Torre's own ideological doubts and scepticism. While the generic use of 'hombre' is in and of itself not necessarily a comment on sex or gender, the shift from 'individuos' to 'hombres' and the use of repetition, particularly in a text centred on feminism, is suspect. On the one hand, this passage chimes with the criticism of androcentric philosophical debates examined at the beginning of this chapter; the self-interested 'hombre' Pulquería criticises, in this sense, can be understood as a reification of a male-centred culture. As Pulquería is here addressing her niece, moreover, there is an implicit sense of female solidarity that unites author, characters and a female reader and, accordingly, hints that the 'moral' solidarity De la Torre endorses should be identified with women.

The notion of a female-centred political structure reminds us of Pulquería's description of women as 'la encarnación perfecta de la democracia y del igualitarismo' (220), examined earlier, and offers insight into the characterisation of De la Torre's protagonist. Not only can Pulquería be read as a mouthpiece for competing feminist discourses, this domineering figure can also be understood as a personification of female — and feminist — political ideals. The character's age — to which she refers repeatedly and, given she has an adult niece and nephew, we may infer to be more advanced than the author's (De la Torre was in her early thirties at the time of writing) — is utilised in such a way as to connote a maturity that, intriguingly, De la Torre identifies with socialism: 'la vejez era igualitaria y sumamente socialista' (54). While the notion that age acts as a 'leveller' is a logical and coherent point, identifying this egalitarianism with socialism conveys that, for De la Torre, a socialist political model is an advanced, sophisticated ideal to which society should aspire. We are reminded here of Pulquería's criticism of the younger generation as inherently conservative. Taking the two in tandem underlines how, in *Jardín*, age functions as a metaphor for degrees of progress; a simplistic yet effective literary strategy that indexes De la Torre's ideological reasoning. Pulquería, then, simultaenously manifests an evolved, nuanced feminist position and, accordingly, socialist values. While such double militancy is common for first wave Spanish feminists — as Roberta Johnson notes, 'Spanish feminist theory is uniquely tinged with social class consciousness' (2019: 89) — what is intriguing about *Jardín* is Pulquería's evidently middle-class perspective, an angle that reflects both De la Torre's personal hang-ups and her ideological blindspots.

In a similar vein to (post-)Francoist socialist feminisms that would view women as a social class, promulgated by the likes of Lidia Falcón,[9] Pulquería recognises women's subordinate place within the social hierarchy: 'Mira: los hombres ricos explotan á los pobres. Y éstos, no sabiendo á quién explotar... pues explotan á las mujeres' (175). Of the topics explored in *Jardín*, it would seem that social class, particularly how class intersects with feminism, causes De la Torre the most turmoil, evidenced in part by a series of miscommunications that lead to an argument between Pulquería and her niece on the subject of working women. Whereas her niece is of the belief that work can be a form of self-fulfilment, Pulquería vehemently disagrees with this stance, arguing that women only work out of necessity. A culture in which women must work is not only a failed societal model but, moreover, a perversion of feminist values:

> Si antes trabajaban algunas desgraciadas, ahora trabajaremos todas, desgraciadas y felices. Es decir, que en vez de pedir y clamar por la liberación de las mujeres que trabajaban, y gastar la energía en demostrar la injusticia de tal estado de cosas, es al contrario: Gastamos toneladas de papel y millones de palabras y armamos tremendas estridencias... para solicitar *el ser cargadas de cadenas todavía más pesadas y más universales*. (167; emphasis added)

Pulquería's stance here is indicative of the inherent conflict between socialist (informed by Marxist) ideation and equality feminism: equal rights and opportunities leave women vulnerable to the capitalist economic model that exploits men, symbolised by the imagery of chains ('cadenas todavía más pesadas y más universales' [167]) that echoes Marxist rhetoric. Pulquería's belief that men are physically stronger (173–74), moreover, means that, to her mind, women are brutalised all the more by manual labour.

Not only does this leave women more vulnerable in the workplace, it also negatively impacts their role within the home:

> trabajan tanto y cobran menos y sufren más... y además de todo esto, ¡tienen sus obligaciones ineludibles y espantosas y transcendentales, que no las dejan cumplir ó las cumplen muy mal! (178)

Rather than fulfil their other duties, which we may infer to include cleaning, cooking and caring for children, working women are distracted by their factory work ('Lo que están es soñando con bombas de dinamita y de trinitoluena' [178]). Such poor working conditions, to Pulquería's mind, at least, galvanise the workers:

> Y son ellas más anarquistas que ellos, sí. Y con razón que les sobra por todas partes, porque ellas están explotadas por todas las fuerzas sociales. (178)

In a clear reference to working class women, who Pulquería identifies with the burgeoning anarchist movement that accompanied the industrial revolution, Pulquería's understanding of female factory workers somewhat misrepresents reality. Work in the tobacco industry, for instance, was a respectable post, with factories 'highly regulated and work conditions particularly favourable to women' (Johnson 2019: 125), while the First World War, to which Pulquería alludes through reference to ammunition factories, revolutionised Spanish women's lives. Whereas De la Torre's contemporaries, including Burgos, Lejárraga and Nelken, would recognise how the conflict liberated Spanish women from the home, a fundamentally feminist advancement, Pulquería is not convinced:

> ¡¡Y yo he oído decir á algunos que esta guerra era el triunfo de las mujeres!!... Y que durante ella habían demostrado su valer y la... universalidad de sus 'aplicaciones' ... A mis ojos no habéis hecho sino 'anularos' en los que valíais y representabais. Habéis hecho... balas. No veo otra labor. ¡¡Y os dais un lustre!!... (67).

Constructing her argument within a differential feminist framework that resonates with contemporary discourses, Pulquería insists that women's inherent moral superiority make them inherently unsuitable for war. Men, in stark contrast, are accustomed to such brutalities; ammunitions factories, like men, are fundamentally 'masculino, es decir, de agresivo y de bárbaro...' (73) and, accordingly, women must avoid such activities, lest they become 'una mujer disfrazada moralmente de hombre...' (73).

Pulquería's arguments reflect both De la Torre's politics and, at the same time, suggest the author's discomfort with middle class feminist perspectives, specifically her own. On the one hand, Pulquería's disgust for ammunition production aligns with the links between the early women's movement; as Estrella Cibreiro and Francisca López outline, 'there is a historical connection between women and non violence' and, accordingly, 'there exists a broad correlation between feminism and pacifism' (2013: 5). At the same time, a broadly anti-war stance aligns with how De la Torre conceived of socialism, at least until the outbreak of the Civil War in 1936. In a speech delivered in 1935, during her tenure as a *diputada*, De la Torre argued that socialism and war were ideologically incongruous: 'la guerra solo sirve para defender los intereses del capitalismo y destruir la Humanidad' ('Actos socialistas en Galicia' 1935: 8; 'Actuación de los partidos' 1935: 12). The characterisation of Pulquería, with this in mind, indicates how the genesis of De la Torre's pacifist beliefs originated from a broadly female-centric standpoint, which, as her career — and the international political climate — progressed, she came to identify more with an anti-capitalist socio-economic argumentation. The link between Spanish feminisms and anti-capitalism, exemplified by the works of Arenal and Pardo Bazán, suggests that, rather than a re-evaluation of De la Torre's ideological priorities, this shift can be seen as an organic evolution of interconnected political objectives.

Bearing in mind that *Jardín* was published during the First World War (in 1917, three years into the conflict), Pulquería underlines the various ways the war has impeded the feminist movement: as well as gravely impacting the lives of women in active countries (specifically listing France, Germany, Turkey, the UK and Russia), Pulquería laments how English suffragettes paused their activism: 'Y el voto se lo regalan á los caballeros, para que se queden con algo...' (71). Rather than be tempted to read Pulquería, in this instance, as simply a mouthpiece for De la Torre, the character's reductionist view of working women — that is, her inability to recognise the feminist capital of entering the workplace — demands a more nuanced interpretation. The ubiquitous tensions between feminist and socialist politics, indeed, are tangible in Pulquería's naïve suggestion that, if women no longer worked (meaning paid employment outside of their home), working conditions would improve for the male worker:

> El día glorioso en que las mujeres digan 'nosotras no trabajamos'... nada de habrá perdido. Se habrán, probablemente, acabado las huelgas [...] Y los jornales subirían, y la obra de mano sería muy estimada, y el obrero mucho más respetado, y su sudor, que ahora está despreciado por el envilecimiento del sudor de la mujer, sería entonces estimado y pagado hasta donde es justo... (177)

Such an interpretation is not only ignorant and fundamentally patriarchal — an uncomfortable hangover of the anti-feminist leftist discourses to which De la Torre was subjected — but also reveals how De la Torre uses Pulquería as a conduit for exploring her own middle class experience. That is not to say, however, that De la Torre is altogether comfortable with her own privilege; rather, there appears to be a degree of (self-)criticism of her own ignorance that the author works through at her protagonist's expense.

The character of Pulquería, then, can be read as a reification of the ignorance of middle class Spanish feminists to the working classes' plight, which was criticised by Spanish feminists from varying perspectives. In 'The Women of Spain' (1889; published in Spanish in 1890), for instance, the aristocratic Pardo Bazán observes how middle class women's snobbery towards manual labour prevents them from earning a living, making them dependent on their husbands, unlike the working class woman who 'considers it her duty to gain her living' (1889: 893; cited in Johnson 2019: 94). Similarly, Nelken, who was working class, argues in *La condición social de la mujer en España* (1922) that, rather than work, middle class women enter marriages that are effectively a form of prostitution[10] and, accordingly, middle class women are 'el mayor *peso muerto de la nación* y al mismo tiempo, lo que hay en ella más enérgico y más valiente' (1922: 56; original emphasis). De la Torre's self-conscious criticism of middle class women is evidenced by Pulquería's idealised image of a society that prioritises 'la belleza de las mujeres, el dinero de los hombres y la comodidad de las cosas' (180); a desire that is evidently incongruous with De la Torre's socialist and feminist ideals.

The narrative, in this sense, can be seen to dialogue with contemporary feminist discourses, acting as a conduit between (arguably valid) criticism and the women at whom it is aimed. While Pulquería exhibits the shortcomings that impeded the Spanish feminist movement and limited middle class women's active involvement, by reinforcing the import of vanity, financial dependence and materialism,[11] the fact that De la Torre's protagonist voices such views avoids alienating like-minded readers. *Jardín* therefore functions as a mediator, echoing the opinions of the female, middle class readers that De la Torre aims to engage and, ultimately, inform. The dialogic quality of the text reflects both how De la Torre's opinions compare with those of her fellow feminists and, critically, charts what we may reasonably infer to be her own ideological shift, as her introduction to more radical ideas (represented in *Jardín* by Pulquería's niece) brings to light how, to the author's mind, her middle class upbringing made her ignorant to the nuances of feminist and socialist politics that Pulquería oversimplifies.

Regrettably, a contemporaneous review of *Jardín* published in the socialist periodical *La Montaña* would reinforce the somewhat perfunctory, emphatically gendered view of women and their output that De la Torre interrogates. Prompted by the commentary published in *La Atalaya* (mentioned at the beginning of this chapter), the piece recognises how De la Torre plays on irony to good effect — which, apparently, 'no siempre ésta fácil a la pluma de las mujeres' ('Una escritora montañesa' 1928: 15) — and the 'gracia' (1928: 15) with which she discusses feminism. Nevertheless, the (male) critic argues, '[e]l feminismo no sale muy bien librado' (1928: 15) in the novel, despite De la Torre's efforts. Making reference to her beauty and pleasant nature ('tan gentil mujer' [1928: 15]), he does, however, recognise her right to 'un buen puesto entre las escritoras españolas y viene a sumarse a ellas sin que éstas la eclipsen' (1928: 16). Though feedback is fundamentally positive, with the critic keen to underline that De la Torre is a local woman, 'hija de Cabezón de Sal' (1928: 15) (which he repeats twice), who should be celebrated, there is sparse evidence that he has engaged with — or even read — the novel. Perhaps the most telling observation to be made about this review is how it exemplifies many of the issues De la Torre navigates in *Jardín*: women's critical output is often downplayed or misunderstood; women are qualified by their appearance; and, crucially, that sex and gender politics inform the reception of female-authored works.

As we have seen, De la Torre's envisaged reader shifts in *Jardín* depending on the matter at hand. It should come as no surprise, then, that Pulquería's concluding thoughts are addressed to her nephew and, accordingly, a male reader, as she demands support from the men who currently hold the power. In her typically domineering style, De la Torre's protagonist implores her nephew, whom she addresses as a representative for all men, using the plural 'vosotros', to facilitate women's emancipation through their own reform:

> Nuestra redención, la redención de las mujeres, no tendrá lugar más que de una manera: Cuando vosotros os civilicéis los suficiente para saber lo que somos y valemos... Y nos dejéis vivir tranquilas y en paz. Cuando nos concedáis la verdadera importancia que, grandísima y transcendental, en realidad tenemos...
> (297)

Through the use of the plural voice, De la Torre concludes her feminist call to arms on a collective, collaborative note. The pluralism of feminist discourses that she negotiates throughout *Jardín* come together, as Pulquería speaks on behalf of all women. Such collectivism not only connotes how socialist ideation can be productively projected onto feminism, it also exemplifies how *Jardín* textualises the way in which De la Torre's core ideological positions intersect. The implied symbiosis between feminist and socialist politics, which are presented as an organic, salient alliance given Pulquería seeming lack of awareness that she is making this link, is illustrated most clearly in the protagonist's thoughts on how to achieve class equality. In a reverse of the above, Pulquería applies a feminist reasoning onto socialist objectives, using scathing irony to underline inequality amongst men.

Again, there is an embryonic form of the (post-)Francoist leftist feminisms that demarcate women as a distinct social class, as Pulquería argues, impersonating the men she critiques, that men lack the collectivism women enjoy:

> ¿Tú eres hombre? ¡Pues yo también!... no hemos hecho nada... ¡Fuera la igualdad! Ni somos iguales ni mucho menos.
>
> Somos tan diferentes que no podemos serlo más. ¡Feminicémonos, feminicémonos muchísimo!... Siquiera para equilibrarnos, señor, que ahora todos nos caemos del mismo lado y vamos cojeando y medio derrengados. (73)

Equating the notion of 'feminising' the male population with engendering equality underscores how applying modes of behaviour coded female, such as deference and respect, to androcentric male political structures could facilitate reform. The call for men to 'femininise', moreover, which De la Torre vocalises through Pulquería's conception of a stereotypical man, can be read as both a facetious attempt to ridicule the masculine voice that silences women and, as evidenced by the fact Pulquería addresses this letter to her niece, an oblique suggestion that women are more capable of realising social revolution. Before De la Torre could self-evidence this in her political career, however, she would have to unpack the male-dominated political models that impeded her, which, as will be argued in the next chapter, she interrogates through a feminist prism.

Notes to Chapter 1

1. The epistolary genre, Elizabeth C. Goldsmith writes, has historically been considered 'particularly suited to the female voice' (1989: vii). Accordingly, as Laura A. Salsini explicates, 'the genre has historically been considered a "female" genre, practised by and most suitable for women authors' (2010: 6).
2. Hereafter, all in-text references to *Jardín* will be to the 1917 edition.
3. See, for example, Aldaraca 1991; Fuentes Peris 2003; Kirkpatrick 2003: 30–36; Nash 1999; Urruela 2005.
4. Though critics rightly note that difference and equality feminisms should be considered in relation to 'a continuum rather than a dichotomy' (Tolliver 2011: 251) and, accordingly, recognise the need of 'reaching beyond the dichotomy equality/difference' (Bock and James 1992: 3), these categories can be useful when contextualising Pulquería's and De la Torre's feminist politics.
5. Proposals concerned single women over twenty-three in municipal elections (Castañada 1994: 121).
6. Given De la Torre was roughly nineteen years old when Pankhurst founded the Women's Social and Political Union in 1903, 'frustrated at the lack of progress achieved by the existing women's suffrage movement' (Bartley 2002: 1), and was raised in a liberal, intellectual family, it is conceivable that she engaged with the suffrage question in her youth. Her evident familiarity with Pardo Bazán's feminism (discussed further in Chapter Three), moreover, can be taken as further evidence De la Torre was introduced to these debates at a young age, as Pardo Bazán considers women's political emancipation in 'La mujer española', first published in Spain in 1890, when De la Torre was still in infancy.
7. As Robert Kern notes, Nelken continued to oppose female suffrage even after it had been granted (1981: 200).

8. The ANME is considered to be the first women's organisation in Spain. Formed in 1918, the group was a relatively moderate association that was dedicated to improving educational and professional opportunities for women and reforming the polemical 1889 Civil Code.

9. In *La razón feminista: La mujer como clase social y económica* (1981), Falcón argues that women share characteristics typically associated with social classes, but their labour is unpaid and socially enforced: 'La religión, la política, la filosofía, la educación, el psicoanálisis, han sido inventados por el hombre, para teorizar la explotación de clase de mujer, convencerla de que así *debe ser*' (1981: 32; original emphasis).

10. Nelken explicates that women's limited professional opportunities mean they must sell their bodies, to a husband or punter: 'La única diferencia es que, en el matrimonio, el agarradero es definitivo y que, una vez conseguido, el comprador, la mujer no se preocupa ya, en compensación, de seguirle agradando' (1922: 51).

11. Carmen de Burgos would later underline such issues in *La mujer moderna y sus derechos* ([1927] 2007), arguing that the vanity and short-sightedness of middle class women impeded the feminist movement: 'La clase media fue más retardataria para enarbolar la bandera feminista, que ahora sostiene con gran entusiasmo. El feminismo lleva implícita la obligación de trabajar y la clase media, inteligente, culta, dotada de un gran respeto a las tradiciones, estaba, sin embargo, minada por la vanidad y la imprevisión' (2007: 66).

CHAPTER 2

❖

Don Quijote, rey de España and *El ágora*: Politics, Philosophy and Patriarchy

After a writing hiatus of over a decade, De la Torre published *Don Quijote, rey de España* (1928; henceforth *Don Quijote*) and *El ágora* (1930), political texts that bear little resemblance to *Jardín* in terms of character or content. Reorientating her focus away from the feminist question, or ostensibly at least, De la Torre examines Spanish political history, scrutinising the interface of the country's political establishment and an abstract manifestation of Spain's collective consciousness. Deftly weaving political analysis with philosophical reflection, De la Torre utilises *Don Quijote* and *El ágora* as a means of interrogating the causes and effects of Spain's recent history. Central tropes that link the two texts include political liberty, Spain's colonial wars, republicanism, nationalism, the conception of the *pueblo* and Spain's *desastre* of 1898. *Don Quijote* and *El ágora* can therefore be read in tandem, as two interlinked interrogations of Spain's complex political and cultural consciousness. The political illiteracy of the Spanish population — whom she refers to as the 'pueblo' — and inability of the political classes to meaningfully engage with their citizens forms the basis of her critique, as the failings of *caciquismo* and the *turno pacífico*, which are condemned through *tía* Pulquería in *Jardín*, are unpacked in De la Torre's own words. The emphasis on dialogue that characterises De la Torre's written output is central to both *Don Quijote* and *El ágora*, as she uses her written critiques as a means of actively engaging with formal political discourses. In reiterating, echoing and reformulating words that she attributes to Spain's leading political and cultural figures, all of whom are men, De la Torre simultaneously joins and interrogates key debates, utilising theses texts as a means of foregrounding her female — and, indeed, feminist — voice. Thus, much in the same way that Pulquería mimics masculinist discourses to reassert female agency in *Jardín*, as we saw in the previous chapter, De la Torre appropriates male voices in order to self-consciously form part of Spain's political history.

   Given *Don Quijote* and *El ágora* are products of an authoritarian Spain, as they were published during the proto-fascist dictatorship of Miguel Primo de Rivera (1923–1930), the texts can be understood as an alternative to the debates from which, at the time of writing, De la Torre was excluded on the basis of her sex and liberal sensibilities. The despondence and melancholy that characterised the Spanish consciousness in the aftermath of the 1898 *desastre* — when Spain would lose its stature as an international colonial power — are tangible in *Don Quijote* and *El ágora*, as the tone of the works captures this sense of collective failure. As De la Torre writes in *El ágora*, Spain 'perdió su imperio colonial. Pasó a nación de segundo orden' (63).[1] An intriguing contrast can be gleaned by comparing *Don Quijote* and *El ágora* with another of De la Torre's narratives: 'La ciudad nueva', a short story published in the *Revista de Santander* in 1930 (repr. in Martínez Cerezo 2000b). Two pages in length, 'La ciudad nueva' is about a boatload of passengers eagerly awaiting their arrival at the unspecified 'Ciudad', a symbol of optimism, promise and opportunity. Bearing in mind that the date of publication suggests that 'La ciudad nueva' was written around the same time as the texts examined here, a dichotomy is presupposed between a hypothetical utopia and the reality of Spain's undemocratic political structures. Juxtaposing the texts points to two important qualities about De la Torre's writing. Firstly, the vast difference in length reflects De la Torre's preoccupation with ideological introspection and critique; while just two pages are dedicated to the prosperous future suggested in 'La ciudad nueva', *Don Quijote* and *El ágora* constitute expansive critiques of Spain's political structures. Optimism and transformation, in this sense, remain moot until present failings are resolved. At the same time, the very existence of 'La ciudad nueva' illustrates how *Don Quijote* and *El ágora* reflect not just De la Torre's objective of scrutinising the past, but also how the ideas she tackles relate to the contemporary political landscape. There is, in other words, an oblique sense of optimism that inspires her decision to examine Spain's political history, seemingly with the objective of looking ahead to a more liberal future.

In the eleven years between the publications of *Jardín* and *Don Quijote*, De la Torre dedicated herself to music and education; likely deterred from political writings and/or activism in the immediate aftermath of the Primo de Rivera *coup d'état* that took place September 1923. As outlined in the Introduction, she founded the 'Academia Torre' in 1925, a mixed-sex school that followed the ethos of the Institución Libre de Enseñanza (Martínez Cerezo 2000a: 16; Olarte Martínez 2010: 23). Founded in 1876, this educational model was inspired by the Krausist philosophy of academic, ideological and intellectual liberty. The teachings of the German philosopher permeated Spain's cultural and political foundation, as the failed Republican experiment of 1868 and subsequent Restoration period proved fertile ground for revolutionary projects that would rid Spain of its supposed 'backwardness' and propel the country towards modernity; an elusive political objective that De la Torre unpacks in *Don Quijote* and *El ágora*. The Krausist school of thought that underpinned the Institución Libre de Enseñanza — and, in turn, the 'Academia Torre' — not only resonates strongly with De la Torre's political philosophy, specifically her resistance to dogma, but also facilitated feminist progress in Spain. As Raquel Vázquez Ramil explains:

> El krausismo español, mentor espiritual e ideológico de la Institución Libre de Enseñanza, dio amplio relieve a la cuestión femenina y fue pionero a la hora de poner en marcha una serie de iniciativas pedagógicas destinadas a mejorar la condición de la mujer española. (2012: 14)

Indeed, the movement resulted in the Residencia de Señoritas (1915–1939), Spain's first university for women, which would lay the ground for the Madrid based Lyceum Club in 1926; 'a site of intellectual practice and collective participation for women' (Leggott 2008a: 95; also see Cole 2000: 11–12; 16; 173; Leggott 2008b: 148) frequented by many of the women who, like De la Torre, would take centre stage during the Second Republic (see Fagoaga 1985: 155). During her career, De la Torre gave addresses at both the Residencia de Señoritas and the Lyceum Club (Mangini 2006: 136), as well as the Asociación Femenina de Educación Cívica (Rodrigo 1994: 241).[2]

The nexus of education, culture and political agency that encapsulates this zeitgeist is fundamental to this analysis, as it reflects both the context in which De la Torre was writing *Don Quijote* and *El ágora* and, consequently, her argumentation. As indicated by the eponymous reference to the fictional fantasist, *Don Quijote* draws on the idealism associated with mythic figure as a means of scrutinising Spain's political history, specifically the Restoration, the Spanish–American war, the *desastre* and the Generation of 1898. The full title of the work — *Don Quijote, rey de España* — evokes De la Torre's republicanism and, through its fifteen chapters, Francisco Layna Ranz proposes that the text 'echa cuentas al decaimiento de un país en sus horas más bajas' (2019: 17). As De la Torre outlines, Don Quijote 'es el perseguidor del ideal caballeresco y por eso fracasa...' (161).[3] Accordingly, 'es la explicación que España da al mundo entero del porqué su fracaso' (140); 'En español, "quijotismo" equivale a "ideal"' (161). In the first edition of *Una mujer por caminos de España*, María Lejárraga contends that *Don Quijote* was unfairly overlooked by critics: 'pasó inadvertido y que hubiera debido ponerla en primera fila entre los ensayistas españoles del siglo XX' (Martínez Sierra 1989: 219). Contemporaneous reviews are equally positive. Just as an editor comments on De la Torre's own discussion of the text in *Vida Económica*, recognising her astute intellect and commending how 'la eximia autora esclarece con la poderosa luz de su entendimiento, puntos de la historia patria, nebulosos' (in Torre 1928: 383), the review in *Nuevo Mundo* is highly complementary, noting how 'los vibrantes capítulos' weave a complex narrative about 'los orígenes de la decadencia de España' (Galvarriato 1929: 3).

El ágora broadly constitutes an ideological commentary on the key political heavyweights of the Restoration: the Liberal Práxedes Mateo Sagasta (1825–1903); the Conservative Party's Antonio Maura (1853–1925); and the Liberal-turned-Radical Santiago Alba Bonifaz (1872–1949). Although Alba, De la Torre acknowledges, would not reach the professional heights of Sagasta and Maura, he embodied this corrupt political system. Alba, she contends, constituted 'un ejemplo doloroso: el del fraude de la ciudadanía' (133) and, accordingly, 'es, más que un político, un símbolo de la política actual' (133). As both Sagasta and Maura were considered architects of the *turno pacífico* and *caciquismo* system that De la Torre wholly condemned, they are discussed both as politicians and symbolic representatives of their opposing political ideations. According to the author herself, *El ágora* was not intended as a political biography *per se*, but rather an attempt to work through the pair's impact on the Spanish consciousness:

> Sólo he pretendido reflejar su influencia personal, el valor ideológico de su 'ademán' ciudadano sobre la marcha de la civilización del pueblo español. (5)

Though De la Torre's prologues typically reveal her political canniness and dry wit — such as the foreword to her scathing satirical critique of the Soviet Union: '"*El banquete de Saturno*" no es más que una novela' (1931: 9) — her reflection here is broadly accurate, as the 'pueblo español', specifically its autonomy, political engagement and consciousness, is most certainly the crux of her political interrogation. Pre-empting criticism from antagonistic conservatives, De la Torre (justifiably) insists that her analysis is not partisan, but rather driven by '[u]n sentimiento de humanización de la política en general' (6) and, so, accusations of '"exagerado antimilitarism", "pusilanimidad" y aun... "antipatriotismo criminal"' (6) will fall on deaf ears.

The use of quotation marks and the specificity of the complaints not only suggests that such admonishments had been levelled at the author through more 'informal' feedback, but also denotes how the texts constitute a communicative channel between De la Torre, her readership and Spain's dynamic political debates. As evidenced throughout this book, the self-conscious manipulation of dialogue that pervades De la Torre's political writings facilitates ideological introspection at an individual and collective level. With the bloody Rif War (1921–1926), which concluded with Spain ultimately retaining its enclaves, in recent memory for contemporary readers of *Don Quijote* and *El ágora*, Spain's colonial legacy is one ideological strand that critics latch on to. The *Nuevo Mundo* analysis of *Don Quijote* enthuses that De la Torre interrogates the impact of Spain's colonial history on the country's collective dissatisfaction with 'brillante sobriedad' (Galvarriato 1929: 3), while Luis Hernández Alfonso's write-up of *El ágora* in *La Libertad* endorses De la Torre's view that the colonial conflicts have permeated cultural and political discourses; '[s]ólo *unos pocos hombres* supieron aprender aquella terrible lección' (Hernández Alfonso 1931: 1; emphasis added). Comparing De la Torre with her male counterparts not only underscores her singularity as a female political critic, but also alludes to the androcentricity of the subject matters that she tackles in *Don Quijote* and *El ágora*, most notably war. Indeed, the few female correspondents that reported on international conflicts were acutely conscious of their sex; Carmen de Burgos, for instance, was sent to Morocco 'to view the war from a feminine perspective' (Pozzi 2000: 188), while Ángela Graupera, who reported on the First World War for *Las Noticias* whilst working as a nurse in Greece and Serbia, makes specific reference to women's experiences.[4]

Throughout *Don Quijote* and *El ágora*, De la Torre makes direct and oblique references to the question of sex. In both texts, she liberally uses 'hombre(s)' as a catch-all term for the mixed-sex population, acknowledging the prevalence of this overlap in *El ágora*: 'la palabra "hombre" se había llegado hasta la palabra "ciudadano"' (53). Though this is indeed an axiom, given 'man' has historically functioned as a gender neutral term for humanity, drawing focus to this oft-subconscious word choice underscores the implications of the linguistic erasure of women from these debates. Such an observation from the pen of a female critic only underlines the point further. At the same time, the word 'hombre' is invested with the tensions between the sexes and the gendered conflict between the 'masculine', political world and the 'feminine', natural environment — 'la Madre Tierra' — that underpins much of De la Torre's ideological introspection in *Don Quijote* and *El ágora*. It is, as she writes in *Don Quijote*, men who engage in war (124; 125), implying an organic conflict between the humanity De la Torre identifies with men and the 'female' natural world. There is, too, a covert — and justifiable — tangible resentment towards the cultural and political spheres from which she was excluded on the basis of sex: in *Don Quijote*, De la Torre interrogates '"los hombres del noventa y ocho"' (58) and '"derechos del hombre"' (161); and, in her foreword to *El ágora*, she refers to Sagasta and Maura as 'hombres' (5), rather than 'políticos' or 'Primer Ministros', for instance. Similarly, the — exclusively male — politicians of the Restoration are characterised as 'los "hombres nuevos"' (101).

Coding the androcentric spheres of culture and politics male, as is also the case in *Jardín*, De la Torre not only takes on a 'male' subject matter, but also utilises the male-dominated genre of political commentaries in order to underscore the masculinist qualities of *Don Quijote* and *El ágora*. Thus, the convergence of genre and topic that we saw in *Jardín* — where De la Torre capitalises on the 'feminine' epistolary format to interrogate feminist discourses — is inverted. (As noted in the Introduction, such eclecticism is perhaps one reason that her work has received little critical attention.) One salient conclusion to be drawn from De la Torre's decision to package her sociocultural and political analyses as straightforward commentaries, unlike *Jardín* and *El banquete de Saturno* which are both clear examples of fiction (albeit starkly different genres), is a clear desire to attract male readers. Rather than sycophantically requesting permission to contribute to these male-voiced debates, however, De la Torre is characteristically scathing and ironic. In the concluding pages to *El ágora*, she facetiously summarises the text as a collection of 'datos puramente biográficos' and 'apuntes de diccionario enciclopédico' (153) that, nonetheless, reveal 'todo el clasicismo de la sociedad política diecinuevina y vigintaria' (153) that characterises 'la historia del "hombre"' (153). It is by examining Spain's androcentric political history from a female perspective, as we shall see, that De la Torre contributes a fresh perspective on well-trodden intellectual ground by incorporating the oft-overlooked female voice.

'"Es preciso regenerarse" dijeron ellos': The Decadence and Decline of Spain

In *Don Quijote*, De la Torre utilises Spain's most well-known literary creation to interrogate the sense of collective failure brought about by the 1898 defeat to the United States. For the author, both Don Quijote and the *desastre* epitomise misplaced optimism. A logical metaphor that taps into the interface of Spain's cultural and political consciousness, the figure of Don Quijote encapsulates a nexus of literary and socio-political commentary that parallels with De la Torre's written output and depicts an imminently Spanish character. Though De la Torre's oeuvre has received little scholarly attention, *Don Quijote* has attracted recent (albeit still sparse) interest from critics, likely due to the eponymous reference to the fictional chivalrous hero. In the prologue to Antonio Martínez Cerezo's 2000 edition, he summarises how, for De la Torre, '[e]l idealismo quijotesco del siglo XX es la industrialización' (2000a: 41), while Francisco Layna Ranz recognises in 'Don Quijote y el error americano' how, in *Don Quijote*, '[l]a hora de Matilde de la Torre es la de la redención, política y económica antes que moral' (2019: 18). In De la Torre's own words, Quijote's futile pursuit of 'el Ideal' (142) was the core of his downfall, as 'no existiendo esa suma perfección, no podía hallarla el triste caballero de la Triste Figura' (142). Having failed 'por su heroísmo, por la excelsitud de sus aspiraciones' (143), Cervantes's protagonist and his characterisation — Quijotismo — therefore connotes 'la derrota, la humillación internacional y la inferioridad política...' (147). Extending the metaphor throughout the text, De la Torre compares the Spanish–American war to Quijote's iconic confrontation of allegorical windmills; '[e]n la guerra contra los americanos España quebró una vez más su lanza contra los molinos de viento' (56). In this battle against 'los elementos' (56), Spain is now in conflict with commerce, business, science and the labour market, the core components of societal and political structures that De la Torre constitutes 'la Naturaleza transformada' (56).

As is the case throughout this book, a closer look at the cultural, political and philosophical influences on De la Torre's writings is revealing. According to Martínez Cerezo, *Don Quijote* bears resemblance to the writings of José Ortega y Gasset:

> Orteguiana en el fondo, más que en la forma, el ideario de Matilde de la Torre es meridianamente claro: España debe olvidar ya de una vez por todas el sueño americano. Y debe olvidar, también, la estúpida ambición de españolizar Europa. Pasado su tiempo, desaprovechada su oportunidad histórica, lo que ahora le cumple el europeizar España. O sea, modernizarla. (2000a: 41)

A somewhat ambiguous descriptor, the characterisation of *Don Quijote* as 'Orteguiana en el fondo' denotes how De la Torre dialogues with Ortega y Gasset's work and emulates his style. Evidenced most clearly by the intertextual link between the title of De la Torre's text and Ortega y Gasset's first publication, *Meditaciones del Quijote* (1914),[5] De la Torre's interest in Spain's most famous philosopher reflects her attraction to philosophical dialogue, as examined in the previous chapter (specifically how it relates to contemporary Spain) and aligns with the core of Ortega and Gasset's academic priorities and political convictions. A supporter of both socialist ideals and the Party (see Dobson 1989: 46), Ortega y Gasset also shares De la Torre's tangible affection for their homeland[6] and sustained, focused analysis of the mutable relationship between the individual and the collective.[7]

The emphasis on political history and intellectualism in Ortega y Gasset's writings chimes with the core of *Don Quijote*, but so does De la Torre's forensic examination of the *desastre* of 1898. John Thomas Graham recognises that a 'loss of religious faith combined with the shock of Spain's national crisis' (1994: 70) resulted in what could be deemed 'an adolescent identity crisis' (1994: 70) for the young Ortega y Gasset. De la Torre, of course, is not the only Spanish female thinker and writer to be influenced by one of Spain's most famous philosophers; as Roberta Johnson notes, both Rosa Chacel and María Zambrano 'identified with Ortega's intellectual leadership in a number of ways' (1996: 54).[8] Whereas both Chacel and Zambrano, Johnson explains, foregrounded the self, utilising 'aesthetic beliefs and practices [that] were patently personalist, "self"-conscious, in direct contradiction to the maestro's dicta about art and literature' (1996: 54), De la Torre's style and form is more distanced and, therefore, more congruent with Ortega y Gasset's tradition. In terms of both subject matter and philosophical approach, however, the author's staunch feminism and her sex problematise De la Torre's discipleship to the proverbial father of Spanish philosophy. Though Ortega y Gasset maintained a felicitous professional relationship with women writers such as Victoria Ocampo and Rosa Chacel, feminist scholars have critiqued his response to feminism. In 'Leyendo a Ortega como mujer', Isabel Navas Ocaña argues that 'Ortega cree que el feminismo está aquejado de superficialidad' (2018: 128), citing his epilogue to Victoria Ocampo's *De Francesca a Beatrice a través de la 'Divina comedia'*, in which he writes that feminist thought lacked 'previsión intelectual' and failed to examine 'la influencia femenina en la historia' (Ortega y Gasset 1924: 134). '[E]l hombre vale por lo que hace; la mujer, por lo que es' (1924: 135), he continues; an observation that Celia Amorós quotes as demonstrative of the patriarcal undertones of Spanish philosophy (2007: 124).

Thus, though it would be reductive to present Ortega y Gasset as a symbol of patriarchal philosophy, there is, nevertheless, a tangible tension in how De la Torre, as a woman and a feminist, engages with his work. Examining the intertextuality between De la Torre and Ortega y Gasset through the prism of critical literature on dialogism illustrates how her engagement with hegemonic discourses problematises a feminist reading. An expressly feminist dialogics, critics argue, should focalise gender (Bauer and McKinstry 1991: 3; Yaeger 1991: 240) and resist patriarchal dominance (see Bauer 1988: 2; Herrmann 1989: 7). At the same time, however, drawing on philosophical traditions can be an effective means of substantiating one's arguments; as Bronwen Thomas explains, '[t]he appeal to tradition seems designed to provide a kind of validation of dialogue and to elevate it beyond the everyday' (2012: 37). *Jardín de damas curiosas* is a salient example of this complex relationship: while the text centres on her objections to the androcentricity of philosophical debate, the use of the epistolary genre suggests that she has taken into account Ortega y Gasset's argument that this literary paradigm is well-suited to women writers.[9] Similarly, *Don Quijote* plays on many of the core themes of *Meditaciones del Quijote*, specifically national reform, modernisation and national culture,[10] alluding to the question of sex, as De la Torre interrogates the intersection of the self, the state and history from an immanently female perspective. As noted above, for instance, the *Generación del 1898* are referred to as 'los hombres del noventa y ocho' (58, 59, 62), often printed with speech marks ('"los hombres del noventa y ocho"') so as to draw attention to the implications of this characterisation. Labelling political leaders as the 'hombres de gobierno' (58), 'los hombres de la "regeneración"' (59) and (the implicitly masculine) '[l]os políticos del noventa y ocho' (60), De la Torre identifies this pivotal socio-political climate with both the men at the forefront and an abstract sense of the masculinity that they embody.

Typically for De la Torre's writings, she plays on dialogue in order to parody her targets and scrutinise their failings. Rather than be (fairly) recognised as 'los hombres de desastre' (59), she notes, those men who dictated Spain's failed political and militaristic pursuits during the Spanish–American War are unjustifiably considered 'los hombres de la "regeneración"' (59). Is it, De la Torre rhetorically asks, because these men successfully realised Spain's so-called regeneration ('¿Acaso porque la llevaron a cabo?' [59])? With her sardonic wit, she facetiously answers her own question: 'No; de ninguna manera. Fue sencillamente que inventaron la frase' (59). As well as drawing focus to the male political leaders' failings and their impunity for these failures, De la Torre emphasises the import of language and dialogue in how this cultural and political narrative was constructed. Accordingly, commentaries on Spain's degeneration that pre-date 1898 are critiqued in such a way as to underscore and undermine discourse. In reference to the writer and diplomat Ángel Ganivet García (1865–1898), considered one of the precursors to the *Generación del 1898*, for instance, De la Torre paraphrases and corrects his core ideas:

> Cuando Ganivet dice que la singularidad de España estriba en su semejanza con los imperios antiguos con la circunstancia nueva de pervivencia después de perder el poderío político, olvidad que la vida nacional española ha transcurrido dentro de la fase de civilización informada ya en líneas generales por el Derecho. (65)

Similarly, she quotes 'Advertencia a España' by Francisco de Quevedo (1580–1645) verbatim in order to suggest that his view on collective hatred ('la fuerza destructiva del odio común' [79]) is ultimately lacking; 'Quevedo se equivocaba' (79). By appropriating the words of men that form part of Spain's cultural consciousness, De la Torre presupposes a broadly feminist position in two senses: not only does she contribute her female voice to phallocentric discourses, but she does so in such a way as to interrogate their failings.

Thus, though speech is evidently vital for De la Torre, she is, nevertheless, keen to scrutinise the hollowness of an unrealised regenerative project that was limited to debate and conjecture:

> 'Es preciso regenerarse' dijeron ellos. Y aunque nunca regeneraron nada, establecieron la necesidad de una regeneración. Solo las sagradas palabras pueden efectuar estos milagros. (59)

Ironically mocking the proposed 'sagradas palabras' (59) and touching on the obscurity and evasiveness of efforts to reform — '"[e]s preciso regenerarse"' — De la Torre underscores how the objective of 'los hombres del noventa y ocho' was fundamentally unclear and, therefore, futile. De la Torre, not unexpectedly, sticks in the proverbial knife, reiterating to the reader her belief that '[l]os políticos del noventa y ocho no entendieron esto' (60). Discourse and dialogue are crucial to how De la Torre formulates this criticism, with her appropriation of the words of the politicians she chastises indicative of how she mockingly mimics those she deems responsible. While there are similar instances in which De la Torre risks prioritising the voices and ideas of the men she is condemning through her disparaging mimicry, which is particularly problematic when a woman quotes the words of men, the ambiguity and vacuity of ' "[e]s preciso regenerarse" ' underlines both the futility of this political project and how speech shapes the cultural narrative.

De la Torre's critique of the failures of '[l]os políticos del noventa y ocho' and 'los hombres del noventa y ocho' are further interrogated in *El ágora*. While her critique in *Don Quijote* centres on how a collective — at points abstract and intangible — sense of failure permeates Spanish society, reflecting the degradation of the country's political structures, the scrutiny in *El ágora* is more focused on Spain's leading political actors. Arguing that 'la "regeneración" ha fracasado' (103), De la Torre alludes to the political corruption and impotence that led to this abortive attempt at political and cultural regeneration: 'Todos los políticos, sin excepción alguna, han defraudado las esperanzas del pueblo' (103). The male politicians that failed Spanish society, according to De la Torre, have therefore not adequately represented the Spanish *pueblo*; a descriptor that speaks to the author's socialist politics. De la Torre's longstanding moral and ideological objection to *caciquismo* is tangible, as will be explored in the final section of this chapter, as she looks beyond the post-1898 decline by acknowledging the failings of the Spanish state during the *turno pacífico* era. Contemplating the turmoil of the Restoration climate, De la Torre reflects on the governments of Sagasta, which she refers to as 'aquellos días nuevos de la libertad' (8), and Maura, who, she writes, rose to power when industrialism and 'el fracas del "hecho" de la libertad política' (74) were taking root.

In accordance with her commitment to writing an impartial critique of the Restoration political establishment — that is, not overly sycophantic or object-ionable — De la Torre's descriptions of both the Liberal Party leader Sagasta and Conservative Maura reflect her insight and candour. Sagasta, she writes, 'fué un político de tragicomedia, como casi todos los hombres diecinuevinos que prohijaron la libertad política' (7). As well as deftly critiquing both Sagasta's career and the illiberal, male-dominated political structures of Restoration Spain, which is connoted through the reference to 'los hombres diecinuevinos', the characterisation of Sagasta's tenure as a 'tragicomedia' illustrates how, for De la Torre, literary and political convention intersect. Slyly excoriating Sagasta's conservatism and ineptitude by noting that 'no era un prodigio como político' (8), she describes him as '[u]n hombre activo, inteligente, travieso, curioso de la emoción de mandar' (8). Rather than focus his attention on his political enemies, De la Torre writes, Sagasta prioritises the needs of the masses: 'Su preocupación es el pueblo, la masa nacional, que bulle y se agita en el ajetreo del diario vivir de su trabajo' (12).

Despite harbouring a moral and ideological integrity that aligns with De la Torre's socialist values, Sagasta was, however, unable to realise his goals. Although, for Sagasta, '[l]a masa nacional le parece un mar navegable para su nave del Progreso' (12), the political climate made such ideals untenable:

> Él es ministro de una flamante República tan llena de ideales que no podía mantenerse a flote. En política se da casi infaliblemente la paradoja de que lo irreal es el laste inexorable de la acción. Un Gobierno muere mucho más por las ilusiones que abriga que por los errores que comete... (12)

Not only does De la Torre critique Sagasta's failings from her point of view, utilising the narrative voice, but so too does she speak on behalf of the Liberal leader in order to convey how he processes his own culpability. Focusing on the country's economic failings, she muses that Sagasta would emphasise how the market restricted his ability to enact effective reform:

> En una defensa a muerte él hubiera siempre podido argüir:
> — Yo no he mejorado la Hacienda pública; pero tampoco la mía privada. Yo no he podido sembrar el suelo de pesetas sanas; pero nunca adquirí ese compromiso, sino el de sembrar sanas ideas... ¡Si no han fructificado, no soy yo el único culpable! El terreno ha respondido mal... (30)

Operating under a spurious democratic system, De la Torre supposes, meant that Sagasta and his fellow politicians lacked the ability to facilitate reform. In a cutting aside that stresses the political capital of language and expression as well as the androcentricity of the Restoration, she argues that '[n]i Sagasta ni ninguno de los hombres que entones se repartieron (¡qué a gusto se encuentra aquí el verbo "repartir"!) el Poder podían ocuparse de aquella mejora' (31). (The emphasis on the meaning of 'repartir' can be read as a sardonic gibe that underlines the undemocratic nature of *caciquismo* and the *turno pacífico*.) Accordingly, a core element of De la Torre's examination is the extent to which these politicians can be held responsible for their shortcomings. Given the political leaders of the Restoration were fully aware that the political structure lacked solid foundations ('[b]ien sabían que el suelo era de arena y guijarros' [31]), there is an ambiguous sense of culpability. Although their theories were relatively sound, an infelicitous political climate ultimately impeded the implementation of effective policies; '[e]llos se limitaban a arrojar puñados de buena teoría en el suelo' (31).

Conflict between ideals and reality is also critical to the outline of Sagasta's Conservative counterpart, Maura, who is presented as intellectual and ideological:

> Un político puro, un filósofo que ha estudiado detenidamente el proceso de las leyes nuevas, se encuentra en posesión de un programa ideológico adaptado a las nuevas conquistas políticas. (74–75)

De la Torre's complimentary take on Maura likely stems from his — albeit unsuccessful — efforts to reform the *cacique* system that she so loathed and his aim to empower the middle classes (see Romero Salvadó 2012). Indeed, Maura's firm belief in democracy, advocacy for Spain's middle class and idealistic approach to politics, believing that 'the people should participate, and that every field in politics should be worked at and dignified' (González 2002: 307), all strongly resonate with De la Torre's ideological priorities. Her emphasis on his intellectualism, moreover, reflects contemporary critics' growing resentment to the Liberals' failings. As Angel Smith explains:

> the image of the archetypal liberal passed from being that of a talented and sincere intellectual and/or activist who was fighting for liberty and an end to the privileges enjoyed by the Church and aristocracy, to that of an electoral fixer in a smoke-filled room who was doing the bidding of the 'oligarchy'. (2016: 55)

Foregrounding the Conservative politician's ideological purity, in this sense, can be read in relation to De la Torre's unwavering belief in the democratic liberty that Maura broadly supported and, at the same time, a way of blurring the presumed identification between intellectualism and the left. Despite Maura's integrity and principles, which De la Torre graciously references as 'su limpieza de ideales' (73) and 'su documentada convicción' (75), however, his ideology fails in practice; 'no bastaron estas dotes para que la huella de su mando sirviera de avance sociológico positivo' (73). Though he presided over 'un régimen de honrado conservadurismo' (75) — an endorsement that almost sounds like an oxymoron coming from a lifelong leftist — Maura, De la Torre deduces, was ultimately unable to realise his ideals.

De la Torre's assessment of Sagasta and Maura's political reigns not only evidences her anxiety with the core of a Spanish political system that stifles progress, but also corrupts those who attempt to reform it. As explored throughout this book, it is this latent conflict between theory and practice that forms the basis of De la Torre's interrogation. Her evident discomfort with political dogma and hostility to ideological introspection, which is fundamental to her novel *El banquete de Saturno*, is hinted at through her reference to Maura's unrealised attempts at reform. (The description of Maura as possessing 'un tipo de virtud marco-aureliana' [73], in reference to the Roman emperor and philosopher, offers another parallel with *El banquete* given classical references pervade the text.) It is in her re-evaluation of Maura's political classification that De la Torre unravels the decadence that underpins the political establishment, sardonically noting that he was 'más bien revolucionario que liberal' (76). Having aligned with the Conservatives out of necessity and practicality rather than a fixed ideological loyalty, Maura and his politics are moulded by a system that he is unable to dictate:

> Maura ingresa en el partido conservador porque, tal como estaba entendido el liberalismo español, su lugar se había desplazado de allí. Fué conservador por adaptación a la necesidad ambiente de gobernar corroborando las conquistas que vacilaban al instaurarse. (76)

As well as revealing De la Torre's (perhaps unexpected) tolerance for politicians with whom, at least in theory, she disagreed on a fundamental level, this observation also connotes how a corrupt regime problematises political demarcation. The salient implication here is that De la Torre's socialist objectives would be untenable in this climate.

Though *El ágora* is centred on Restoration Spain, there are critical parallels to the climate in which it was written that denote a more overtly contemporaneous political commentary. As outlined at the beginning of this chapter, both *Don Quijote* and *El ágora* were published during the Primo de Rivera dictatorship, when Spain was experiencing a political reconfiguration and collective identity crisis that reflects many of the core debates of the Restoration period. Not only does focalising a historical political period (rather than the current administration) eschew any difficulties with censorship, but so too does it afford De la Torre a means of drawing out parallels, however obliquely, that continue to plague Spanish political structures. One example is her consideration for the country's financial burden after the *desastre* (127),[11] given economic stagnation was a central obstacle for the Primo de Rivera regime.[12] Questions of how best to rehabilitate the country also persisted, as the promise of reformation by way of a republican administration was within touching distance. With this in mind, *Don Quijote* and *El ágora* should be understood not just as historical political commentaries, but also dialectics that indirectly outline the systematic failures that must be addressed before progress is possible. Both works, indeed, were published just a year before the inauguration of the Second Republic.

While *Don Quijote* establishes a historical interrogation of the abstract concepts that shape Spain's collective political consciousness, it is in *El ágora* that De la Torre confronts ways of overcoming key obstacles. Dialoguing with debates surrounding the shortcomings of Spanish liberalism and iterating revolutionary discourse, she simultaneously appraises, endorses and refracts Maura's position:

> Maura ha sido más bien revolucionario que liberal. Ha preconizado la necesidad de una revolución y aun la ha definido en una frase lapidaria: 'Si el Poder no la verifica desde arriba, el pueblo la verificará desde abajo'. (11)

Drawing on Maura's policy of revolution 'from above' — 'revolución desde arriba' — De la Torre utilises her political analysis as a means of obliquely inciting revolution. It is by echoing what is perhaps the Conservative leader's most preeminent political argument that De la Torre is able to shift focus from Spain's political structures to its citizens. What is ostensibly a citation, in this sense, can be understood as an oblique suggestion; given we know that Maura's approach ultimately failed, the logical alternative is revolution 'desde abajo'. By attributing a quotation to Maura in such a way as to reframe the objective so that it more closely aligns with her own ideological loyalties, De la Torre simultaneously foregrounds her own political strategy and scrutinises the limitations of established — and well-known — tactics, policies and ruminations.

It is when De la Torre revisits Maura's conceptualisation of revolution 'from above' that she is more explicit in her scrutiny of how best to transform Spain's retrograde political system. In what can conceivably be understood as an attempt to engage her reader in the task of introspective political analysis, De la Torre lays out her thought process, effectively scripting her deliberation:

> Maura comprende la necesidad de una transformación violenta, ya que la inercia política no parece alterable por reflexiones filosóficas...
> — 'Si vosotros no hacéis la revolución desde arriba, el pueblo la hará desde abajo'.
> Ahora bien: ¿Qué idea tenía Maura de una revolución?
> Acaso una idea física aplicada a la mecánica. Una revolución era, desde luego, una vuelta entera de un disco.
> ¿Pero... en qué sentido?
> ¿Hacia la derecha? ¿Hacia la izquierda? Desde luego, el disco se considera fijo sobre el eje. No cabe la idea del desplazamiento. (78)

The inherent futility of political philosophies that cannot be realised under a restrictive, impotent governmental system, she proposes, demand a more robust response. Given the suggestion of a 'violent' revolt ('una transformación violenta') appears to be at odds with De la Torre's pacifist tendencies (which is discussed in Chapters One and Three), we should perhaps understand this descriptor as a hyperbolic use of revolutionary rhetoric that aims to underscore the need for radical, rather than bloody, reform. Simultaneously dialoguing with Maura's politics and De la Torre's internalised political dialectic, the narrative navigates between the two in such a way as to invite the reader to interrogate Spain's political structures. The rhetorical questions (¿Qué idea tenia Maura de una revolución?; ¿Pero... en qué sentido?; ¿Hacia la derecha?; ¿Hacia la izquierda?), in this sense, indicate the reflections and doubts of both De la Torre and the reader, connoting an extratextual political dialogue that links author, reader and the political establishment.

'La Patria es hembra': Sexing Spain's Political History

Despite the fact that De la Torre underscores the androcentricity of Spain's political system and cultural output through frequent, albeit subtle, references to the salient fact that these political leaders and commentators were — almost without exception — men, an overt feminist critique is not always tangible in *Don Quijote* and *El ágora*. There is, for instance, no explicit engagement with how Spanish women fare within these male-dominated spheres, nor is there a concrete argument that details the benefits of women's political participation. To some degree, this reflects how De la Torre's texts prioritise specific ideological questions; having explored feminism and women's rights in *Jardín de damas curiosas*, her attention in *Don Quijote* and *El ágora* shifts to political history, a field that is undeniably centred on men. Nevertheless, there are various inklings that suggest a female critique. Not only does De la Torre's nuanced, thorough interrogation constitute an implicit feminist statement, given her knowledge and intellect evidences women's capability for political analysis, but her use of symbolism and language also suggests an attempt to utilise what could be interpreted as a female — or even feminine — writing style.

On the one hand, her characterisation of the Spanish political structure is often invested with sexual politics and gendered imagery. The political climate when Sagasta takes power, for instance, is described in *El ágora* as a period in which '[la] libertad era una virgen' (8) and, yet, those in charge were ignorant to the difficulties this presented: 'España ignoró que había pasado el puente del fracaso político, arribando a la cuestión social *con la virginidad* de sus males' (68; emphasis added). Similarly, the failure of previous Spanish rulers to recognise the impact of the Monroe doctrine, which considered interference in the Americas by a European nation as a sign of hostility, is mockingly lamented; 'ningún gobernante *ha desflorado su virginal ignorancia* sobre la legitimidad del coloniaje centralista' (38; emphasis added). Sardonically musing about Spanish politicians' illiteracy of US political history and this critical policy ('[n]ingún gobernante ha perdido el tiempo averiguando quién fué Monroe' [38]), De la Torre indirectly proportions a degree of blame to those who could have anticipated the fallout of the Spanish–American war. The doctrine, indeed, was drafted in response to Spain's colonial interest in the

Americas.[13] It is, therefore, conceivable that more awareness of the implications of the Monroe document could have mitigated the brutal impact of the *desastre* that, as discussed above, De la Torre saw as a symptom of broader political failings.

In all these examples, the well-established metaphor of conquering 'virgin' land is used in such a way as to reframe it in order to focalise what can be understood as intellectual 'territory'. Rather than foreground, and implicitly endorse, a nationalistic appetite for acquiring land, in other words, De la Torre's focus is on cultivating an academic, political and international awareness. The use of a metaphor that is intrinsically linked to imagery of sexual domination brings to mind the author's sex. Drawing on such imagery as a means of scrutinising the intellectual and political shortcomings of men constitutes a hyperbolic criticism of their capability for office that connotes a conflict between De la Torre and the subjects of her critique that is centred on sex. There is, moreover, the suggestion of strategically subverting this symbolism given it is invested with patriarchal supremacy. De la Torre, in other words, mocks the 'virginal' ignorance of Spain's male politicians in order to underline not just that she is a competent analyst in spite of her sex, but that she possesses added insight *because* she is a woman. The author's idiosyncratic wit is tangible throughout, however, as De la Torre's implementation of sexed metaphors about state and nation is invested with a tongue-in-cheek undertone that leaves the distinct impression that, despite capitalising on the affective capital of such imagery, she does so with a degree of critical awareness.

Even when recognising the strengths of male politicians, De la Torre describes the androcentric political sphere in relation to the feminine. Acknowledging Sagasta's sensitivity to the corruption that permeates the Spanish political system, for example, she commends him for understanding how, 'en política, como en amor, no hay palabra; que todo ardid es permitido' (11). In a consideration of Catalonian independence movements that continues to resonate in the present-day landscape, De la Torre extends the metaphor of sexual conquest. Before examining her use of imagery, it is worth underlining how this reference to Catalan nationalism exemplifies the contemporary pertinence of De la Torre's political writings, given debates and conflict continue to dominate twenty-first century Spanish politics, and illustrates how her political concerns blur the boundaries between the abstract, theoretical argumentation and shifts in the political climate. By linking political philosophy to current circumstance, in this sense, De la Torre effectively demonstrates the practical application of political theory. Despite her evident interest in the progress of Catalan nationalism, however, the thorough dissection apparent in relation to other political questions and matters is wanting here; a lack of conviction that could be a result of both geographical and ideological distance.

Focusing this section on to Maura's tenure, De la Torre recognises how it is impossible to predict how these tensions will play out with her observation that '[l] o cierto es que ni el gobernante ni los gobernados saben la finalidad de movimiento catalán' (90). As well as providing a salient example of how De la Torre's political observations, read retrospectively, often prove to be even more prophetic than she could have envisaged, her thoughts here also conflate the political leader ('el gobernante') with the Spanish proletariat ('los gobernados') in such a way as to connote both the turbulence of the situation and imply that, in instances such as this, leaders do not necessarily have greater foresight than common citizens. The implicit egalitarianism of this parallel can also be read as an oblique critique of the asymmetric power dynamic of the governor and the governed. Though her personal opinion on the consequences if Catalonia were to secede is relatively ambiguous, what is clear is De la Torre's discomfort with the misrepresentation of leftist ideals and violent fallout of 'la Semana Trágica'. Lamenting how the confrontations reflected 'un desorden de carácter socialista, anarquista y hasta quién sabe si republicano...' (90), all ideological positions that De la Torre broadly supports,[14] she concludes that, though 'Barcelona da entonces un grito justo' (91), it was, fundamentally, 'tan prematuro que no puede tener eco' (91).

In a visceral, resonant description of the violence that encompassed the city, De la Torre utilises imagery that evokes the female body. Underscoring the violence of the revolts, she summarises 'la Semana Trágica' as follows:

> Una imprescindible y sana lógica de pervivencia nacional ahoga en sangre el movimiento barcelonés, porque es nada más *el aborto del futuro aun en gestación normal* en el resto del mundo. (91; emphasis added)

The use of symbolism that evokes pregnancy and gestation relates the country's national history to the female body by drawing on the sexed metaphor of nature as feminine.[15] Likely taking inspiration from Ortega y Gasset, who also linked women and nature (see Navas Ocaña, 2018), De la Torre taps into the concept of a failed pregnancy (bearing in mind that 'aborto' could translate to mean both 'miscarriage' and 'abortion') in order to convey the futility of the uprisings. The haunting image of Barcelona drowned in blood ('pervivencia nacional ahoga en sangre el movimiento barcelonés') reinforces this metaphor, recalling the biblical mythology of Eve's treachery in the Garden of Eden. There is, in this sense, an oblique suggestion of sexing the revolutionary (which spurred 'la Semana Trágica') as female and the hegemonic establishment (the 'pervivencia nacional') as male; a dichotomy that brings to mind the socialist narrative of the conception and metaphorical birth of systemic reform. Though this example failed to be realised, identifying the revolt with pregnancy, albeit abortive in this instance, suggests an organic, productive quality of revolt. (As will be discussed in the next chapter, reproduction and birth as a metaphor for the revolution and a clear objection to violent revolts are also alluded to in *El banquete de Saturno*.)

While the association between the feminine and nature is not limited to female authors or philosophers, it does, nevertheless, come with added significance when this is the case. De la Torre's approach to sexing the natural world, that is to say, is shaped, to some degree, by both her sex and her feminist politics. A salient point of contrast to illustrate this point is Ortega y Gasset: though the male philosopher scrutinised the symbolic femininity of nature, his ambiguity on feminist issues (noted in the previous section) means that his take is likely inflected by stereotypical feminine traits. As a woman and a feminist, on the other hand, De la Torre is well-placed to make use of this firmly established cultural trope. At the same time, interrogate the implicit patriarchy that underpins it. Her depiction of 'la Semana Trágica' as akin to an unsuccessful pregnancy, with this in mind, can be read as a sardonic subversion of the socialist narrative of 'birthing' the revolution. Indeed, investing the abortive uprising with an unorthodox take on womanhood (that is, a failed pregnancy) suggests an authorial desire to not simply reinforce sexed symbolism, but rework it.

On one level, De la Torre works within the established binary of the feminine natural world and masculine political sphere. In both texts, the land is identified with the female and maternity through references to 'la Madre Tierra'; an allegory that is invested with the notions of genesis and regeneration that underpin De la Torre's political philosophy. In *Don Quijote*, colonisation and conquest are interrogated in relation to the sexed metaphor of penetrative invasion and, yet, the matriarchal, natural order prevails. The fact that conquests are not fully realised, with usurpation never absolute, given the inevitable miscegenation that it entails, is indicative of the land's inherently female power: 'Una ley biológica esencialmente matriarcal, hace predominar los caracteres de la tierra sobre la influencia del conquistador' (129). Though this argumentation lacks a degree of cultural consciousness, and does little in the way of critiquing discourses of racial or cultural hierarchies (as illustrated by the following: 'que la conquista no llega a ser étnicamente absoluto porque la energía raza conquistadora se diluye en la raza conquistada, naturalmente superior en todo caso' [129]), De la Torre's conceptualisation of a matriarchal, biological law delineates a primitive, moralistic protector that resists colonial domination.

The symbolic undertones of sexual purity and virginity noted at the beginning of this section are reinforced here in such a way as to present an inherently female defence against foreign aggression. Establishing that '[l]a tierra es hembra' (129), De la Torre reasons that it therefore 'conserva sus características necesarias en una virginidad siempre renovada' (129). The oxymoronic construct of a 'regenerative' virginity ('una virginidad siempre renovada' [129]) offers an intriguing insight into how De la Torre grapples with the implications of a patriarchal concept, as she re-conceptualises 'virgin' land in such a way as to present the notion of remaining untouched as an active, almost empowering quality. Rather than a passive state of being, in other words, virginity functions as a fitting metaphor for a dynamic resistance to an invading force that is intrinsically linked to the female sex.

Developing this point, De la Torre elaborates on how she draws a distinction between invasion and conquest:

> La diferencia entre la invasión y la conquista es puramente étnica. Los pueblos invasores acaban, al final de siglos, por sustituir una raza por otra (grandes emigraciones mongólicas, germanas, etc., que dieron fisonomía a los actuales países). Los pueblos conquistadores (los macedonios en Asia, los árabes en España, los españoles en América..., etc.) acaban siendo absorbidos por la Madre Tierra. (130)

With the primordial 'Madre Tierra' serving as a counterbalance to military intervention, sexual politics plays out on an international scale. Indigenous women, De la Torre argues, maintain a natural connection to the land and, accordingly, resist total domination. Explaining this through a metaphorical marriage, she concludes:

> Son los movimientos de conquista guerrera desplazamientos incompletos en el estricto sentido de la palabra: Van los hombres solos. Apenas establecidos en el nuevo país fundan allí su hogar emparejando con la hembra indígena. *Es decir: se han casado con la Madre Tierra y ya jamás conquistarán la tierra.* (131; emphasis added)

The gender and sexual politics function on two levels here, as De la Torre considers both how the male invaders and local women converge and utilises the gendered metaphor of the male foreign force and native female land. (The brutality experienced by women in this context is explored later in the chapter.)

Though explicating this micro and macro union in relation to marriage implies harmony, and arguably an oblique conservatism, the defensive, protective character of women who are empowered by the intrinsically female 'Madre Tierra' delineates a degree of equity. An organic, intrinsically female strength is delineated in such a way as to presuppose a balance and form of resistance, underlining how the indigenous land is ultimately impenetrable:

> En esta lucha hay por fin una asimilación: es la Madre Tierra la que se apodera del invasor. Se apodera de la acción física y le infiltra su espíritu indígena. (132)

Just as marriage serves as a symbolic representation of the miscegenation of two cultures through invasion and conquest, the act of copulation and the sexual encounter conveys the complexities of foregrounding a gendered equilibrium in this context. On one level, the empathically sexed roles of subject and object are reinforced in De la Torre's reasoning: 'El varón es elemento dinámico; la hembra el elemento estático: tierra y semilla' (130). Conception is depicted as a violating exploitation by which the male invader is victorious, with the fusing of different races and lands presented as interrelated. Fertilisation, De la Torre explicates, 'se verifica a expensas de los elementos maternales' (130) and, so, 'la raza pervivirá a través de la invasión conquistadora' (130).

While this conceptualisation of '[e]l movimiento de germinación' (130) seems to contradict the understated dynamism of the 'Madre Tierra' that De la Torre heralds, there is a somewhat rational acceptance of the asymmetric power imbalance of the conqueror and the conquered. Nevertheless, control remains ultimately — albeit subtly — with the female and the feminine world that she represents. Rather than subvert the foundations of the active and passive roles, De la Torre imbues the stagnant object with an ethereal potency:

> Pervivirá en una aclimatación siempre contraria al elemento masculino dinámico. Tomará de él en una selección instintiva, los caracteres necesarios de agresividad y los encauzará en una reacción conservadora del elemento estático indígena. (131)

Though the sexed binaries of active/passive and subject/object are upheld, an intrinsically female sovereignty is presupposed by the act of natural selection ('una selección instintiva'). There is an inevitable tension to this reframing. Not only does it rely upon a fundamentally conservative understanding of the female as (at least ostensibly) passive, but it also presents a moderating force ('una reacción conservadora') as both beneficial and indispensable. The result is to the convergence of two rivalling tribes, 'el indígena, amparado por la Madre Tierra y el extraño, cultivado por la acción del invasor' (131), which De la Torre describes as 'dos "movimientos" contrarios' (131).

As well as relating these ideas to an abstract understanding of colonial invasion, De la Torre also applies these immanently sexed theories to Spain's political structures. In *El ágora*, for example, the primitive insight of the female natural world is used as a means of characterising Sagasta's premiership: the Liberal Party leader, De la Torre writes, cultivated political ideals ('las más puras concepciones idearias y sentimentales en la política' [68]) borne out of nature, 'la tierra madre' (68). That is not to suggest, however, that De la Torre presents this as a positive influence. Indeed, she expounds, Sagasta's legacy is fundamentally that of well-meaning failure; despite possessing 'la extraña virtud' (68) that should facilitate political innovation, his intervention was ultimately abortive due to the *caciquismo* system that 'aisló a España de la universal ilusión entonces ambiente: la eficacia del sistema puramente parlamentario para lograr el progreso social' (68–69).

On the other hand, Maura, the Conservative leader, represents the masculine interloper; 'el hombre político' (84) who, having assumed power in 1907, is unable to realise his objective of enforcing reform. The incertitude as to how to accomplish this feat prompts De la Torre to invite her readers to reflect on the intricacies of this aim: 'No es fácil reorganizar la fuerza, porque... observamos. ¿Qué es Fuerza? (así, con mayúscula)' (84). Drawing attention to what she deems Maura's desire to engender restructure through undemocratic means, De la Torre breaks her narrative flow in order to engage the reader and, critically, alludes to the potency of language when interrogating political endeavours. We may conclude, in accordance with De la Torre's solicitation, that Maura lacked the foresight to determine how to implement this restructuring, given the political establishment ('[la] Fuerza') lacked a clear model. Echoing the imagery that she utilises in relation to invasion, De la Torre considers how the core of Spain's political system is centred on the armed forces and, accordingly, men. As a means of underlining this point, she leads the reader through her thought process by transcribing her reasoning: 'Suponiendo que fuerza sea ejército y escuadra, el ejército está compuesto por... hombres' (84). Despite her ostensive effort to explicate this position, De la Torre arguably skips a proverbial step; from Maura's political objective of the reconstruction of Restoration Spain to the male-dominated armed forces, the logical link between the two rests on the implicit parallels of the state and military. Taken in conjunction with De la Torre's politics, it would appear that this linkage, which is particularly cogent in the context of a Spain grappling with its domestic and international interests, is underlined as a means of underscoring the androcentricity of Spain's power structures.

Though De la Torre refrains from directly associating her sexed metaphors of colonial invasion with the political positions of the Restoration leaders, identifying Sagasta with the 'la tierra madre' and Maura with the masculinist invader hints at the male/conservative female/liberal dichotomy that is critical to De la Torre's political tensions. Perhaps the most salient point is the implicit identification of the

Liberal Sagasta with the feminine and the Conservative Maura with the masculine; a parallel that would suggest a more accommodating take on the Liberal leader's politics than is immediately obvious. Though tempting to overstate De la Torre's apparent preference for the feminine, in accordance with her liberalism, her ample contempt for the *caciquismo* system suggests that this contrast delineates an academic observation, rather than a means of criticising the implicit machismo of conservatism. Indeed, given that a major concern of De la Torre's is the limited ideological distinctions between two parties both repressed by an undemocratic process, it would be reductive to assume a feminine/reformative masculine/repressive binary, at least in this instance. There is, in other words, no reason to infer that her identification of Maura with the masculine evinces an objection to his politics or career. Instead, we can read this comparison as a commentary on how his style maps onto the sexed imagery that forms a core component of the political consciousness.

It is the examples in which De la Torre relates sexed metaphors about the state and nation to women's experiences that she most effectively capitalises on the affective potential of this symbolism. Reflecting on the War of Independence in *El ágora*, De la Torre considers the female — and feminine — role in the conflict. The women play a supporting role that is based on nurturing and caregiving; with 'un sublime arranque del ternura maternal conmovedora' (49), those 'mujeres caritativas' (49) care for the injured soldiers. In *Don Quijote*, similarly, she considers how Spanish soldiers are likely shaped by the homes — and, implicitly, mothers — that raise them: 'Es muy posible que en muchos hogares españoles, cunas de futuros soldados se leyese por la noche al amor de la lumbre algún libro de caballerías' (116). The narratives of the *conquistadores* are also considered in relation to women in *Don Quijote*. Quoting the work of contemporary historian Francisco López de Gómara (c.1511–1559), De la Torre cites a passage from his hugely successful *Historia general de las Indias y conquista de México* (first published in 1552) that focalises the experiences of the women who chaperoned Atahualpa, the last Inca emperor. The dialogue with Gómara's work is underlined through quotation marks, with De la Torre pointedly quoting the eminent historian:

> 'Hallaron en el baño y real de Atabaliba cinco mil mujeres que aunque tristes y desamparadas, holgaron con los cristianos; muchas y buenas tiendas; infinita ropa de vestir; servicio de casa y lindas piezas y vasijas de oro y plata, una de las cuales pesó ocho arrobas de oro. Valió en fin, la vajilla de Atabaliba cien mil ducados...' (Gómara). (115)

While there is no explicit acknowledgment of the patriarchal culture that puts (presumably prostituted) women in this desperate position from Gómara, De la Torre's reiteration of this passage implies a reorientation of focus that foregrounds the anonymous women. Despite the abundance of luxuries and opulence that surround this multitude of women, they are ultimately dissatisfied and powerless ('aunque tristes y desamparadas') in an environment centred on men. Seemingly without endorsing Gómara's polemical work,[16] which was criticised by many of his contemporaries (including those who used his writings as a source),[17] De la

Torre distils this canonical political text in such a way as to highlight the female experience.

Remembering that both *Don Quijote* and *El ágora* were published when the Second Republic was within reach, it stands to reason that De la Torre was quietly optimistic that women would soon become more prominent in Spanish public life. Her decision to write the texts would suggest as much, as the subject matter denotes a self-conscious delineation of women's political engagement. In *Don Quijote*, De la Torre's eulogistic endorsement of Elizabeth I (of England) alludes to women's political perception. Pre-empting an attack by the Spanish Armada (patriotically referred to as 'la Invencible' [121]), De la Torre details how England's monarch sought support from Parliament as she was acutely aware of the potential threat to her country: 'Sabe del poder español más que nadie; lo teme más que nadie' (121). An astute female political leader who, in this case, is not Spanish, connotes women's capability for international politics without undermining the characterisation of the Spanish political system as fundamentally androcentric. The author's concerted effort to underscore this point to her reader is illustrated through the somewhat sycophantic adulation of a Spain once feared by its (or perhaps *her*) enemies. Read within the melancholic philosophy of a country recently humiliated on the international stage, reference to the now impotent 'poder español' serves as an oblique reminder that Spain is at a critical juncture in its social and political development.

As examined in the previous section, the fallout of the Spanish–American War, specifically its impact on the collective political consciousness, is fundamental to De la Torre's analysis of Spain's tumultuous climate. Referencing the conflict in *El ágora*, De la Torre scrutinises how the press utilised sexed and sexual imagery to galvanise the Spanish people and, accordingly, shape the way in which the defeat was perceived. It was, she reasons, imperative to inspire the population ('excitar al pueblo' [57]) and so inflammatory headlines were used, such as: '¡¡Los asesinos de nuestros pobres soldados quieren violar la metrópoli!!' (57). The concept of a metaphorical, political rape is reiterated, as De la Torre notes how 'la violación de las metrópolis' (57) evokes 'el machismo su integridad más brutal y genésica' (58). Logic dictates, then, that '[l]a Patria es hembra' (58) and so the patriotism inspired by this incendiary imagery reinforces, rather than subverts, an implicit machismo. Much in the same way that the political system is literally and metonymically coded male, then, the *pueblo* relates to Spain's domestic and international enterprises through a sexed lens. If, as De la Torre argues, 'el valor mítico de ese término "patria violada" enciende la ferocidad sexual del patriota' (58), sexual and state politics intersect in such a way as to facilitate the public's understanding of and interest in the formal running of the country. That is not to suggest, however, that political engagement is strong, but rather that sexual imagery proves an effective means of conceiving of a structure and phenomenon that, for many, remains elusive.

'La "política"... no le importa al pueblo': Political Disengagement and the *Pueblo*

As De la Torre's distaste for the *caciquismo* system indicates, a central theme of her political discontent stems from the disconnect between Spain's leadership and its citizens. On one level, this could be resolved through a redistribution of power that empowers the people, in line with a core objective of socialist ideation. Leftist doctrines, indeed, are typically united in their desire to overturn the exploitative capitalist model. Most socialist and Marxist philosophers, however, favour a strong — oft-authoritarian — state, with anarchism a notable exception to this trend. It is this component of socialism that De la Torre finds the most unpalatable; as examined throughout this book, the inevitable tension between individual autonomy and a leftist state frequently arises as a source of introspection for De la Torre, on both a personal and theoretical level. The socialist revolution that De la Torre evidently covets is therefore problematised by her somewhat paradoxical principles, which aim to prioritise both the individual and the collective. Rather than view her compatriots as a means to revolutionary ends, De la Torre also seems to harbour a desire to foment an academic — even philosophical — interest in her political ideals. Her aim to engage the populace, in other words, goes beyond a cynical interest in mobilising the masses simply as a means of engendering reform; rather she foregrounds the political imperative of ideological consciousness raising.

In order to underscore the contemporary relevance of her focused interrogation of the breach between Spain's political establishment and the *pueblo* it is supposed to represent, De la Torre details how political disengagement made the Primo de Rivera regime possible. Not only was the Spanish population politically ignorant, as she explains in *El ágora*, so were the politicians:

> El pueblo no creía ya absolutamente nada cuando vino la Dictadura...
> Mas lo verdaderamente terrible fué que... ¡los políticos tampoco creían ya en nada! (146)

Rather than an isolated phenomenon, this sense of disaffection is historicised. Echoing the pathological imagery used by many of the 1898 Generation, including Ortega y Gasset and the intellectual Joaquín Costa,[18] De la Torre describes Spain's debilitating political fragility and inertia as a form of sickness. Sagasta, she outlines in *El ágora*, witnessed the Republic die of an obscure illness: 'Sagasta ve morir la República de muerte extraña. Consunción o apoplejía. Entre los dos extremos, ningún médico puede deslindar la enfermedad' (13). Whereas Costa (in)famously called for an 'iron surgeon' to cure Spain of its ills, a call to arms that Primo de Rivera used to justify his dictatorship (see Britt-Arredondo 2005: 43), De la Torre makes use of this metaphor to critique the failure of the political system to engage its citizens, effectively subverting Costa's rationale. In *Don Quijote*, she writes that Spain 'padecía un absentismo espiritual; pero no era el religioso ni el político; era el absentismo de la ciudadanía' (86). It is this dearth of citizenship, which we could also infer to mean a lack of solidarity and political awareness, that permeates Spanish culture. As Francisco Layna Ranz proposes in his analysis of *Don Quijote*, the analysis 'denuncia el absentismo ciudadano que señala como culpable de los problemas nacionales tras el llamado desastre del 98' (2019: 15).

Accordingly, De la Torre historicises the conceptualisation of nation and the sense of socio-political cohesion it foments. A relatively recent notion, she muses, nationhood is central to an understanding of society:

> *La idea de la Patria es muy nueva.* Hasta el siglo XV no se aclara exactamente. Y solo con un especial cultivo logra después convertirse en un sentimiento elevado y abstracto.
> Cuando a partir del siglo XIV comenzaron a dibujarse claramente las ideas del antagonismo 'geógrafo nacional' la nueva disgregación fue un elemento de progreso. Ya no era *la 'clase social' hermana* en un sentimiento de orgullo universal (feudalismo) o humillada en sentimientos de inferioridad (vasallaje), *sino una verdadera nación agrupada bajo un ideal común, una bandera y una política más o menos definida.* (72; emphasis added)

Noting the impact of two fundamentally undemocratic systems, feudalism and vassalage, on the collective political consciousness, De la Torre considers how disaffection and antipathy has been cultivated over centuries. In *El ágora*, she reflects on the context of the Peninsular War, specifically the 1808 'Dos de Mayo' revolt that saw citizens in Madrid rise up against the French occupying army. An implicit nationalism inspired this mass resistance, which, nevertheless, does not equate to engaged political activism:

> El pueblo, no solamente no tomó nunca parte en la política, sino que mira hacia otra orilla, todavía difusa entre la niebla de lo porvenir. El pueblo español se siente latir como conglomerado étnico, pero en modo alguno como nacionalidad consciente de su marcha política. (36)

Not only does the comparison with a 'conglomerado étnico' allude to the latent discord between the individual and the collective that characterises De la Torre's fundamental ideological tensions, but so too does this image evoke the colonial discourses examined above. The sexed imagery that De la Torre capitalises on to work through (inter)national conflicts, as discussed in the previous section, is utilised in this passage to detail the bravery with which the rebels faced the firing squads (commemorated in Goya's eminent painting, *El tres de mayo de 1808 en Madrid*), which cumulates in '[l]a última sacudida del machismo histórico' (36).

Rather than frame this nationalistic revolt in positive terms, De la Torre presents it as but one in a series of pivotal historical events that have shaped the collective psyche and the construction and conceptualisation of the Spanish *pueblo*. In an acerbic allusion to the absolutist monarchy of Fernando VII, which usurped the liberal Cadiz Constitution of 1812 when it was re-established after the French retreat, she wryly muses how Spain's citizens fare no better; ¿qué le van a pedir a aquel pueblo que huyendo del fusil de Murat se encontró con la horca de Fernando VII?' (36). Two key questions underpin De la Torre's reflections on Spain's disaffected *pueblo: how* the *pueblo* is conceptualised and *why* the state fails to engage its people in political dialogue. At numerous points throughout *Don Quijote* and *El ágora*, the concept of what the *pueblo* signifies and entails is considered from different perspectives. On one level, as proposed in *Don Quijote*, it connotes a degree of militancy and nationalism that is invested with comradeship: 'El soldado es el pueblo' (107). At the same time, and in accordance with De la Torre's staunch belief in individual agency, she recognises how conceiving of the *pueblo* in this way quells citizens' liberty. Social hierarchies and national identity intersect, as the two shape how the understanding of citizenship evolved:

> Hay un principio de ciudadanía que ensalza la unidad en el mando, la ponderación del Poder Real como medio único de salvación. El pueblo siente que mesa menos la mano del rey que la del señor feudal [...] *El individuo pierde una importancia y su funde en el anonimato de la nacionalidad. La palabra 'pueblo' adquiere un significado político.* (103; emphasis added)

De la Torre's reasoning here critiques the immutable power structures that dictate the lives of the Spanish people in such a way as to connote a socialist philosophy. Not only does the politicisation of the word 'pueblo' strongly resonate with the leftist ideation, but so too does the emphasis on the subordination of the masses. Thus, despite not explicitly referencing how shifting understandings of the *pueblo* relate to socialist principles, the salient conclusion of De la Torre's critique is that a more egalitarian society would propagate political awareness and engagement.

With regards to what causes this political detachment, De la Torre logically concludes that illiteracy and ideological ignorance are critical. Writing in *El ágora*, she argues:

> Sobre un pueblo analfabeto, sólo puede contarse si se agitan los sentimientos, porque *las ideas no tienen fuerza.* El pueblo español estaba agotado en el impulso instintivo y en cuanto a las ideas... Pues *todavía no las había conocido.* (36; emphasis added)

Much in the same way that De la Torre's conceptualisation of the *pueblo* evokes socialist politics, her interrogation of the 'pueblo analfabeto' evokes the leftist notion of consciousness raising. Similarly, in *Don Quijote*, she recognises how ineffectual political leaders stem from and result in an uninformed population: 'El pueblo era ignorante; los políticos desorientados; el mal desconocido de sus causas...' (59). Critically, it was the undemocratic *caciquismo* system that cultivated the masses' political disengagement, with the blame firmly squared on egregious state structures. As De la Torre explains in *Don Quijote*:

> España estaba harta de ejercitar esa ciudadanía clásicamente viciada por *la falta de ideales políticos populares y por la opresión económica.* El resultado negativo de su experiencia, la desanimó de usarla. Aquella dejación general del derecho de votar, aquella dejación que la ley de Maura haciendo el voto obligatorio, era el síntoma que acusaba el gravísimo estado del espíritu nacional. Un pueblo 'que no intenta siquiera» intervenir en sus destinos, demuestra su escepticismo en cuanto a la eficacia de su esfuerzo.' (61; emphasis added)

The emphasis on economic subordination ('la opresión económica') and a lack of appealing political alternatives ('la falta de ideales políticos populares') connotes that socialist reformation could facilitate a means of repairing this breach between the Spanish state and its people.

It is in reference to Sagasta's premiership that De la Torre considers this asymmetrical power dynamic from the perspective of a political leader aiming to resolve this structural and ideological failing. Political discourse and dialogue with the contemporary climate pervade this passage, as a focused interrogation of language is central to how De la Torre unpacks the causes and ramifications of political antipathy. As she expounds,

> He aquí el verdadero 'delito político' en su fase más odiosa.
> Cuando se aspira al Poder, todo ambicioso tiene un programa de elevación moral para su pueblo. Según él, los políticos 'pueden' verificar la regeneración de las sociedades decaídas y aguijarlas en su camino del progreso...
> Cuando 'llegan'...
> El verbo 'Llegar'.
> El rey de los verbos.
> Es rey, porque tiene en realidad un valor abstracto. ¿Llegar adónde? No se expresa el punto de destino. (26)

The reiteration of 'llegar', underscored through the use of quotation marks, places emphasis on the unrealised potential of the current situation; as De la Torre herself explicates, the verb indicates an abstract, ambiguous resolution. Referring to 'llegar' as '[e]l rey de los verbos' evokes the full title of the text — *Don Quijote, rey de España* — which, as Francisco Layna Ranz notes, is invested with a 'carga antimonárquica' (2019: 17). In this sense, there is an ironic undertone to this description of 'llegar' that evokes how De la Torre's core ideological pillars and dry wit inflect the way in which she delineates her critique.

With Sagasta recognising the failings of faux democracy, under which 'el voto popular era un mito' (27), methods of reform are considered:

> Si el pueblo era analfabeto, podía habérsele enseñado a leer.
> Si era esclavo el caciquismo... podía haberse intentado su libertad.
> Si carecía de instrucción cívica, podía habérsele facilitado...
> El sistema parlamentario es precisamente eso: el parlamentar del pueblo. Si la redención de España estaba en la libertad política, 'hacer llegar' esa libertad al pueblo era el deber primero de los redentores. (27)

Though Sagasta, to De la Torre's mind at least, has insight into the oppression of the *pueblo*, she concludes that 'no fué más que el continuador del despotismo... "relativamente" ilustrado' (27–28). Thus, despite the fact that the Liberal leader's core political philosophy, at least ostensibly, centres on empowering the people, his methods and vision still ultimately rest on undemocratic, autocratic means. Revising the iconic political adage ' "[t]odo por el pueblo... pero sin el pueblo" ' (28), which has been applied to authoritarian and absolutist regimes since the eighteenth century, De la Torre summarises Sagasta's approach as follows: 'El axioma de libertad sagastina pudo expresarse así: "¡Todo por el pueblo, pero 'sobre' el pueblo!" ' (28).

It is worth dwelling on this play on political dialogue, not just because it exemplifies how De la Torre repeatedly illustrates her vast knowledge of ideological discourses, but, critically, because she does so in such a way as to engage in debates from which she would be otherwise excluded. By rewriting a well-known political slogan, as she does in relation to Sagasta in the above example, De la Torre pointedly appropriates and reworks the words in order to self-consciously participate in this political rhetoric. Rewording the famous adage only serves to underline the significance of language and discourse. Much in the same way that De la Torre unpacks the layered meaning of 'pueblo', as discussed above, she scrutinises the significance of 'política' by focusing on Maura's premierships. Just as it was noted earlier that Sagasta's identification with the feminine, in contrast to Maura's links to androcentric politics, could be read as an indirect endorsement from De la Torre, the parallels of Sagasta with the *pueblo* and Maura with 'la política' further indicates that De la Torre is more sympathetic to the Liberal leader. At the very least, an implicit connection between the *pueblo* that Sagasta aimed to engage and his Liberal ideation is suggested through this linkage.

With a loyal commitment to the law a core component of Maura's political philosophy (79), the Conservative leader was poised with to govern the *pueblo*, or '[l]a masa nacional' (80), 'a que Maura trata de obligar a la ciudadanía' (80). In this context, citizens are entirely disillusioned, as De la Torre outlines:

> Es, sencillamente, que el pueblo se desliga del interés pueblo, no ya un movimiento de desconfianza, como sucedió ante el derecho del sufragio, sino en un franco movimiento de desdén.
> La *'política'*... *no le importa al pueblo.* (82; emphasis added)

The shift from mistrust to disdain is intriguing as it connotes that the Spanish people are, in fact, acutely aware of the political culture and, as such, a tangible contempt for the undemocratic *caciquismo* process can be understood as a reaction against a crooked system. Disinterest, in other words, does not necessarily denote a lack of awareness or understanding, but, on the other hand, it could reflect an awareness of the failings of suffrage under the Restoration. Nonetheless, such apathy makes politics an obscure concept for the *pueblo*:

> El pueblo, siguiendo una trayectoria inesperada para el gobernante tipo Maura, se ha desplazado de su radio de acción. No opina; es decir: opina una sola cosa.
> Y esa cosa... no se refiere a la política. (82)

De la Torre's conception of 'la política' as a formal state structure, rather than a social movement or manifestation of collective protest, is revealing, as it is suggestive of how she considers political engagement at this point in her career.

There is, then, a sense of alienation on De la Torre's part, as, like the *pueblo*, she feels disconnected from Spain's ineffectual political establishment. That is not to say, however, that De la Torre necessarily understands politics in such limited terms; rather she acknowledges how the government views the system that it has created and upholds. As she muses:

> Claro que sí la palabra «política» tuviera un sentido menos restringido, su amplitud cobijaría también el movimiento de progreso social. Pero no sucede así. Para el gobernante retrasado (todos los gobernantes de la Europa actual, por ejemplo), política es todavía... 'seguridad política'. (82–83)

Just as understated, perhaps even subconscious, allusions to socialist ideation are tangible in De la Torre's deconstruction of the *pueblo*, the reference to 'el movimiento de progreso social' also evokes the author's socialist sensibilities. There is, indeed, the implication that politics *should* have a broader meaning ('un sentido menos restringido'), which resonates with a leftist conception of empowerment and engagement of the masses. With the potential for political reform on the horizon, interrogating and reworking how the *pueblo* and politics are conceptualised is not simply a means of historicising the collective political consciousness, but a method of unpacking ideas that can be rebuilt under a revolutionary government. Accordingly, and as we shall see in the final section of this chapter, ways of realising reform that correlate with socialist — and in many cases feminist — ideals are woven through her analyses in *Don Quijote* and *El ágora*.

'¿Y quiénes son los hombres capaces de traer esa libertad?': Republicanism, Liberty and Socialism

While the political landscape of nineteenth-century Spain proved fertile ground for an interrogation of how the constructs of political liberty and agency evolved, international discourses were also influential. A salient example is the work of John Stuart Mill (1806–1873), the English political philosopher and Liberal Member of Parliament who authored the seminal *The Subjugation of Women* (1869), which was translated by Emilia Pardo Bazán and published in Spain in 1892. (As noted in the next chapter, there is ample evidence that De la Torre was well-versed in Pardo Bazán's works.) Bearing in mind that Mill's ideas and political writings were disseminated in Spain, it stands to reason that his work on liberalism, even indirectly, shaped De la Torre's approach. Lorenzo Benito y Endara's Spanish translation of Mill's *Essays on Liberty*, for example, was published in 1890 and well-received by Ortega y Gasset (see Trincado and Ramos 2011: 516), whose impact on De la Torre is considered above. When Spain introduced liberal male suffrage in 1870, moreover, the politician Ángel Carvajal Fernández de Córdoba frequently referenced Mill whilst debating the Electoral Law bill (see Trincado and Ramos 2011: 517–18). For Mill, as he writes in *On Liberty* (1859), political liberty entailed 'protection against the tyranny of the political rulers' (1993: 3) and was sought by implementing two elements: 'political liberties or rights' (1993: 4); and 'constitutional checks, by which the consent of the community, or of a body of some sort, supposed to represent its interests, was made a necessary condition to some of the more important acts of the governing power' (1993: 4). In *Considerations on Representative Government*, Mill further argues that 'the rights and interests of every or any person are only secure from being disregarded, when the person interested is himself able, and habitually disposed, to stand up for them' (1861: 54). Accordingly, Mill, like De la Torre, was a staunch advocate of political engagement; as Dale Miller outlines, 'Mill holds that widespread political participation helps to ensure that no one's interests are neglected in political deliberation' (2000: 90; also see Thompson 1976: 9).

   As the foregoing illustrates, the question of political agency formed part of a global dialogue. For De la Torre, a republican regime is a critical precursor to engendering a functioning liberal democracy. Given the title of *Don Quijote, rey de España* evokes De la Torre's antimonarchism, it stands to reason that it is in this text that the author most explicitly engages with her republicanism. Factionalism, inequality and injustice are rife under monarchist rule, as '[n]o hay reyes compañeros sino reyes enemigos o reyes esclavos' (64). Such despotism, De la Torre reasons, can only be overturned through the inauguration of a Republic, which is organically more accommodating to political liberty and socialist ideals. That is not to suggest, however, that De la Torre proposes that a republican model would be faultless; '[n]o hay para qué hablar de la perfección de los regímenes políticos ni de la República Universal' (70). Nonetheless, republican governments, De la Torre believes, will expedite social reform:

> Es cierto que esa República Universal es el desiderátum de la sociabilidad humana, pero el camino para conseguirla no es el de las grandes agrupaciones a priori, sino el de las menudas disgregaciones autónomas. (70–71)

To some degree, the reference to a 'República Universal' could be taken as evidence that De la Torre was inspired by international writings on liberalism, such as Mills's work. As we shall see in the next chapter's analysis of *El banquete de Saturno*, the tensions between a Universal Republic and autonomous states is a critical ideological stumbling block for De la Torre. While the plot of *El banquete* evidences that, within three years of writing *Don Quijote*, De la Torre was entirely disillusioned by the notion of an international republican alliance, there is a sense here that she is still processing how individual and collective needs can coexist.

One core ideological misgiving that De la Torre has about the throne is how it enables absolute, unquestionable rule. In *El ágora*, she reflects on monarchical powers; the King, she notes, is charged with sanctifying the Constitution, a document that is therefore known as a 'carta otorgada' (18). Commending Sagasta for his own commitment to republicanism, De la Torre recognises a link between political liberty and a republican political model:

> Después de todo, él piensa (y tiene toda la razón política y filosófica) que el ideal republicano ostenta una finalidad definida, moldeable por las leyes. (15)

> República indica algo así como cosa lograda en la libertad popular. El universal derecho, 'consciente de su derecho y capaz de ejercerlo'... (16)

In the first passage, in which De la Torre differentiates between political and philosophical thought, the fixed framework of the republican model is alluded to in relation to legal reform; both details that echo the analysis of *Jardín de damas curiosas* in the previous chapter. Identifying a republic with 'la libertad popular', as evidenced in the second extract, not only underscores how De la Torre envisages a republican government as a felicitous opportunity to engender political agency, but also how she links republicanism with democracy.

On one level, it is worth pointing out that De la Torre's belief that a republican government was an essential precursor to fair elections is broadly accurate. As Stanley Payne explicates, 'the fundamental pattern of electoral control would never be altogether broken under the constitutional monarchy' (1993: 11).[19] In order to differentiate between the faux democracy of *caciquismo* and legitimate electoral reform, De la Torre underscores how suffrage can only be considered an effective right when the *pueblo* is '"consciente de su derecho y capaz de ejercerlo"' (16). The use of quotation marks serve to present this stipulation as if it were legal rhetoric. The emphasis on being sufficiently informed and competent to effectively exercise this right, moreover, resonates with the socialist paradigm of enlightening the masses. Under the Restoration model, however, political liberty was weak and ineffectual:

> En su fragilidad estaba reflejada la infancia de la libertad española. Nada más representativo de aquella paz política recién conquistada, de aquel sistema, constitucional recién afianzado, que aquella pequeña vida balbuciente y débil. (18)

Though Sagasta, De la Torre proposes, feigned implementing 'las doctrines liberales' (24), his efforts were ultimately futile given how, in this context, '¡La Libertad es... un mito!' (25). Along with Cánovas, Sagasta was charged with cultivating how liberty was conceptualised in the founding years of the Restoration. The two political leaders, she writes, 'condujeron de la mano aquella infancia de la libertad' (19) and, therefore, '[l]a robustecieron en la ideología; la consagraron en un empirismo no por negativo menos sagrado' (19).

Again focalising the linguistic and rhetorical connotations of political discourses, De la Torre reflects on how Sagasta — and his contemporaries — were stifled. Not only was the political agency of the *pueblo* repressed, but so too was the power of Spain's political leaders. Appropriating and assuming Sagasta's reasoning, De la Torre writes in *El ágora*:

> Claro es que *el verbo 'gobernar'...* también se acomodó a las circunstancias.
> Sagasta gobernó con el apotegma ecléctico:
> 'Gobernar es transigir'.
> Es la filosofía del vencimiento.
> ¡¡Transigir!!
> Y, en efecto, se transigió. No sólo Sagasta. Transigieron todos los políticos de la época. Fué una transacción general, de la que *no se libraron ni las fórmulas de gobierno ni los principios* que, si no fueron puestos descaradamente en la balanza, se traicionaron de hecho con todas las hipocresías y salvedades. (24; emphasis added)

Not only does De la Torre note how compromise is often prioritised over ideology, a common political quagmire, but she considers how this is inflected in notions of liberalism and liberty. Describing this compromise as transactional ('una transacción general'), she recognises how such a restrictive environment is corruptive and, consequently, undermines the liberal political project. That is not to say, however, that 'la esclavitud política' (20) is unavoidable, rather it is 'un viejo sentimiento arraigado en la antigua utilidad de caudillaje' (20). Structural changes are, therefore, a prerequisite so that 'las nuevas "ideas" respecto del gobierno de los pueblos' (20), 'el proceso evolutivo' (20) and 'la "revolución"' (20) can be reified.

With the conflict between the individual and the collective considered on a macro scale in relation to the development of republican state(s), it also functions on a micro scale when De la Torre is working through how she conceptualises socialism. In a chapter entitled 'El Quijotismo industrial', which we may understand to mean industrial — or capitalist — idealism, she argues that poverty is a social concern, 'un deshonor colectivo' (157), that is not indicative of an individual's failings. The political ramifications and significance of poverty are further unpacked in *El ágora*, as De la Torre recognises how socio-economic inequality is intrinsically linked to power: 'El dinero otorga el poder, ¿no es verdad?' (29). Money, she writes, is 'una carga molestísima' (29) and, in line with her philanthropic philosophy, she underlines her disinterest in wealth; rather than have money for herself, De la Torre's priority is possessing 'la manera de poder otorgarlo...' (30). An increased awareness of how poverty strips individuals of their agency is central to De la Torre's review of Panait Istrati's *Rusia al desnudo* (printed in *El Cantábrico*), which was published, like *El ágora*, in 1930. De la Torre focuses her review on the pitiful conditions of the Russian people and concludes that 'el gran delito del capitalismo es su fuente restrictora [*sic*] de la producción, que basa el escandaloso porcentaje de su dinero en el negocio seguro de la carestía' (1930: 1). (As will be examined in the next chapter, a social and political critique of Soviet Russia and De la Torre's dialogue with travelogues is central to *El banquete de Saturno*.)

Echoing her critique of Istrati's *Rusia al desnudo*, in which she notes the failings of an unachievable utopia (which is critical to the analysis of *El banquete de Saturno*), she argues that political pragmatism must be prioritised over ideological purity. Political liberty, in turn, will organically lead to a socialist government. The potential for change is within reach, as De la Torre reasons in *El ágora*:

> Muy cerca de nosotros está aquella época que pudiéramos llamar 'de transición' de la libertad política al socialismo. Absolutamente desacreditada la una, apenas balbuciente el otro, mecido todavía en la cuna de la utopía, la sociedad sufría el desbarajuste de un fracaso irremediable: el de los ideales políticos. (31)

Perhaps the most intriguing element of the latent parallel that De la Torre draws between liberty and socialism is how, for some, this is somewhat of a political paradox. For De la Torre, however, the two share ideological common ground, which is an position that is likely shaped by Ortega y Gasset. The Spanish philosopher, whose thought Ángel Peris Suay's describes as 'sin excepción liberal y democrático' (2014: 61), believed socialism to be both a democratic and liberal political philosophy (Dobson, 1989: 55–56). It is in working through the connotations of 'política' that De la Torre presents socialism as a fundamentally democratic ideation. Writing in *El ágora*, she reflects:

> ¿Pero *qué sentido tiene entonces la palabra 'política'*? Muy sencillo.
> Consiste en un tejemaneje de comadres de vecindad.
> Combinaciones de gobernadores (medio de satisfacer ambiciones incipientes).
> Traslados de jueces que prevarican... contra el Gobierno (venganza de agravios pequeños).
> Manipulación de empleos administrativo-lucrativos (satisfacción de ambiciones grandes).
> Manipulación de empleos de módico lucro (cumplimiento de pequeños compromisos).

> Establecimiento de monopolios sobre artículos necesarios... (Grandes fraudes).
>
> Y luego... *lo más importante, lo necesario, lo 'básico' de la libertad política: hacer las elecciones.*
>
> Esta era *la ocupación cumbre de los hombres públicos.* (31–32; emphasis added)

The democratic elections that De la Torre identifies as a key element of political liberty are, of course, within reach at the time of writing: 'Hoy (final de la Dictadura) se habla del restablecimiento de la Libertad' (148). It is, in part, for this reason that De la Torre uses both *Don Quijote* and *El ágora* as a means of distilling the country's core socio-political conflicts and prioritising the ideological goals that should be implemented; '[s]e pide otra vez el sufragio universal; se habla de "elecciones liberales" y de "política de partidos"...' (148).

A salient obstacle, however, is 'la vieja política' (149); the androcentric political establishment that is resistant to reform:

> ¿Y *quiénes son los hombres capaces de traer esa libertad?*
>
> He aquí lo enorme. Lo que justificará muy pronto el final violento del régimen: *Son precisamente 'aquellos' mismos hombres; aquellos mismos nombres*; aquellos fracasados discurseadores [*sic*] de Congresos y Senados; aquella legión de ex ministros semidioses de la cosa pública... [...]
>
> ¿*Acaso es que esos hombres 'no tuvieron tiempo' de darnos la libertad o la justicia y siquiera el pan de cada día?* Veamos cómo todos ellos han pasado por la vida pública y todos dejaron los errores tales y como los encontraron; todos sufrieron la malsana influencia del Poder y la seducción de «lo más alto», como «le» llaman los parlamentarios. (148–49; emphasis added)

Though public opinion is shifting, De la Torre argues, 'los viejos fantasmas del convencionalismo político' (158) linger and so it is yet to be seen whether full reform is possible. Perhaps, she muses, they will return to retain power after the dust has settled:

> ¿Volverán?
>
> ¡Acaso!... ¡acaso! [...]
>
> Acaso vuelvan, sí; porque es posible que su acción guarde todavía una suprema utilidad: la de ser ese fulminante necesario al verdadero progreso del mundo. (158)

In a tone that is as audacious as it is derisive, De la Torre concludes that these political leaders may in fact be politically apt: 'Todos esos hombres, probablemente, tienen buenas ideas' (152). Nonetheless, the implicit suggestion is that new blood with fresh ideas is needed. As those who devised and maintained the cataclysmic Restoration regime are dismissively described as 'esos hombres', there is an oblique suggestion that this could include women. Indeed, these failed, male politicians had ample, wasted opportunity to enact reform and so it therefore stands to reason that history would be destined to repeat itself should they retain power. As De la Torre wryly observes, 'serán cobardes ante la acción renovadora. Tan cobardes como lo fueron antes' (152).

Notes to Chapter 2

1. Hereafter all in-text references to *El ágora* will be to the 1930 edition.
2. Antonia Rodrigo explains that the Asociación Femenina de Educación Cívica was founded in opposition to the 'el espíritu elitista del Lyceum Club, que se había convertido en lugar de encuentro de las señoras elegantes de la sociedad madrileña' (1994: 240).
3. Hereafter all in-text references to *Don Quijote, rey de España* will be to the 2000 edition.
4. In her newspaper column for *Las Noticias*, for instance, Graupera laments how women are often accused of treachery or espionage without justification, stereotyped as disloyal by the biblical Delilah (Graupera 1918a: 3), and implores Spanish women to empathise with the Greek women who suffer violence, brutality and loss (Graupera 1918b: 3). In *El gran crimen: Lo que yo he visto en la guerra*, which is based on her war-time correspondence, she details the suffering of women whose partners or sons are sent to fight (Graupera 1935: 4–8, 18–19, 46–47) and recounts the empathically gendered violence women endured (1935: 2, 7, 17, 25, 37, 41, 43, 85, 87, 94–95, 110, 130, 133, 198, 207, 245, 287).
5. As Alejandro de Haro Honrubia observes, *Meditaciones del Quijote* constitutes, 'de forma más o menos explícita, una serie de soluciones al que denomina — siguiendo toda una tradición — como problema español' (2018: 192). Inspired by 'filosóficos deseos' (2018: 177), Haro Honrubia explicates, Ortega y Gasset reflects on 'el denominado problema español que no solamente es un problema político e histórico, sino que también se hace sentir con fuerza en el orden de las ideas o intelectual' (2018: 177).
6. An intriguing indicator of Ortega y Gasset's loyalty to his homeland is found in an interview printed in the *Times Literary Review*, as Ortega y Gasset is commended for not appearing 'ashamed of being a Spaniard' (10 July 1959: 414; as quoted in Dobson 1989: 11).
7. Salient examples from Ortega y Gasset's oeuvre include *La rebelión en las masas* (1930) and *El hombre y la gente* (1957), which was based on lectures delivered in 1949 and 1950. John T. Graham notes that, while *La rebelión en las masas* 'captivated readers' (2001: 96), *El hombre y la gente* failed to attract the same degree of enthusiasm. Graham suggests that a likely reason for this is that the latter was 'written for academic specialists, in effect if not by design' (2001: 96), which, as developed in the Conclusion, is a logical explanation as to why De la Torre's work lacks much critical attention.
8. Also see Shirley Mangini (1987) for an in-depth analysis of Rosa Chacel's relationship to Ortega y Gasset's work, specifically her novel *Estación: Ida y vuelta* (1930).
9. In 'La poesía de Ana de Noailles', Ortega y Gasset notes how women writers monopolise the epistolary paradigm, deeming it an apt example of the 'private' genre (1924: 118–19), which, as Isabel Navas Ocaña observes, connotes the hegemonic association between women and the private sphere (2018: 128).
10. See Tatjana Gajic (2000) for a detailed analysis of how *Meditaciones del Quijote* and Ortega y Gasset's speech 'Vieja y nueva política', both published in 1914, conceived of national reform and Spanish culture.
11. Obliquely alluding to her socialist socio-economic beliefs, she notes how greed spurred Spain's desire to retain control of its colonies and, consequently, obliterated the country's well-being. Had vast financial provisions not been dedicated to the war, 'aquel desastre se hubiese reducido a un combate episódico en el que la victoria o la derrota no hubieran sido mortales' (127).
12. James H. Rial recognises that the fallout of Restoration politics continued to impact the Spanish economy during the Primo de Rivera dictatorship, as it 'promoted governmental activism' which was inadequate and limited given the 'state's poverty' (1986: 26).
13. In his analysis of US foreign policy, Willem Theo Oosterveld writes that the Monroe doctrine was drafted with Spain in mind; 'the emphasis on non-colonization appears to be primarily aimed at powers like Spain and Portugal' (2015: 309). Similarly, Martin Sicker notes that the policy was a formal articulation of 'President Monroe's increasing concern that France might intervene to help Spain recover its colonies in the Western Hemisphere' (2002: 18).
14. As discussed in Chapter Three's analysis of *El banquete de Saturno* (1931), De la Torre presents anarchism positively and draws out ideological parallels with socialism.

15. Kate Soper discusses the universality of the identification of nature with women and details how it stems from the female connotations of reproduction: 'The association of femininity with naturality represents a more specific instance of the mind-body dualism brought to conceptions of nature, since it goes together with the assumption that the female, in virtue of her role in reproduction, is a more corporal being than the male. If we ask, that is, what accounts for this coding of nature as feminine — which is deeply entrenched in Western thought, but has also been said by anthropologists to be crosscultural [sic] and well-nigh universal — then the answer, it would seem, likes in the double association of women with reproductive activities and of these in turn with nature' (2000: 139).

16. Though *Historia general de las Indias* was 'an instant success' that spurred five Spanish-language editions and numerous translations (Schroeder 2010: 3), it 'acquired notoriety for its unyielding portrayal of imperialism' (Roa-de-la-Carrera 2005: 3) and Gómara's ultimately futile effort to construct 'an ethically persuasive argument' (2005: 2) for Spain's colonial expeditions.

17. Cristián A. Roa-de-la-Carrera notes how contemporary historians Gonzalo Fernández de Oviedo y Valdés (1478–1557) and Bartolomé de las Casas (ca.1484–1566) criticised Gómara's work as it 'elevated Cortés to the stature of a great leader and hero' (2005: 3). Bernal Díaz del Castillo (ca.1495–1584) and Inca Garcilaso de la Vega (1539–1616), on the other hand, 'left compelling testimonies of the conquistadors' discontent about Gómara's disregard for the honor and merits of some individuals who served in Mexico and Peru' (2005: 3).

18. Salient examples include Ortega y Gasset's 1914 essay in *Ensayos sobre la generación del 98 y otros escritores españoles* (1981; see Balfour 1997: 67) and Joaquín Costa's seminal *Oligarquía y caciquismo como la forma actual de gobierno en España: urgencia y modo de cambiarla* (1902; see Balfour 1995: 412).

19. Payne elaborates as follows: 'Elections did slowly become more genuine in some of the larger cities, however, and after a few years somewhat broader representation was allowed to third parties, some of them republican. Between 1907 and 1923, these republicans would be allowed to hold between 2 and 4 percent of the seats in parliament, even though registered abstentionism increased after the turn of the century' (1993: 11).

CHAPTER 3

El banquete de Saturno: Novela social: Sex, Socialism and Soviet Russia

Of De la Torre's eclectic, emphatically politicised written output, *El banquete de Saturno: novela social* (1931; henceforth *El banquete*) is undoubtedly her most complex, multifaceted text.[1] Fundamentally a satirical account of a failed Marxist-socialist dictatorship that bears strong resemblance to Soviet Russia, the very existence of *El banquete* is indicative of political change. The novel's blurb states it was written 'hace ya algunos años, cuando aun nadie creía en la posibilidad de una República española' (4), while a newspaper report in *El Sol* published in September 1931, just five months after the establishment of the Republic, explains that the work was penned under the dictatorship of Miguel Primo de Rivera, but that the author had refrained from publication 'por el temor a la misma, temor muy justificado' ('Libros' 1931: 2). As noted in the previous chapters, De la Torre's (relatively limited) publications all coincide with key moments in Spanish political history: *Jardín de damas curiosas* (1917) with the national strike, *Don Quijote, rey de España* (1928) and *El ágora* (1930) with the death throes of the Primo de Rivera regime and, in the case of *El banquete*, the birth of the Second Republic. While De la Torre's socialism and feminism were the core ideologies that defined her political career and literary output, it is important to remember that she was also a staunch republican. In May 1932, for instance, she publicly declared her support for the Second Republic alongside María Lejárraga,[2] the year before she was elected, and, after taking office in November 1933, she was described as a '[r]epublicana de siempre' in the press ('Sobremesa' 1933: 3; also see Domingo 2004: 25).

Despite vocally defending the republican project, De la Torre attracted criticism for refusing to back a unified women's Republican movement that surpassed individual party loyalty;[3] a conflict that evidences tensions between her feminist convictions, support for the Second Republic and her lifelong socialism. Perhaps one of the most intriguing elements of De la Torre's outlook is how, rather than view the restructure of the Spanish political system for which she had long hoped optimistically, *El banquete* reveals her trepidation of how a revolutionary government is susceptible to corruption. An ominous account of a proletarian uprising that results in a corrupt, authoritarian regime, the novel defies categorisation, as it incorporates a multitude of genres, political theories, literary tropes and classical references. Interspersed with infrequent, surreal extracts that allegorise the principal failings of the post-revolutionary regime, such as a fantastical depiction of ancient gods goading the strikers during the violent uprising and a satirical depiction of the Wall Street crash that critiques the capitalist model, the narrative is, nevertheless, a relatively straightforward account of a proletarian revolution that spurs a series of uprisings across the world, resulting in an international socialist alliance that is ultimately doomed to fail.

The reader is granted intimate access to the revolution and the inner workings of the regime through one of the male factory workers who becomes a politician under the new administration, Julio Miroles, whose surname — a play on "les miro" — is invested with the omniscience and totalitarianism that characterises the uprising and subsequent "República Social-comunista" (186, 208, 253, 258).[4] A committed socialist who supports the revolution, Julio grows increasingly disillusioned with the corrupt, tyrannical regime, with his doubts exacerbated by his personal loyalties to the Fornés family, Miguel, Lena and Jaime; lifelong friends of the protagonist who oppose the strike and insurrection. Following the success of the Spanish revolution, a series of uprisings occur across the world and an international socialist alliance is formed. The Spanish government falls under a coup d'état, led by a disillusioned group who had once fought for the revolutionary forces, and the international community fails, splintered by different aims and expectations that lead to a horrific war and results in devastation and millions of deaths.

The titular reference to the god Saturnus encapsulates the nexus of satire and (anti-)utopia that characterises the work; as Robert C. Elliot explains: '[U]topia and satire are ancestrally linked in the celebration of Saturn' (1971: 24; also see 1971: 21–23; Kumar 1987: 104–05, 109). The eponymous deity is usually portrayed holding a sickle and wheatsheaf (Berens 2007: 18), evoking Marxist imagery, while the feast in his honour encompasses egalitarian principles (Berens 2007: 200; Elliot 1971: 10). As this outline suggests, *El banquete* is as much a boastful display of the author's creative skill and breadth of knowledge as it is a complex political satire. The early decades of twentieth-century Europe proved fertile ground for satirical texts and dystopian fiction, as the Soviet Union prompted a wealth of fictionalised critiques that scrutinised the Russian regime. Although the most (in)famous example of literary condemnation of Soviet Russia to be born out of the Spanish context is undoubtedly George Orwell's *Animal Farm: A Fairy Story* ([1945] 1951), De la Torre's *El banquete* would engage with the same questions of totalitarianism, individual autonomy and political integrity more than a decade earlier.

As scholarship of the genre indicates, anti-Soviet literature is typically identified as 'anti-utopia', rather than dystopian, as it connotes a nightmarish, satirised perversion of utopia (see Hillegas 1967: 147; Kumar 1987: 49, 381–83; also see: Stites 1989: 13; Suvin 2016). For De la Torre, her vision of an anti-utopia is a society in which socialist and feminist values are disregarded and, critically, a socialist government in Spain is dictated by the Soviets. In an interview with *La Calle*, De la Torre clarifies that the eponymous reference to Saturn devouring his sons symbolises the repression of liberty that leads to the downfall of the fictitious Republic in the novel. *El banquete*, she explains, is an intellectual exercise, a means of illustrating that '[s]e puede ser científicamente pesimista, sin traicionar a la Causa' ('Las mujeres de la democracia: Matilde de la Torre' 1931: 11); a reflection that evidences how De la Torre uses the novel as a means of unpacking the ideological inconsistencies or blind spots of socialist doctrine without, to her mind, undermining her convictions. Rather than acknowledge the loaded political potential of the work, however, De la Torre, somewhat wryly, insists in the book's title page that '*"El banquete de Saturno"* no es más que una novela' (9).

Her hesitance to admit that, as with all of her oeuvre, *El banquete* is as much a contribution to political dialogue as it is a work of fiction can be read in two ways. On the one hand, it corresponds with advertising for the novel, noted above, that suggested De la Torre was wary to publish under a reactionary government. At the same time, as this analysis will demonstrate, De la Torre is also cautious of overtly criticising her socialist allies, both in terms of ideological objectives and contemporaneous political debates. One way De la Torre could mask her evident discord with the current state of socialist politics in Spain was through the satirical, often fantastical, narrative. Indeed, De la Torre is keen to package the novel in this way, referring to 'la sátira de "El Banquete de Saturno"' (276) in a footnote that momentarily drops the fictional façade. Though there is little consensus as to the ideological leanings of satire,[5] and some critics argue against its didactic potential (such as: Feinberg 2008: 255, 259; Griffin 1994: 154–55), the genre is, nevertheless, typically associated with political and/or social critique (see, for example: Anderson 1982: 184; Bohnert 1995: 163; Feinberg 2008: 37). In particular, satirical tropes are often utilised in relation to Roman literature (Coffey 1976: 3; Rudd 1986: 1), specifically in reference to the fall of the Republic (Knoche 1975: 71; Van Rooy 1966: 59); a link that exemplifies how De la Torre's political ideals and literary strategies coalesce.

The dialogic quality of *El banquete*, with the narrative and political voice fore-grounded, as is the case in all of De la Torre's work, therefore functions to bridge the gap between contemporary Spain and De la Torre's anti-utopian hypothesis. Satire is key. As touched on in the Introduction, a core component of Mikhail Bakhtin's theory of dialogism in the novel is humour. For Bakhtin, the multivalent nature of the novel allows it to subvert homogeneous discourses through heteroglossia, often aided by forms of laughter; in novelised forms of other genres (such as satire), 'language renews itself by incorporating extraliterary heteroglossia', becoming 'dialogized, permeated with laughter, irony, humour, elements of self-parody' (1981: 7). In *El banquete*, De la Torre's scathing wit extends beyond a conspicuous critique of Stalinism and corrupted reifications of socialism, as she subverts the generic conventions of socialist realism, a genre that became increasingly popular throughout the 1920s and 1930s (see Fuentes 1980: 31, 35, 38; Purkey 2013: 13). Evoking the socialist literary paradigm, De la Torre subverts it from within through her depiction of a failed, unscrupulous revolutionary government and a disillusioned, passive socialist antihero, as her resistance to uniformity and solidarity is manifest in the very structure of the novel.

Characteristically for De la Torre, the narrative is insistently self-reflective about its rejection of the socialist model, as evidenced when a revolutionary sardonically underlines the most salient flaw of literary propaganda: 'Los que no conocen a Tolstoi ni a Andreiew ni a Gorki ni a Trotski ni a Lenin siquiera, son los mujika. No los han leído nunca, entre otras razones, porque no saben leer' (40). The brief appearance of a fictionalised Emilia Pardo Bazán, who takes the form of a conservative aristocrat Dama Parda (84–85), grounds this criticism in a contemporary Spanish context, as the subject matter of *El banquete* echoes Pardo Bazán's 'La Revolución y la novela en Rusia' (1907), a series of lectures that interrogates the links between society, revolution and literary output (delivered and first published in 1887) that has been credited with popularising Russian literature in Spain (Purkey 2013: 14).[6] The leftist reader that this presupposes is further implied by De la Torre's publisher, the Barcelona based Mentora that, capitalising on what Víctor Fuentes describes as a '"boom" del libro de la izquierda" from the late 1920s (1980: 34–38), printed numerous works that centre on international politics.[7] As this analysis will demonstrate, *El banquete* is a novelistic form of interrogating socialist doctrine and policy and, crucially, women's place within it. The text, in this sense, constitutes a self-conscious contribution to contemporary socialist discourse that suggests a re-conceptualisation of socialist rhetoric that benefits from female and feminist input.

'No estamos en el caso de Rusia': Satirising the Soviets

The sense of foreboding that the events in Russia evoked on an international scale was particularly acute in Spain as the Spanish left looked to Russia for a revolutionary model. The Revolution aroused 'great sympathy' from Spanish socialists and anarchists (Alba and Schwartz 1988: 4) and left-of-centre political groups such as the anarchists, communists and radical-socialists saw the Bolsheviks as an example to be followed (Gómez 2002: 67). Spaniards' interest in Russia, Víctor Alba explains, was logical given the two countries had much in common: labour movements primarily organised by the anarchists rather than Marxists; political control exercised by an elite, with limited democratic reform; and, above all, the fact that in both Spain and Russia 'the peasant was reduced to almost servile status' (1983: 1). The Bolshevik Revolution galvanized elements of the Spanish left to such an extent that 1917 marked the beginning of a three year period which would become known as the '"*trienio bolchevique*", the end of which coincided with the founding of the Communist Party in 1920' (Gómez 2002: 66; also see Fuentes 1980: 30).

   Against this political backdrop, De la Torre constructs a narrative that hypothesises a scenario in which the Russian revolutionary model is transposed onto a contemporary Spanish context. Following a workers' strike which leads to an October revolution, the new government becomes more oppressive than the previous regime; a distortion of ideological convictions that is typical in anti-utopian works from the beginning of the twentieth century (Franková 2013: 212). Following the revolt, the new 'República Social-comunista' enacts a series of Marxist/socialist policies: there is a redistribution of wealth (214), a national bank is introduced ('Banco Social-comunista Español') (218) and personal property is seized by the state (213). The regime's economic model is thus a realisation of a

Marxist economic model, as *The Communist Manifesto* argues for the '[a]bolition of all rights of inheritance' and the '[c]entralization of credit in the hands of the State, by means of a national bank with State capital and an exclusive monopoly' (Marx and Engels 2009: 28). It is worth clarifying here that socialism and Marxism can be understood interchangeably in this context. From a historical perspective, Paul Thomas explains that 'the sharpness of the distinction between socialism and communism came to be blurred' as the nineteenth century progressed (2008: 14);[8] an observation evidenced by the fact that the PSOE manifesto was modelled on Marxist discourse (Esteban and López Guerra 1982: 120).

In *El banquete* specifically, moreover, there are two scenes in which characters identified with Marx, one through his name (201) and another through his facial hair (16), are termed 'socialists' rather than 'communists' in the narrative. It is, therefore, unexpected that De la Torre's portrayal of the socialist values she would spend her life defending are unequivocally negative. Ironically, or perhaps not, the socialist regime's egalitarian reforms only serve to worsen the proletariat's plight as wide-spread hunger, a concern that plays a key role in initiating the uprising, becomes a national concern (7, 31, 49, 50, 52, 57, 110). The government's response is a typically ineffective take on socialist rhetoric that is depicted satirically. Communal eating halls are opened and made obligatory for all citizens, while cooking and eating in private is banned. Rather than resolve the crisis, the national canteens only serve to dehumanise the citizens, which is illustrated in a strikingly poignant scene in which an elderly woman pitifully laments that she can no longer cook for her family (256–57). The reference to communal canteens is telling, as it emulates both Thomas More's *Utopia* and the Spanish travelogues about post-revolution Russia (see Purkey 2013: 30), exemplifying the eclectic array of sources that inform the novel and, accordingly, the multiple intertextual dialogues at play.

The conspicuous critique of the Soviet Union is evidenced by the name of the police force, 'Ejército Rojo' (190, 209, 227, 293), and De la Torre depicts the regime's leader César in such a way as to make his identification with the corrupt, hypocritical Soviet regime unmistakeable. Described as a dictator (209, 259, 278), echoing his Roman namesake, who enforces 'la Tiranía Socialista' (255), César mimics Soviet rhetoric. The plot's setting, Urba, can also be understood as an oblique reference to the authoritarian nature of Ceśar's rule, as it evokes the Latin for 'city', alluding to Livy's *Ab Urbe Condita Libri*, a history of Rome in which Livy writes repeatedly of the need for one man to take control, 'be he [a] dictator or individual of extraordinary courage' (L'hoir 1990: 240). César's musings about how to manage '[l]os indeseables' (191), moreover, echo the Soviet policy of 'stamping out' opposition deemed 'enemies of the people' (Čavoški 1986: 22–23), while Lenin's belief that people needed an *intelligentsia* to guide them (Ferré 2011: 56) is evoked by César's objection to suffrage, as he believes that the *pueblo* is 'socialmente niño y necesita tutores' (177).

A tension between the author's attempt to present her own (female) opinion on the tyrannical socialist regime, both within the diegesis of the novel and De la Torre's political circles, and desire to present her reflections in an authoritative way is tangible in the intertextual dialogue she constructs with male-authored works.

The most salient example is *Setenta días en Rusia: Lo que yo vi* (1925; henceforth *Setenta días*), the travelogue by Ángel Pestaña, a member of the anarcho-syndicalist Confederación Nacional del Trabajo (CNT), that documents his experiences in Bolshevist Russia. De la Torre includes a fictionalised recreation of Pestaña in *El banquete* who takes the form of Agustín Espada, a young anarchist doctor. Initially a supporter of the regime, Espada is the only character in the novel who is not ridiculed or undermined by the author in one form or another. He acts as the voice of reason in the narrative, publicly criticising the regime and highlighting inconsistencies and hypocrisy. He accuses the government of taking political prisoners and 'persiguiendo al pueblo mucho más crudamente que nunca lo hicieron los burgueses' (255) and condemns the power driven leaders he calls 'proletarios endiosados' (256), an ironic slight given the secularism of Marxist doctrine.[9]

While Espada's vocal opposition to César's government mirrors the objections of many Spanish leftists who travelled to Russia, there are various intertextual references that suggest De la Torre consciously draws on *Setenta días* in an attempt to imbue her opinions with a sense of veracity or legitimacy. The most persuasive evidence to suggest that De la Torre had Pestaña's travelogue in mind when writing the novel is the similarity between the titles of De la Torre's work and a chapter in *Setenta días* entitled 'Gran fiesta y banquete' (1925: 92–99), as she appears to make this link clear to her readership. The workers' debates about the Russian economy (21), furthermore, chimes with Pestaña's references to Russia's failing economy (1925: 56; 90; 130; 156), while the examples of Russian words in *El banquete*, such as 'muljik' (42), also echoes Pestaña's work. The character of Espada most closely resembles Pestaña when criticising the state-run communal eating halls that dehumanise and oppress the citizens. He openly criticises the canteens for inhibiting individual liberty and sardonically muses about the meaning of 'igualdad' (257), in line with Pestaña's observations about citizens' hunger (1925: 196), collectivised food rationing (1925: 133) and regimented eating schedules (1925: 16–17, 46), a focus that, read retrospectively, captures the political climate more accurately than De la Torre could have envisaged, as it reflects recent historical accounts and would foreshadow the Soviet famine of 1932–1933 that immediately followed the publication of the work.

Though innumerable (mostly left-wing) Spaniards travelled to Russia,[10] including leftist women, such as María Teresa León and Dolores Ibárruri, there is no evidence to suggest that De la Torre visited the socialist state. It was, therefore, critical travelogues like *Setenta días* that most likely shaped her perception of Soviet-ruled Russia. Unlike her political allies, including Lejárraga, who was a member of the *Asociación de Amigos de la Unión Soviética* group founded in April 1933 (Alba 1983: 153), De la Torre evidently opposed what she deemed to be a distorted manifestation of socialist values. Her decision to draw on Pestaña's work specifically is curious, as there were examples of popular travelogues authored by members of the PSOE, such as Fernando de los Ríos's *Mi viaje a la Rusia sovietista* (1921) and Julio Álvarez del Vayo's *La nueva Rusia* (1926),[11] for her to reference. Characterising Espada as an anarchist makes De la Torre's apparent rejection of socialist-authored works appear pointed. The fact that her flawed protagonist shares the name of Álvarez del Vayo, whose work, as Lynn Purkey notes, commends 'the rapid growth in electrification and industrialization during the decades following the Revolution' (2013: 25), would suggest that, having consulted a range of these travelogues, the author has formed her own opinion that is not always in consonance with her socialist comrades' views. Rather than 'toe the "party" line', then, De la Torre draws on the work of an anarchist as it most closely mirrors her perspective.

The fact that the author looks to an anarchist is particularly significant as it implies a tolerance towards the socialists' greatest opponent on the left, and, typically for De la Torre, reinforces her political point, as it alludes to the anarchists' fundamental ideological priority: individual autonomy. The characterisation of Espada, that is, is doubly invested with a sense of personal liberty as he defends these values and is identified with a political ideology that is characterised by these beliefs. The author's tacit approval of anarchist ideals is evidenced elsewhere in *El banquete*, most notably the reference to the French anarchist Louise Michel (24) and in a debate about divorce (69); a topic that further illustrates the forward-looking nature of the work given divorce would be legalised in Spain just four months after the novel's publication.[12] De la Torre, nevertheless, was a committed socialist, and would formally join the PSOE shortly after writing *El banquete*. Whether her loyalty to the socialists suggests admirable conviction or, as is also likely, stemmed from her desire to become a *diputada*, which would not have been possible given anarchists typically reject government structures in all forms,[13] what is clear is that De la Torre often disagreed with her socialist comrades on two key points: female suffrage and Socialist Russia.

Grounding *El banquete* firmly within its historical context illustrates how the author uses the novel to add her (female) voice to contemporary socialist debates, offering what to her mind was a much needed directive to her socialist colleagues. As noted at the beginning of the section, Spanish socialists looked to Russia for a revolutionary model given the social and political parallels between the countries. Communication between socialists in Russia and Spain was first established on 24 January 1919 in an address directed explicitly to the 'leftist elements of the PSOE' (Alba 1983: 3); a specification that reflects the tensions within the author's Party. Although the PSOE and *El Socialista*, the Party and paper of De la Torre, were generally more cautious than others on the left, maintaining a 'dignified silence' following the Revolution in Russia (Gómez 2002: 67), there were more extreme factions of the Socialist Party. The Unión General de Trabajadores (UGT), the trade union allied with the PSOE, for instance, was headed by Francisco Largo Caballero, a figure deemed 'the Spanish Lenin' for his revolutionary stance (Gunther, Ramón Motero and Botella 2004: 35). The period immediately preceding the publication of the novel was particularly pertinent, as debates surrounding how the Party would respond to Russia intensified. Although the majority of Spanish socialists condemned the regime in Russia in the immediate aftermath of the Revolution, basing their opinions on De los Ríos's *Mi viaje a la Rusia sovietista*, which is highly critical of the regime,[14] there was a tangible shift during the late 1920s and early 1930s as attitudes to Russia began to relax and the socialist press began to 'express a good deal of enthusiasm' for Soviet policies (Gómez 2002: 71).

Against this backdrop, De la Torre constructs a novel that is insistently self-conscious about its contribution to these debates. There are explicit references to the Russian government (42, 77, 226) and, alluding to the communication between Soviet Russia and Spanish socialists, the rebels in *El banquete* are directed and informed by their Russian comrades. The uprising is initiated at the Russians' behest (89) and, after the successful revolt, César continues to look to Russia for guidance (192). In the chapter 'Los indeseables', an overt reference to the Soviet purges, César reveals his admiration for the ruthless methods employed by his Russian mentors:

> No estamos en el caso de Rusia, desgraciadamente. Rusia pudo matar o desterrar a los que la estorbaban, porque ella tuvo la ventaja enorme de constituir una excepción y su lucha pudo desenvolverse en una libre eliminación de sus propios venenos... (192)

The forward looking quality of the novel, which is the only detail that José Domingo notes in his brief summary of *El banquete* (1973: 149), implores the reader to consider César's reflections as a very current, critical political concern. The relevance of the work is evidenced by the numerous anti-Soviet works published in Spain around this time. Another anarchist, Vicente Pérez (Combina) published *Un militante de la C.N.T. en Rusia* in 1932, which condemned the limited democratic process (Purkey 2013: 22), while a work of fiction from the same year, Ilia Ehrenburg's *España: República de trabajadores* (1932), pointed to the 'factionalism and individualism lacking in Soviet politics that so disturbed Spaniards' (Purkey 2013: 23). The allusions to individual liberty in *El banquete*, then, point to one element of post-Revolution Russia which was frequently condemned by Spaniards, while the dates of these other works, particularly Ehrenburg's novel, indicate that De la Torre was ahead of the curve.

The contemporaneous quality of the novel is emphatically underlined in the narrative, as the rebels' musings about the Russian government imply that the action takes place in 1932 (226),[15] suggesting an imminent potential future for Spaniards. The date given for one meeting, '20 de octubre de 193...' (122),[16] more-over, underscores impending doom by connoting that this dystopian political project could occur at any point in the coming years. Fundamentally, the tyranny, hypocrisy and brutality of the socialist regime in *El banquete* is a critique of the dangers of collaborating with the Russians, in the narrative and in reality; a view that is also articulated by Jardeña, one of the few socialists who tries to maintain his ideological integrity under the regime: 'No; no hablemos de Rusia cuando tratemos de la actual transformación del mundo' (226). Through these self-reflexive references, De la Torre addresses her readership directly. In this instance, her envisaged reader is, conceivably, a member or representative of the PSOE; as noted earlier, the publishing details of the novel strongly suggest a politically engaged, internationally aware left-wing reader and, as indicated by the Party's intrigue in Russia at this time, De la Torre evidently felt compelled to voice her opinion.

It is worth underlining here that, although various (male) characters make explicit references to Soviet politics, Julio — De la Torre's male narrator — docs not offer any views on Russia. The protagonist's silence can be considered an acknowledgement by the author that, given his identification with the fictional regime, a reader would be unwilling to follow his directive. While the callous dictator César reflects favourably on the Russian model and Jardeña, a minor character, is more prudent, Julio's position is unclear. Reading the characters' prominence in the text as symbolic of their political agency, with César in a position of authority and Jardeña a fleeting, ineffective participant in the debates, suggests a worrying indictment from De la Torre about the current climate: extremist voices are dominating socialist dialogue and, alarmingly, they are looking to Russia. Remembering that *El banquete* was written before De la Torre was elected for the PSOE, fiction proves a useful medium through which De la Torre can navigate the tensions between her desire to contribute her female voice to the plethora of male voices, both in the narrative and in real life. Her foreword to the work, with this in mind, is as provocative and sardonic as the narrative itself: '"*El banquete de Saturno: novela social*" no es más que una novela' (9). Rather than passively accept her implied inferiority, as she seems to imply through this preface, De la Torre uses her male characters as puppets for her bidding, which is evidenced most clearly by the double-edged — or double-voiced, to use Bakhtinian terminology — meaning of César's reflections: 'No estamos en el caso de Rusia' (192), as the author makes a self-reflexive pun at the tyrant's expense.

As detailed in Chapter One, one of the most polemical questions for the newly founded Second Republic was female suffrage. Not only was women's political emancipation at the forefront of feminist debates, socialists were also divided on the matter. On the one hand, De la Torre's sharp, insightful critique of Soviet Russia can be understood as an indirect commentary on women's political parity. Indeed, it seems almost incredulous that debates surrounding women's ability to reason and their suitability for political debate were rife at this period in history. Interrogating current ideological and policy issues, De la Torre can be seen to remodel and critique socialist discourses in such a way as to disassociate her own views from the failed, corrupt socialist experiment that she documents in *El banquete*. As we shall see in the next section of the analysis, it is through her male narrator that De la Torre simultaneously adds a veil of authority to her views and interrogates the gender politics of contemporary socialist ideation.

'¡Hermano centinela... fraternidad! ': Male-voiced Socialism

Given *El banquete* is one of relatively few socialist works to be authored by a woman, and certainly one of the earliest in Spain, it is somewhat unexpected that the author chooses to mediate the narrative through a male narrator. The inevitable tension that arises when a female author explores her own political convictions through a male protagonist is particularly pertinent for a work that was published at a time when women's right and capability to participate in political dialogue was central to feminist and socialist debates. Julio's references to Marxist discourse exemplify how textual crossdressing — a female author voicing her ideas through a male protagonist — can simultaneously (re-)assert and undermine the woman writer's ideological autonomy. The protagonist's critique of 'Capital Vampiro!' (32), for instance, which draws on the 'vampire' analogy employed by Marx in *Capital* (1976: 416, also see 342), along with Julio's disparaging retort that his friend and colleague Miguel allows himself to be 'bought' ('comprado') by refusing to join the strike (37), echoing the slavery imagery that is employed in communist writings,[17] illustrates both the female author's nuanced knowledge of political theory and implies a not unproblematic attempt to eschew the issue of gender.

While it is, arguably, not possible to overlook the significance of gender or sex when considering the 'formal' political domain in any geographical or historical context, De la Torre's decision to make use of a male narrator in a work published at a time when anxieties surrounding women's political subjectivity were heightened appears particularly pointed. Rather than depict a positive account of a socialist revolution told from the perspective of a female protagonist, the author uses the narrator's sex as a way of distancing herself from the failed, corrupt regime in *El banquete*. Julio can be seen to personify the uprising and government, which is illustrated by charting the character's development throughout the narrative: initially identified as a socialist (33, 52, 92, 238), worker (199, 217) and union member (27, 37, 52), Julio confesses how his personality changes after the rebels take control of the state: 'Amo mi profesión gubermental sobre todas las cosas y a veces... (¡perdón!) he desgustado la embriaguez del triunfo de los héroes y, acaso, me tuve por un semidiós...' (283).

Not only does the protagonist's transformation from an egalitarian idealist to an egocentric narcissist reflect the shift in the character and mood of the revolutionary regime, Julio also functions as a mouthpiece for the ideology and rhetoric that underpins the uprising. There is a clear emphasis on dialogue in the novel, which is particularly striking in the opening pages in which Julio recounts his recollections of an exchange between the male workers and factory boss, Pepet Espalter:

> [Espalter] — ... El capital que yo heredé en esta fábrica, era de diez millones de pesetas. Ahora bien: entendedme: Este capital no es solo dinero. No os vayáis a figurar un montón de pesetas más alto las chimeneas de la fábrica [...]
>
> (El pueblo oyente: — ¡Ah, ladrón! Confiesas que somos materia capitalizable! ¡Que tu padre nos dejó en tu poder como si fuéramos máquinas...!) [...]
>
> — Esperad un momento. Tenéis razón. Vosotros, mis obreros de 'La Jereza' sois partes de mi capital. Pero yo, a mi vez, soy vuestro capital único: ¡Yo soy rico!
>
> (— ¡Ah, bandido! ¡Y lo confiesas!) (8–9)

In this 'back and forth', which continues over four pages, the workers answer Espalter in unison, as one homogenous mass. The group mimic a Greek chorus, in line with the classical homage of the novel; a literary or theatrical device that depicts typically a 'homogenous group' that 'consists of non-individualized and often abstract forces [...] that represent higher moral or political interests' (Pavis 1998: 53). The dialogic quality that characterises the narrative conveys the collective reasoning that spurs the revolution:

— ¡Quién lo diría del patrono Espalter?

— ¡Ahora se verá en pequeño qué es la Revolución Social!

— ¡Siempre fué Pepet muy socialista!

— ¿Socialista? ¿Por dónde?

— ¿Sabéis? Esto es sencillamente lo que él dijo: Que está cansado de ser rico.

— Mejor para nosotros, que estamos cansados de ser pobres. (10)

As evidenced in the citation above, the visual layout of the text emphasises the significance of the dialogue, which critics observe is a key characteristic of the dialogic novel (see Thomas 2012: 38). These convoluted debates mirror the claustrophobic, tense atmosphere in the build-up to the uprising, while the dialogue, which is visually jarring to the reader, connotes the fast-paced surge of activity and textually inscribes the tension between the individual and collective that underpins *El banquete* through the innumerable, nameless (male) voices that contribute to a continuous stream of dialogue. Again, this structure alludes to the classical sources that inform De la Torre's literary strategy, notably Macrobius's *Saturnalia*, which focuses on a banquet to celebrate the festival of Saturnalia and is comprised of a series of male-voiced dialogues.

Acting as a spokesman for the rebels, the protagonist's speech is invested with the notion of collectivism and egalitarianism that sparks the revolution. When trying to coerce Miguel to join the strike, for instance, Julio uses the third person plural ('nosotros') (96, 130) to present himself as the voice of proletariat and, in a particularly tense scene during the violent uprising, Julio must convince an armed, unidentified soldier that he is also a revolutionary. He achieves this through strategic use of language, calling out '[p]ueblo' several times (141), and clarifies that the two men are fighting for the same cause by shouting '[e]res tú *nuestro...* ¿verdad?' (142; emphasis added). Julio's ideologically loaded language exemplifies the emphasis on dialogue in *El banquete* and underlines the link between the character and the revolution he (initially) supports. Not only does the author present her male protagonist as a personification of this flawed socialist model, she also uses Julio as a mouthpiece to criticise the government; an example of Bakhtin's doubled-voiced discourse. Through this double-edged approach, De la Torre is able to condemn the events in the narrative and, at the same time, maintain a critical distance from the perverted form of socialism that is portrayed in the novel. Self-reflexive prompts that implore the reader to pay attention ('entiéndase'), such as when Julio describes the success of the revolution (183) and a failed attempt to overthrow the new regime (194), make the author's intentions emphatically clear.

The protagonist can be seen, on the one hand, to internalise the tensions between individualism and collectivism that characterise the failings of the socialist experiment in the narrative. An illuminating example is found during the uprising, as Julio's shift from the third-person plural ('nosotros') to the singular voice ('yo') illustrates this conflict. Although his stream of consciousness begins by considering the views of his comrades, Julio's thoughts are interrupted by his sudden musings about a public bus he uses frequently and therefore considers his personal property: 'Siento algo así como la propiedad de un medio de locomoción que me sirve y me espera con fidelidad consciente' (106). Reading the protagonist as a personification of the revolutionary rhetoric he espouses here would suggest a lack of self-awareness that the author is only too keen to highlight, as Julio's sense of ownership of the bus is incongruous with Marxist doctrine.[18] The fact that his doubts occur during the revolution, before the rebels' objectives become distorted under the new regime, connotes an ideological ambiguity that a reader does not automatically identify with the author. Julio's lack of conviction, in this case, could reflect both the flawed ideology that underpins the uprising and De la Torre's own reflections on the nature of socialist revolution and collectivism.

In another, more visceral, example from the narrative, Julio describes the rebels as one homogeneous mass — '[t]enemos hambre canina. Siete horas de trabajo en la Casa del Pueblo nos han secado la garganta y el estómago' (105) — before becoming overwhelmed by a sense of isolation: '¡Soy solo! ¡Si triunfo... para mí; si muero... no dejo lutos ni lágrimas detrás de mí' (105). The literary strategy employed to reflect this ideological tension can be read in relation to Bakhtinian theories of dialogism. An understanding of the self, Bakhtin writes, is cultivated through dialogue with another: 'I achieve self-consciousness, I become myself only by revealing myself to another, through another and with another's help' (1981: 117). The socialist subtext to Bakhtin's notion of self-identification through external communication is, however, disrupted in El banquete, as Julio's efforts to harmonise his individual and collective needs is unsuccessful. For Dale Bauer, as she argues in Feminist Dialogics: A Theory of Failed Community (1988), the oppressive nature of hegemonic, authoritative, and therefore masculinist, dialogue inhibits intersubjectivity, silencing the female voice. By attributing not unreasonable misgivings about individual autonomy to a male figure associated with a failed socialist uprising, De la Torre is able to process these issues without undermining her own commitment to the cause. It is, of course, the author's sex that underscores this disidentification with her male narrator.

Another, more creative, means that De la Torre plays on the characterisation of the protagonist to make her own political point is through the echoes of socialist realism in El banquete. The author's resistance to uniformity and solidarity is manifest in the very structure of the novel as she evokes the socialist literary paradigm and subverts it from within. Drawing on a genre that was becoming increasingly popular in Spain at the time,[19] the author satirises the ideologically resolute socialist hero through her depiction of Julio. While the protagonist's role as a spokesman and advocate for the uprising mirrors prototypical traits of the socialist hero (see Clark 1997), Julio's faltering commitment to the collective and gradual disillusion with the revolution reads as a conversion narrative in reverse. As noted at the beginning of this chapter, the narrative is insistently self-reflexive about its subversion of this paradigm, as characters openly criticise the irony of politicised literature aimed at a predominantly illiterate proletariat. The literary context at the time of the novel's publication would suggest a conscious effort on the author's part to resist literary convention that engenders the depersonalisation and unification she aims to critique in the narrative. As Katerina Clark notes, there was a discernible shift from the late 1920s as socialist fiction became 'more closely controlled, and a narrower range of literary approaches was allowed' (1981: 32),[20] further demonstrating the contemporaneous quality of *El banquete*.

As well as using her male protagonist as a symbolic rejection of the sense of homogenisation and conformity that De la Torre problematises in *El banquete*, the author also makes use of the character to verbalise what, in all probability, is her own critique of the international socialist alliance. This is evidenced by juxtaposing De la Torre's views with Julio's criticism of the international congress. In a speech delivered in 1935, the author would underline how, to her mind, socialism and individual liberty are analogous, arguing that socialism will triumph, as 'las masas lo que quieren es libertad' ('Los partidos proletarios' 1935: 6), while Julio's condemnation of the regime in the narrative illustrates how the administration impedes individual liberty: 'Cuánto más socialista sea ese Congreso, más tendrá a intervenir en nuestros propios asuntos' (295). Juxtaposing Julio's critique of the international alliance with Marx's aim of achieving 'equality through the abolition of the principle of personal property and an absolute community of wealth' (1971: 79)[21] illustrates how the narrative dialogues with, rather than simply echoes, communist rhetoric. The protagonist, in this sense, functions as a mediator, allowing the author to work through her doubts about Marx's ideas without undermining the cause; reflecting De la Torre's own intentions for the novel. Although socialism is, in Julio's opinion, inherently flawed, as evidenced by his critique of the international congress, De la Torre's position is more nuanced and, arguably, suggests greater conviction. The conclusion to *El banquete* supports this reading, as the protagonist wants to return to his former work in the factory (289, 305) and quits his political activism: 'Y la sociedad... ¡que la arregle otro! Yo he puesto ya mi grano de arena. Estoy cansado' (304). If we understand Julio's departing remarks self-reflexively, the activist who would take his place was, conceivably, De la Torre herself given the publication of the novel preceded her impressive political career. The ambiguity of 'otro' can be read in relation to the author's role in *El banquete*: an allusive figure who informs Julio's political rhetoric and, at the same time, can be seen to undermine her fictional creation by chronicling his faltering commitment to achieving egalitarian reform.

Comparing the character of Julio with the protagonist in De la Torre's epistolary novel *Jardín de damas curiosas*, examined in Chapter One, accentuates how the author uses sex as a means of underlining her detachment from the protagonist in *El banquete*. Unlike Julio, the female protagonist in *Jardín* is almost demanding to be read as a fictionalised (re-)creation of De la Torre when debating key issues, particularly as she advocates suffrage and women's education.[22] Although both protagonists broadly share the author's ideological convictions, it is De la Torre's female character who most clearly evokes the author's position, whereas Julio, conversely, is identified with the problems the author associates with her socialist convictions. Rather than (re-)construct a fictionalised version of herself, as she appears to do, to an extent, in *Jardín*, the author uses the protagonist in *El banquete* to underline key details and work through her own ideological doubts in such a way as to not undermine her own commitment to socialism. The male protagonist, in this sense, functions as a proverbial scapegoat, tarred with the failed regime he embodies, allowing the author to avoid the sense of 'guilt by association' that Krishan Kumar notes plagued many left-wing writers in the climate of post-revolution Russia (1987: 382). One obvious benefit of using a male protagonist to achieve this sense of disidentification is that it discourages a reader from unduly conflating the author and protagonist, which is particularly tempting when the two share broadly the same ideological convictions.

Rather than a tacit acknowledgement of women's lack of political agency or a suggestion of resigned defeat, De la Torre, somewhat paradoxically, makes an emphatically feminist point through her male-dominated narrative that reads as a derisive critique at her male characters' expense. By creating a distance between the author and the protagonist in *El banquete*, De la Torre invites the reader to collude in her critique of the perverse socialist revolution that Julio personifies. As observed earlier, Mentora, the publisher of *El banquete*, presupposes a left-wing reader, an inference that is supported by the parallels with the socialist realist genre. The fact that De la Torre was a woman writer, however, problematises any assumptions about the sex of the readership. Her decision to publish *El banquete* under her own name, rather than use a male pseudonym or gender-neutral initial ('M. Torre'), could be understood as an understated invitation to women readers, as she effectively markets the work as relevant to women. In doing so, she ensures that her novel would reach the highest possible readership, many of whom would have had little interest in feminist or female-centric issues and, more significantly here, a female-authored socialist novel. Thus, although a consideration for the publisher's other output indicates that *El banquete* would likely reach the author's intended market of left-wing intellectuals who were conscious of the international political context, it also implies a largely male readership; a detail that De la Torre seems to acknowledge through the emphasis on male voices.

The sex of the author's envisaged or intended reader, however, is ambiguous. Despite crafting a narrative that is undoubtedly more accommodating and familiar to a male reader given it centres on male characters in an almost exclusively male work environment, De la Torre's personal convictions and professional trajectory make it unfeasible that she did not at least hope for her work to reach a female readership. As women and men's relationship with formal political debate was so starkly different in this context (and with Marxism in particular, as will be seen in the next section), it stands to reason that the reader's sex would have shaped their interpretation of the novel. For a male reader to collude in the female author's critique, he must assume an ideological agency to the author that supersedes that of the protagonist. He could, furthermore, be inclined to identify with the protagonist, whose development throughout the narrative would function as a mirror that critically reflects the male reader's doubts, failings and inconsistencies. In this sense, De la Torre's narrative affords her an ideological superiority over her male protagonist and reader that would go some way in explaining her seemingly conciliatory use of a male protagonist.

A female reader, on the other hand, is, perhaps, more willing to approach the flawed hero critically as, like the author, any sense of identification between reader and protagonist is immediately problematised by sex. The solidarity amongst left-wing women that characterised De la Torre's political career is, therefore, manifest here, as female reader and author collude, sharing in their critique of a male socialist who personifies a corrupt androcentric doctrine. The dialogic quality of the work accentuates the male-dominant nature of the failed regime in the narrative because, of the plethora of voices that engage in heated debate and ideological discussion in *El banquete*, all but two are male. The sex of the protagonist, in this sense, serves a double purpose, as it functions as a metaphor for the 'other', subverting the male-female power dynamic through the author's implied disidentification from the corrupt socialist dictatorship that is personified by the male protagonist, and underlines the predominance of male voices in socialist discourse.

'[N]o comprendemos vuestros derechos': Emancipation of Women and the Worker

Despite a shared belief in social reform and equality, Marxism and women's eman-cipation have a complex relationship. Although communist discourse proposes that women's emancipation is a natural consequence of workers' liberation, suggesting that the capitalist economic system is responsible for class and gender inequality,[23] feminist critiques of Marxism observe that conflating capitalist and patriarchal social structures occludes problems which specifically or disproportionately affect women. Marxism's focus on the economic system, critics have argued, distracts from a genuine aim for women's emancipation (see, for example: Guettel 1974; Hartmann 1981: 2–3; Haug 2015a: 81);[24] a tension between the emancipation of women and the worker that was debated by De la Torre's Party in the early decades of the twentieth century. Although the PSOE established a secretariat for 'women's issues' in 1918, as Frances Lannon notes, 'there was always a debate about whether a preoccupation about women was a distraction from the primary concern with class' (2011: 277). Perhaps most critically, *El banquete* was published just a month before the polemical vote that saw the only three female *diputadas* in the Cortes divided on the question of female suffrage.

As evidenced throughout this book, one of the most common leitmotivs in De la Torre's work is the political capital of voice and, by extension, political emancipation. While voicing socio-economic discourse through a male protagonist could, on the one hand, be a conscious effort on the part of the female author (at least ostensibly) to attribute a sense of authority, veracity or legitimacy to her views, De la Torre's decision to use Julio as a mouthpiece for a flawed application of her beliefs suggests a power play between author and protagonist that, in this instance, is invested with sexual and gender politics, as the author emphatically reasserts her own ideological stance over that of the protagonist. De la Torre, in other words, possesses a critical awareness and sense of justice that the male socialist lacks, affording her the moral high ground. In *El banquete*, there are two prominent female characters whose dialogue in the novel can be seen to index their political agency: Lena Fornés, a factory worker who opposes the strike and revolution, and María Zarja, a revolutionary and leader of an all-female union.

Of the two women, Lena features most frequently in the narrative as she is the object of the protagonist's affection. The character can be seen to personify the conflict between Julio's personal desires and ideological beliefs because, like her brothers, she opposes his revolutionary politics. The two engage in frequent debates about the strike, with Lena refusing to take part as she believes work is an honourable endeavour: 'No se puede dejar de trabajar, Julio... Como se pueda, donde sea y como sea... cuanto se hace por lograr trabajo honrado es honroso' (61). Although Lena's brothers share in her objections to the strike in *El banquete*, which invalidates a simplistic female/conservative male/revolutionary binary, it is, nevertheless, curious that the most prominent female character in the narrative is opposed to the strike. Through her romanticised depiction of hard work, Lena simultaneously underlines her emphatic rejection of socialist principles and evokes the Marxist concept of 'false consciousness', considered by Engels, which denotes an uncritical acceptance of the capitalist economic model: 'He works with mere thought material which he accepts without examination as the product of thought, he does not investigate further for a more remote process independent of thought; indeed its origin seems obvious to him' (Engels 1968b: np).

Reading Julio as a manifestation of the communist rhetoric he espouses, the pair's arguments invoke the problematic link between emancipation for women and the worker that characterises Marxist doctrine. Lena's objection to the uprising and strike implies a tension or disharmony between women and the left, with the pairs' heated debates illustrating the animosity between women and the socialist doctrine that Julio represents. The dynamic between the pair during their debates reads as an allegory for the limited recognition of women's ideological agency in communist rhetoric. Just as Julio makes strategic use of language to index socialist ideology figuratively, speaking for and on behalf of the worker, when arguing with Miguel, as noted earlier, he again employs the first-person plural to reinforce his point: '¿Quieres dar a entender que yo, que "nosotros" en nuestra inferioridad mental no comprendemos vuestros derechos?' (64). When speaking to Lena, the use of 'nosotros' is invested with gender-political significance as his initial lapse into the first person, emphasised by the use of quotation marks, implies that he prioritises his personal affection for Lena over their ideological conflict. The contrast between the singular (tú/yo) and plural voice ('nosotros'/'vuestros derechos') connotes how the characters' relationship functions as a microcosm for the broader ideological divide, while Julio's (accurate) use of the generic masculine and the ambiguous way he identifies Lena with the opposing side, through his description of 'vuestros derechos' (rather than 'vosotras/os'), encapsulates women's unstable relationship with socialist discourse.

Juxtaposing this exchange with a similar back and forth in *Jardín* would suggest that the ambiguous depiction of gender is strategic on the author's part. As examined in Chapter One, the significance of gender in *Jardín* is immediately obvious to the reader as, when debating feminist issues with her nephew, Pulquería underlines how their personal disagreement relates to a broader ideological divide by using the first person feminine plural ('nosotras') and addressing her nephew as 'vosotros'. Switching focus from a hypothetical woman-centric initiative in *Jardín* to a contemporary political reality in *El banquete*, De la Torre plays on language to explore women's experiences and roles within this context. The lack of clarity in the text as to whether, to Julio's mind, he considers Lena amongst a female, male, or mixed group could be read in relation to the dearth of female-specific legislation in socialist doctrine. That is to say, the character's linguistic ambiguity, which stands out when compared with his specificity elsewhere and the examples found in *Jardín*, textually inscribes the absence of female-specific concerns in the socialist rhetoric that he represents. The sex of the protagonist here is critical, as it suggests that, for De la Torre, this erasure constitutes a form of patriarchal oppression.

There are other, more allusive, ways that Julio's speech serves to undermine or negate Lena's ideological agency. His refusal to facilitate or reinforce Lena's point of view during their debate, for instance, could be read in reference to the unrealised expectation of support and guidance that is implied in Marxist doctrine: 'Quiere saber si yo adivino el resto. Pero yo no la ayudo' (61). Julio's retort to Lena when she tries to impress upon him the difficulties faced by non-strikers, furthermore, can be understood as a tacit acknowledgement of the absence of meaningful consideration of women's rights: '[N]o comprendemos vuestros derechos' (64). De la Torre, in this instance, can be seen to voice a critique of socialist discourse through her male protagonist, emphasising the patriarchal (or at least androcentric) nature of the theory and undermining the male figure who embodies it through a satirical self-reflexive critique at the character's expense.

As well as highlighting a conceptual flaw in socialist doctrine, Julio's perception of Lena as an uncritical conduit for conservative rhetoric taps into the interface of socialist and feminist discourses, specifically women's suffrage and relationship with leftist politics. Julio's reflections when Lena is defending her decision to break the strike illustrate this point as his inner thoughts suggest an unclear or inconsistent understanding of her ideological agency. Although Lena is speaking, Julio contemplates how the Sindicato de Empleados Libres is flailing due to Miguel's resistance (61), apparently oblivious to the impact of Lena's abstention. By associating Miguel's actions with Lena's speech, the protagonist attributes an ambiguous level of political agency to Lena that echoes the commonly used argument against women's suffrage which centred on the reasoning that women already contribute to political matters by influencing their male relatives. Concepción Arenal, for instance, made this argument in her seminal *La mujer del porvenir* in 1884: 'Cuando sea ilustrada, influirá en la política en el voto del hermano, del esposo, del hijo, del padre y hasta del abuelo' (2009: 87). What is interesting here is how Julio's perception of Lena's agency highlights a patriarchal undertone to feminist and socialist discourses, as he acknowledges that she is defending the views he opposes (indeed, he argues with her frequently) but does not appear to hold Lena responsible for her actions.

The fact that his ignorance is probably self-imposed so as to avoid viewing the object of his affection in a negative light underlines the paternalistic undertone of the protagonist's perception of Lena. Grounding this reading firmly within its historical context, Julio's inability to recognise Lena as an autonomous individual with her own views alludes to female socialists' objections to female suffrage. As outlined in the Introduction and Chapter One, Kent objected, believing Spanish women were not yet 'politically sophisticated enough to support the socialist cause' (Tolliver 2011: 247), while Nelken did not think that Spanish women were sufficiently prepared or experienced to vote. In *El banquete*, De la Torre appears to imply a patriarchal and paternalistic undertone to the arguments presented by Kent and Nelken which, again, is emphasised by the protagonist's sex. In many ways, Lena and Julio's relationship functions as an ideal microcosm for this conflict as the sense of ambiguity or understanding that characterises women's place in and relationship with Marxist rhetoric is reflected in their relationship: it is never explicitly stated that the two are romantically involved. Rather the reader sees Lena through Julio's eyes, meaning her views, behaviour and character are mediated through a socialist male figure. The leading female character in *El banquete*, in other words, is reduced to what the male socialist thinks or assumes about her.

What is particularly curious about the depiction of Lena is how the figure is, on the whole, portrayed in a favourable light by the author. When describing her opposition to the strike, for instance, Lena's reasoning is logical and, arguably, admirable, as she emphasises the honourable nature of work ('trabajo honrado es honroso') (61). The female/conservative male/revolutionary binary that is implied by the Lena/Julio dynamic suggests friction between the author's socialist and feminist beliefs. Although De la Torre was not, at this point, elected to office, evidence of her support for women's suffrage is found in *Jardín*, published over ten years before the 1931 ballot. It stands to reason, therefore, that, on this issue, De la Torre would have differed from her socialist colleagues who prioritised their socialist beliefs over women's rights. Other than the obviously problematic nature of assuming political convictions based on a voter's sex, Gerard Alexander also provides a nuanced, convincing argument to disprove any trend, focusing on claims that the electoral victory of a right-wing coalition in 1933 (when De la Torre was first elected) was due to women disproportionately voting for conservative parties (1999). It could be argued, based on this close reading of Julio and Lena's relationship, that De la Torre was, unlike Nelken and Kent, more optimistic about women's potential for political debate and critical reasoning, whatever their view.

De la Torre's efforts to involve women in socialist initiatives would suggest that the author was conscious of this tension and sought to account for this potential problem in her political career, while her collaboration with other left-wing female politicians implies that, unlike her socialist colleagues, De la Torre prioritised her feminist loyalties over an uncritical loyalty to socialism. A close reading of one exchange between Lena and Julio is evidence of this point. Although Julio is pointedly silent, refusing to engage with Lena when she is critical of the uprising, she continues, undeterred:

> Pero yo no la ayudo y ella continua. Y espera un momento mi réplica, que ella conoce; mi réplica en defensa de los derechos del trabajador, que tantas veces hemos discutido en nuestra larga amistad. (61)

As the protagonist's lack of assistance does not deter or impede Lena's dialogue, in the diegesis and at a textual level, De la Torre implies a victory for female-voiced ideological debate, no matter what the point of view. The fact that the first female socialists elected to office opposed women's suffrage, fearing that women lacked the critical faculties to process political debates is, therefore, undermined by Lena's confident display. The male protagonist can be seen to internalise this paradox, as despite his earlier claim that he appreciates her 'pensativa cabeza' (27), in practice, Julio does not credit Lena with having thought-out, reasoned opinions, and views her as an uninformed extension of her brothers and male colleagues. The implication here is that, despite a shared belief in social reform and equality, socialist and feminist objectives are often incongruous and, crucially, the intersection of the two can be seen to highlight a fundamental flaw inherent to both: prioritising the collective good over individual liberty.

While a tension between women and leftism is implied by Lena's opposition to the strike, the relative absence of the only female socialist character in the narrative, María Zarja, connotes women's isolation within socialist circles. An advocate for social(ist) justice (89), María is the leader of an (exclusively female) union for seamstresses (10),[25] who is celebrated for achieving concessions from the factory boss during a strike (10, 23). The details of María's activism, however, are not revealed. Considering the depiction of María's ideological autonomy alongside her textual subjectivity illustrates how the author draws the reader's attention to the character's virtual absence in the novel as a comment on women's role in socialist activism. The character's limited role in *El banquete* is emphasised by the fact that she speaks at the Sala de Conferencias (122) and, although she loses out on the role of socialist (anti-) hero to Julio, María documents current events (258). There is a tangible contrast, in other words, between how much impact María seems to have in the diegesis based on what the reader can piece together and how much information is outlined by the male narrator. Bronwen Thomas observes that this is commonplace in the dialogue novel, with readers having to 'work especially hard to unearth even the most basic information about characters' (2012: 67).

Dialogue, Thomas adds, is therefore critical to characterisation, as we are conscious of how utterances 'may be manipulated by others' (2012: 73). For María, she is misrepresented in as much as she is overlooked in the narrative, with the voices of her male comrades prioritised. Paradoxically, then, María is at the same time exposed and unseen, effective and powerless, articulate and mute; functioning as a convenient metaphor for women's relationship with socialist thought and activism at this point in Spanish political history. At the same time, the character's socialist activism, union involvement and flair for writing brings to mind the author herself, with María a fictional manifestation of her exclusion from political circles (remembering *El banquete* was written before De la Torre was elected to office). The character's name is likely in homage to Lejárraga, De la Torre's personal and political ally who, like De la Torre, would not take her seat for the PSOE (in Granada) until 1933. It is by mediating the description of María through Julio that the misogynistic undertones of socialism are suggested, as he focuses on her beauty and sensitivity (10, 24, 241), suggesting that, for the protagonist, María is a woman first and a political figure second. She therefore acquires a double subalternity that is imposed on her by the protagonist and the author as she is objectified by her socialist (male) colleague and through her (in)visibility within the narrative.

For Julio, there is a discernible tension between the way he views María as a woman and as a socialist. The undertones of misogyny that are suggested by Julio's comments about María's beauty are mitigated somewhat by his positive description of her as comparable with famous female figures known for their involvement with social change, such as Carlota Carday, a figure of the French Revolution, Louise Michel, a French anarchist who fought for a social revolution, and Saint Teresa de Ávila, the Spanish mystic and writer (24). The ideological, temporal and geographical gulf that is implied by comparing contemporary French revolutionaries with a Spanish figure who, despite her monumental contribution to feminist thought in Spain, is nevertheless associated with Catholicism and a more moderate approach than is implied by the French revolutionaries illustrates how, in Julio's eyes, a politically engaged Spanish woman is a rara avis. The author herself evidenced women's involvement with socialist activism, as did several other famous figures, underscoring how Julio's suggestions are intended critically to highlight the limitations and blind spots of socialist thought.

Viewing the character of María through Julio's eyes, the latter functioning here as a critical conduit for leftist activism in a practical sense, could suggest that De la Torre's envisaged readership were predominantly the revolutionary men that she associated with the foundations of socialist thought she displaces in the novel. While readers of both sexes would have understood how the description of María relates to her sex, particularly given De la Torre underlines this point through references to her appearance, the impact on a female reader would form an intratextual female solidarity between reader, author and character. Thus, a male reader is forced to confront his own ignorance, whereas a female reader is inclined to identify with the overlooked, yet politically articulate and morally just, figure of María. There is, furthermore, an undertone of ridicule at the protagonist's expense that invites the female reader to collude with the author as, despite Julio's nuanced ideological views and important government work, his perception is clouded when it comes to women. While his adoration of Lena gives the reader a sense of a lovesick adolescent, the protagonist's attraction to María implies that Julio's critical faculties, and, by extension, those of the socialist male workers he represents, are tainted or weakened by his sexual and romantic desires. Although the nuances of this reading would almost certainly be lost on a male reader at the time of publication, Julio's unsatisfied longing would likely amuse a female reader more familiar with romantic fiction.

The protagonist's description of María's professional accomplishments exemplifies how the coming together of socialist doctrine and women's ideological agency, represented allegorically by Julio and Lena's relationship and internalised in the characterisation of María, functions as a catalyst for highlighting the failings inherent in socialist and feminist discourses. For Julio, María's ability is notable even when compared with her male colleagues: '[U]no de nuestros más puros prestigios societarios; *uno de los mejores oradores*, además, que hablan español en el mundo...' (10; emphasis added). Julio's insistence that she is impressive on an international scale suggests both the protagonist's admiration for the female activist and her competence, as he uses the generic masculine plural ('uno de nuestros') to both negate Lena's individual agency and celebrate María's successes. Although women of both political viewpoints are relegated to the shadows by men, Julio's recognition of María's ability suggests that if a truly exceptional left-wing woman is able to 'join the party' (practically and figuratively), she may be as equally competent as men and, crucially, her accomplishments will be acknowledged alongside those of her male comrades. Rather than undermine María's accomplishments by considering her a leading 'female' voice, a limiting compliment frequently attributed to the author by contemporary and present-day critics, Julio compares her favourably amongst men.

Comparing the two female characters illustrates how, in both cases, rejecting or dismissing women's ideological agency can be damaging to the socialist cause: Lena opposes revolutionary politics and María, who is evidently skilled and capable, is ignored. De la Torre can be seen to try to harmonise the conflicting socialist and feminist values that she herself embodied through María. Whereas Lena is identified with her brothers and potential lover, María is aligned with her male colleagues suggesting that workers' activism *could* be a more tolerant environment for professional women. Socialism, in this sense, could be a natural ally of the workers' movement under the right circumstances, while it categorises women in relation to the family. Lena's rejection of revolutionary politics, however, affords her a liberty not available to María, who must negotiate her dual lack of political voice as a female socialist, as the female characters' degree of ideological agency is paralleled with their visibility in the narrative.

'[L]a Minerva de la Casa del Pueblo': Feminising Socialist Discourse

Arguably the most obvious advantage of exploring the re-conceptualisation of political ideologics through literature is its multiple interpretative layers, which leave room for the nuances, contradictions and depth of political discourse; a quality we could describe as elasticity. Harbouring the potential to reflect, instruct and hypothesise, fiction can function as an experimental testing ground for working through different resolutions to the problems of society. As the analysis thus far has demonstrated, De la Torre uses the narrative as a means of exploring the failings of socialist discourse, intimating that women's exclusion from revolutionary politics undermines the socialist cause. While it has been argued that Julio attempts to undermine Lena's political agency, mirroring the practical and symbolic silencing of women in socialist discourse that was heightened at this juncture in Spanish political history, she does, nevertheless, function as a catalyst for the protagonist's ideological development. The author can be seen to play on hegemonic gender norms and the (hetero-)sexual dynamic to denote Lena's indirect influence over the protagonist's gradual disillusionment with the socialist revolution in such a way as to underline how, rather than being a hinderance, gender is key to her political agency.

In an exchange more befitting of romantic fiction than an ideologically loaded political commentary, Lena and Julio share a tender moment during the violent uprising that alters the protagonist's perception on the revolution. The pair take shelter and, visibly frightened, Lena seeks comfort from Julio by holding onto his arm: 'Lena tiene miedo. Siento que su mano tiembla sobre mi brazo y me arrastra en un movimiento de retroceso hacia el fondo del pasadizo' (119). Though this scene appears to be a hyperbolic account of the narrator's romantic fantasy, reinforcing a patriarchal dynamic of men protecting vulnerable women, it is an important turning point in Julio's ideological development. Through his emotional connection with Lena, Julio begins to empathise with the opposition he had previously considered a 'montón idiota' (105), reflecting on the suffering and terror that the uprising causes. Although Julio's close friend and Lena's brother, Miguel, dies tragically during the fighting, the protagonist's thoughts are centred solely on protecting Lena. He pointedly avoids any discussion about Miguel's fate in order to 'tranquilizarla' (120) and, rather than join his comrades, he prioritises Lena's well-being by finding her a safe hiding place away from the violent clashes, a kindness that Lena acknowledges and appreciates (121).

Though the chaotic nature of the revolt mean that Lena's vulnerability and fear are undoubtedly justified, the significance of gender is emphasised by the fact that Julio reveals his own fears and trepidation during the uprising (105, 114, 150). Rather than being genuinely heroic and courageous, that is to say, Julio effectively fulfils the role expected of him as a man. While this scene is undoubtedly problematic from a feminist perspective, since it appears to reinforce a paternalistic male/protector female/victim dynamic, the protagonist's reactions are more akin to a lovesick adolescent than a domineering figure of patriarchal authority. The sense of sexual tension between the two, implied by Julio's comment that he feels Lena's hand 'tremble' (or, perhaps 'quiver') on his arm, furthermore, suggests the protagonist's sexual frustration rather than a brewing romantic encounter. Whether we understand this scene as a genuine, albeit poorly executed, attempt at writing romance or a further example of the satire that pervades *El banquete* (I am inclined towards the latter), what is clear is that the author plays on gender politics in order to imply that Lena has some impact on the protagonist's unravelling commitment to the revolutionary cause. If De la Torre wrote this scene with a female reader in mind, drawing on the formulaic romance novels demarcated for a female audience that were hugely popular in the early decades of the twentieth century (see Ávila 2005; Navajas 1991), Julio's account is more likely to invite a wry smile at the male protagonist's expense than invoke a romantic — or sexual — fantasy.

Situating this reading with its historical context illustrates how De la Torre taps into the tensions between socialist and feminist beliefs in such a way as to satirise an assumed lack of ideological agency based on gender, suggesting a degree of political influence that is consubstantial with prototypically 'feminine' characteristics, specifically sensitivity and vulnerability. It is precisely because of her anxiety and fear, that is to say, that Lena prompts Julio's flailing commitment to social revolution.

This episode mirrors an earlier exchange in which Julio dismisses Lena's opposition to the strike by insisting that she speaks out of fear ('miedo') (62), revealing his paternalistic understanding of Lena and her views. While Lena's behaviour appears to prove Julio's reasoning, De la Torre shifts the emphasis from Lena's anxieties to the protagonist's flailing commitment to his socialist convictions. The implied lack of autonomy that speaking out of fear would suggest is subverted, as the character is afforded a degree of textual agency that effectively compensates for the way Julio, and the socialist doctrine he embodies, dismisses her critical ability.

Lena's impact on the protagonist, thus, influences the progression of the narrative, with this scene constituting a pivotal moment in Julio's character development. The implied link between political and textual agency that this suggests is illustrated by the tangible shift in Lena's language that occurs after this point. Although she evades subjectivity through the use of the impersonal during an early debate, using 'se puede' and 'se hace' even though she is referring to Julio (61), Lena pointedly aligns herself with the anti-revolutionaries during a later argument: ¿Tú crees que solo tú sufres en esta lucha social? Piensa que nosotros... también sufrimos, Julio...' (178). Capitalising on politically loaded language, Lena uses Julio's strategy against him, subverting his paternalistic reactions to her anti-revolutionary views by identifying conservatism with a mixed-sex collective ('nosotros') and socialism with a singular, male voice ('tú'). Lena's *political* impact here, therefore, relates to socio-economic theories and sexual politics in equal measure.

By implicitly affording Lena an autonomous political identity that is invested with (hetero-)sexual politics, the author depicts how patriarchal convention engenders conservative rhetoric. Julio's treatment of Lena appears to undermine communist discourse at a base level, as the protagonist's perception of their exchange effectively counters Engels' argument that communism would revolutionise relations between the sexes, believing that the abolition of private property, which made women reliant on their husbands, and the introduction of communal education, Marxism would 'transform the relations between the sexes into a purely private affair' (1971a: 185).[26] Not only does Julio describe himself in the protector role but his commitment to the cause falters. The fact that this scene is told from the protagonist's perspective only serves to emphasise the hypocrisy of socialist doctrine that this implies. Considering De la Torre's understanding of feminism in relation to Julio's thoughts at the end of the narrative exemplifies how the interface of gender and government politics is borne out in *El banquete* in such a way as to underline how socialism hinders its own development by excluding women. As indicated earlier, the novel concludes with Julio planning to leave his political activism behind, hoping instead to start a family life with Lena. Drawing on a common trope in Soviet literature (Purkey 2013: 117), Julio believes that his dream of having children with Lena will lead to the metaphorical birth of the revolution: '[M]i estirpe de revolucionario transmitiendo a nuestros hijos todo su talento y toda mi ánima de luchador impertérrito...' (304).

By envisaging Lena as the mother of ideologically committed offspring, the protagonist can be seen to quash her political agency, as both a socially engaged worker and a woman. Although the narrative charts his ideological development, then, the notion of women's ideological autonomy continues to elude him. Not only are her views dismissed as inconsequential, she also becomes a vessel for the socialist revolution that she does not support; a fate that encapsulates the conflict between leftist and feminist discourses that is interrogated in the narrative. Alluding to Gorky's *Mother* (1906), an author and text popular in Spain at this time (see Purkey 2013: 16, 48), De la Torre touches on the critical impact of a maternal figure on the evolution of socialist thought in *El banquete* through the singular reference to Julio's mother, as the protagonist recalls how her death due to employers' negligence emboldened his revolutionary convictions (32). The inevitable tension between De la Torre's socialist and feminist loyalties, however, is tangible, as the impact of Julio's mother on the development of Julio's ideological consciousness, and, by extension, socialist thought, is sacrificial rather than empowered.

An allegorical reading makes clear the symbiotic link between the development of socialist and feminist discourses, as the child that Julio envisages would combine the notion of women's ideological autonomy associated with Lena with the socialist thought personified by the protagonist. Synthesising these oppositional, inherently paradoxical ideologies through biological reproduction rests on the assumption that this fusion is organic and instinctive, as motherhood functions as a metaphor that bridges the gap between a feminist and socialist initiative. Bearing in mind how a comparison of the characters of Lena and María would suggest that leftist politics are more open to less prescriptive roles for women, the fact Lena's greatest impact of political development is through her hypothetical child reinforces how the conservative view she is identified with is invested with hegemonic gender norms. As *El banquete* was written after De la Torre's brief marriage in 1917, which was annulled after fifteen days and produced no children, it is likely that, at this point in her life, De la Torre considered socialist activism and motherhood as two distinct paths, with each of her female characters following alternative routes.

The merging of feminist and socialist concerns is made manifest in the characterisation of María. Given that she embodies the author's fundamental ideological principles, it is not unexpected that the ideas she proposes are presented favourably. During pivotal debates about how to approach the uprising, María voices her belief that a just society should be achieved without bloodshed:

> Pero es espantoso que necesitemos del laboreo de los cañones para poder sembrar la justicia social... Es como si se preconizase el suicidio para la curación de las enfermedades. (89)

María's hope for a non-violent revolution directly opposes Julio's support for 'un socialismo revoltoso' (32), a contrast that implies that armed struggle identified with men (Julio) and peaceful reform is associated with women (María). Since the subsequent rebellion results in a bloody, violent conflict, a counter narrative is implied in which socialist revolution is engendered by a peaceful, female-led uprising. By questioning any organic link between socialism and armed conflict, the narrative points to another ideological failing of Marxist writings which, in this instance, has a gender-political subtext. A female (or 'feminine') perspective, this implies, is crucial to the re-conceptualisation of socialist thought, as qualities traditionally associated with 'femininity', such as tenderness, docility and nurturing, are positively projected onto (male) political doctrine.

Just as Lena's influence over the protagonist relates to gender and sexual politics, then, so too does María's understanding of socialist reform. The nexus of prototypically 'feminine' behaviour and critical reflection that this suggests is reflected in María's nickname in the factory, where she is known as 'la Minerva' of the Casa del Pueblo (24, 308), a reference to the goddess of learning, useful arts and 'feminine' accomplishments (Berens 2007: 47) and 'the thinking, calculating, and inventive power personified' (Smith 1881: 449). In *Jardín*, Minerva is described as the goddess of wisdom who, nevertheless, had to be considered beautiful ('hubo, para dar idea de ella, necesidad de figurarla hermosa' [1917: 231]), unlike Venus, the goddess of beauty, who need not appear intelligent; a contrast that exemplifies how powerful female figures (real or not) were viewed in relation to femininity.

María's suggestion of a non-violent revolution in *El banquete* evokes an extra-textual female-voiced socialist dialogue as De la Torre uses the character means of expounding her own opposition to violent conflict and, at the same time, points to a distinctly female — and feminist — socialist network. For the author, socialism and war were ideologically incongruous, as she believed bloodshed only served to fuel the capitalist machine: 'la guerra solo sirve para defender los intereses del capitalismo y destruir la Humanidad' ('Actos socialistas en Galicia' 1935: 8; 'Actuación de los partidos' 1935: 12). This idea is tangible in *El banquete*. Although the male strikers endeavour to carry out an uprising which does not adhere to the 'obscuro dogma de Moloch' (123), the subsequent revolution is allegorised in the narrative in a fantastical scene in which the spectre of Moloch, symbolising war, conflict and violence, oversees the uprising. Moloch's description of his callous domination over the population suggests that he is orchestrating, rather than passively witnessing, the brutality: 'Yo que tengo siete hornos de fuego para consumir la Fuerza humana [...] ¿No veis cómo yo me río de vuestras precauciones?' (307). The workers' collectivised struggle for justice, this suggests, is an illusion, pointing to the powerlessness of the revolutionaries, dictated by a ruthless, parasitic force, alluding to a Marxist understanding of a capitalist employer. De la Torre appears to emphasise how the revolutionary model suggested by María, and undoubtedly supported by the author, constitutes a more authentic and productive realisation of socialist values.

The most immediate concept evoked by the link between non-violence and a female character is the historic relationship between women and pacifism, as anti-war movements were an early means through which women could participate in public activism (see Chapter One). Although a reader may be tempted here to oversimplify De la Torre's depiction of women, given Lena's fear and María's opposition to violence appear to reinforce expectations of female behaviour, her criticism of the assumed link between women and pacifism suggests otherwise. As evidenced throughout this book, it is important to understand De la Torre's views on pacifism, war and women diachronically: as examined in Chapter One, De la Torre plays on discourses of women's vulnerability and sensitivity to decry violent conflict, while, as we shall see in the next chapter, the Spanish Civil War, not unexpectedly, hardened De la Torre, as she came to see war, and women's role in it, as tragically necessary in some cases. Women, she would argue in 'Feminismo y pacifismo', a speech delivered in 1933, are not 'pacifistas por doctrina y ni aun por sentimiento' (1934: 57–58).

Rather than simply a mouthpiece for the author's views or an embodiment of the female-centric pacifist movement, the character of María calls to mind a pioneering figure who was influential in the development of socialist and feminist theories: Flora Tristan (1803–1844). Tristan's seminal *L'Union ouvrière* (1843) would encourage a united workers' movement five years before the publication of *The Communist Manifesto*. Tristan calls for 'l'UNION OUVRIÈR' throughout her manifesto, emphasising the need for female and male workers to unite: 'UNION UNIVERSELLE DES OUVRIERS ET OUVRIÈRES' (1843: 4). Intriguingly, Marx always refused to meet Tristan in person and would rubbish rumours that began circulating in 1925 that her writings had influenced his ideology (Collins and Weil-Sayre 1973: 229, 230).[27] Unlike the writings of Marx and Engels, Tristan's work makes specific reference to female workers, which she emphasises in the section 'Le *pourquoi* je mentionne les femmes' (1843: 43–70). While Tristan's emphasis on female workers mirrors De la Torre's commitment to involving women in socialist and union causes, which is to be expected of female socialists, her revolutionary manifesto differed crucially from Marx and Engels on one fundamental point: her staunch opposition to violent revolution. The immanently gendered contrast between violent conflict and peaceful reform that is personified by Julio and María, then, can be applied to socialist doctrine on a broader, more conceptual level, as Julio and María, on this issue at least, can be considered fictional re-creations of Marx and Tristan. Julio's frequent mimicking of communist rhetoric would support this reading, as would the comparison between María and French female activists in the narrative (24).

María's lack of visibility in the text should, with this in mind, be read as a symbolic reference to Tristan's erasure from the history of socialist discourse; a parallel that implies that *El banquete* taps into a socialist feminist network that is made manifest in María. Just as María's vision for a humane socialist uprising constitutes a female-led alternative to the nightmarish, male-voiced anti-utopia that occurs in the narrative, the character's (and author's, in this case) ideation also point to a female-voiced socialist discourse that has, like María, been silenced by more vocal male comrades. For De la Torre, the successful realisation of revolutionary, egalitarian values would only be achieved thanks to women's active contribution to socialist doctrine and activism and, before she would dedicate her political career to defending these ideals, fiction would afford her a means of making her contribution to socialist and feminist debates. Not unexpectedly, the only contemporary (male) critic to review the work overlooked such nuances:

> Though she has intended the volume as propaganda for her special political creed, the author recognises that there is a mountain of human weakness made up of selfishness, ignorance, lack of perspective, unpreparedness to face ideal

> conditions, etc. which must be levelled before her Utopia can become fact. The
> novel does not have a single character who has enough energy to be propelled
> by his own legs, and is almost destitute of gripping incidents. (Fucilla 1932: 210)

The entrenched bias of male critics at this time, along with the unjustifiable criticism that *El banquete* is 'almost destitute of gripping incidents' (Fucilla 1932: 210), not only brings to mind one possible reason for De la Torre's limited recognition today, it also suggests that the text would be misjudged and/or misunderstood by male readers. For a female reader, *El banquete* would have almost certainly harboured an extra nuance or subtext, which, given De la Torre's political career and literary output, we may infer was an intentional convergence of her literary strategies and ideological ideas. Perhaps the most meaningful conclusion to be drawn, therefore, is that the narrative engages with and exemplifies the notion of an isolated female, socialist voice in male-dominated debates, a concern De la Torre would devote her life to tackling.

Reading *El banquete* as a barometer of De la Torre's ideological evolution denotes how, on the cusp of her political career, she was evaluating contemporary socialist discourses and, critically, examining the gender and sexual politics of socialism in such a way as to carve a space for her views. Understood within its broader literary context, moreover, this fictionalised political project can be considered a prescient precursor to a later body of female-authored texts that reject Soviet communism, both as a viable governmental model and a blueprint for Spanish republicanism. As well as reflecting the 'spontaneous, revolutionary subjectivity experienced by many during the Spanish Civil War' that Gina Herrmann (2005: 105) observes in relation to Ibárruri and Teresa Pàimes (another leading female communist in Republican Spain), the novel also functions as an intergenerational, transnational link between fictionalised exemplars of socialist feminism in Soviet Russia and Spain. Indeed, *El banquete* can be considered the missing link in the intertextual dialogue Lynn Purkey (2013: 120) observes between Alexandra Kollantai's *Vasilisa Malygina*, the tale of a Bolshevik activist published as *La bolchevique enamorada* in Spain in 1927, and Luisa Carnés's *Tea Rooms: Mujeres obreras* (1935), which depicts the lives of working women in Madrid. While De la Torre's characterisation of María lacks the eminence of Kollantai's empowered protagonist (whose ideological convictions cause tensions with her increasingly conservative husband), Carnés's female lead, who also rejects marriage, offers a metafictional homage to De la Torre, as suggested by the character's name: Matilde. The socialist feminist consciousness developed in *El banquete*, then, not only forms part of a network of female-authored political narratives in Spain, but can also be understood as a seminal literary and political text that shaped the works that would follow.

Notes to Chapter 3

1. Research for this chapter also forms the basis of an article published in the *Journal of Spanish Cultural Studies* (Madden 2021).

2. 'En Madrid y provincias: Varios actos de propaganda política y social' 1932: 4; 'En Madrid y provincias: Varios actos de propaganda política' 1932: 6; 'Propaganda republicana feminina en Ávila' 1932: 4.

3. Lorenzo 1932a: 3; Lorenzo 1932b: 3.

4. Hereafter, all in-text references to *El banquete de Saturno: Novela social* will be to the 1931 edition.

5. Though it had been argued that satire is traditionally conservative, seeking to retain the established order (Elliot 1971: 215), Dustin Griffin notes that critics are undecided on the political leaning of satire (1994: 133). Similarly, George Austin Test offers examples of satires that suggest 'conservative' or 'liberal' ideals (1991: 13). For Griffin, there is an inherent progressive quality to the genre, as 'satire thrives in the face of — or because of — censorship or political reprisal' (1994: 139).

6. There are further intertextual links to Pardo Bazán's extensive output in *El banquete*. Pardo Bazán's 1903 articles on Práxedes Mateo Sagasta (1972: 149–54) and Joaquin Costa and *caciquismo* (1972: 155–61), for instance, focus on the same subject matter and figures as De la Torre's political biography *El ágora* (1930), while the tensions between individual liberty and a united workers' movement in *El banquete* echo Pardo Bazán's reports on strikes in Germany. Her observation that the political Right successfully quashed or undermined strike actions by putting an emphasis on individualism (1972: 73) seems particularly pertinent.

7. Examples include Mario Aguilar's *El proceso Dreyfus* (1931), Giuseppe Torre's *El fascismo al desnudo* (1931) and Grigorii Zinov'evich Besedovskii's *Memorias por un diplomático soviético* (1931) The political character of the Mentora editorial during the Second Republic is noted by Mónica Baró Llambias, who notes that many texts focused on international politics, including commentaries on China, the United Kingdom and the Soviet Union (2006, 91).

8. See the 'Principles of Communism' for Friedrich Engels's explanation of how communism differs from socialism (1971a: 186–87).

9. Karl Marx famously declared religion 'the opium of the people' and argued that '[t]he abolition of religion as the *illusory* happiness of the people is the demand for their *real* happiness' (1970: 131; original emphasis).

10. Accounts of the socio-political climate in Russia also came from the political right. The right-wing press interpreted the October revolution 'as the triumph of evil over good' (Gómez 2002: 67), and travelogues by conservative authors were published in the 1920s, such as Vals i Taberner's *Un viatger català a la Rússia de Stalin* (1928) and Diego Hidalgo's *Un notario español en Rusia* (1929) (see Gómez 2002).

11. Mayte Gómez calls these examples 'landmark books' as, unlike earlier Spanish writings on Russia, they 'were written by political leaders who travelled to the country personally' (Gómez 2002: 68).

12. Divorce was legalised under the Constitution of the Second Republic promulgated in December 1931 (Art. 43).

13. Federica Montseny is one clear exception, as she became Minister of Health in 1936.

14. As Maite Gómez notes, De los Ríos 'condemns post-Revolutionary Russia for 'sacrificing individual freedom and for lacking real democracy' and many socialists attributed a legitimacy and veracity to De los Ríos's travelogue given his standing within the PSOE (Gómez 2002: 71).

15. The characters note that the Russian government has been in power for three 'lustrums'. As the Revolution took place in 1917, this would mean the narrative is set in 1932.

16. The date '193...' points to a possible source of influence on *El banquete*. In his study of science fiction in Spain, Carlos Sainz Cidoncha mentions 'La República Española de 191...' by Domingo Cirici Ventalló and José Arrufat Mestre. The work, Sainz Cidoncha explains, is a satire, and was published in 1911 in anticipation of a republican government in Spain (1976: 10).

17. For instance, in *Capital*, first published in 1867, Marx argues that the workers must pass a law to create 'an all-powerful social barrier by which they can be prevented from selling themselves

and their families into slavery and death by voluntary contract with capital' (1976: 416). In relation to slavery, it should be made clear that Marxian ideology did not class the proletariat as slaves, rather it argued that the two were comparable. Friedrich Engels explains that whereas a slave is sold 'once and for all', the proletariat sells himself 'by the day' and 'by the hour' (1971a: 172; 1971b: 165).

18. As stated in *The Communist Manifesto*: 'The distinguishing feature of Communism is not the abolition of property generally, but the abolition of bourgeois property. But modern bourgeois private property is the final and most complete expression of the system of producing and appropriating products that is based on class antagonism, on the exploitation of the many by the few. In this sense, the theory of the Communists may be summed up in the single sentence: Abolition of private property' (Marx and Engels 2009: 20).

19. Critics note how socialist literature became popular in Spain in the late 1920s and early 1930s (Fuentes 1980: 31, 35, 38; Purkey 2013: 13).

20. Clark attributes this to the 'cultural revolution' launched by Stalin in Russia in 1927 (1981: 31). For further details of literary and artistic propaganda in Soviet Russia, see: Dobrenko 2011: 398; Ferré 2011: 50, 63–64; Lodder 2011: 109.

21. This quotation is taken from *The Revolutions of 1848–49*, based on writings published in the same year as *The Communist Manifesto*. It is worth highlighting that Marx differentiates between socialism and Marxism in this context, explaining that the aim of socialism is 'the realisation of the idea of equality by means of the equal distribution of goods, dependent on labour' (1972: 79). My justification for often conflating the two in this analysis is explained earlier.

22. For her work on this initiative, according to Susana Tavera, the author was (almost certainly sardonically) dubbed 'Platón con faldas' (2005: 214); as noted in the Introduction, it is possible that De la Torre was aware of this nickname given the similarities between *El banquete* and Plato's *Republic*.

23. In *The Communist Manifesto*, the bourgeois are blamed for women's oppression as it is claimed that they view wives as 'a mere instrument of production', and it is argued that communists would eradicate this problem (Marx and Engels 2009: 25). Citing Charles Fourier, Marx outlines how, at least in theory, social reform and gender equality are inherently interrelated: 'The degree of emancipation of woman is the natural measure of general emancipation' (1957: 259). This quotation has been reproduced as printed, although critics who cite the same sentence write '[t]he degree of female emancipation' (Haug 2015b: 39; Meyer 1977: 86).

24. Michèle Barrett, for example, states, in reference to 'the oppression of women by men', that Marxism 'has tended to pass over [it] in silence' (1988: 8), while Catherine V. Scott refers to the doctrine's 'blind spot about gender' (1995: 88).

25. The name of the union, 'Obreras filadoras', is intriguing, as it suggests that De la Torre had Catalonia in mind when writing the novel, as 'filadora' is Catalan for 'seamstress' ('hiladora' in Spanish). Bearing in mind that De la Torre was from Cantabria and represented Asturias, it is possible that the reference to Catalunya links to the Semana Trágica, a week-long series of violent clashes in 1909 between the army and a combination of workers, anarchists, socialists and republicans. It is likely that the bloody, violent nature of this conflict inspired De la Torre's description of the uprising in *El banquete*.

26. Engels argues a similar point in 'The Origins of the Family, Private Property and the State' from 1884, stating that communism will create 'a generation of men who never in their lives have known what it is to buy a woman's surrender with money or any other social instrument of power; a generation of women who have never known what it is to give themselves to a man from any other considerations than real love, or to refuse to give themselves to their lover from fear of the economic consequences' (1968a: 508).

27. See Marie Collins and Slyvie Weil-Sayre, 'Forgotten Feminist and Socialist' (1973), for an in-depth summary of the parallels between Marx and Tristan.

CHAPTER 4

❖

Mares en la sombra:
Gender, Collectivity and Trauma

The interface of the personal and political that characterises De la Torre's writings would be fundamentally transformed by the outbreak of the Spanish Civil War (1936–1939). Growing resentment towards the Second Republic's liberal, secularist policies would boil over on 17 July 1936, when Francisco Franco's Nationalist rebels revolted. The bitter, bloody conflict that followed would permanently disrupt De la Torre's life, as she was forced to leave her beloved Asturias to seek sanctuary in Mexico and her political career was prematurely cut short. In February 1936, she had retained her seat for the PSOE in an election narrowly won by the left-wing Popular Front coalition, a result that, along with the assassination of the proto-fascist José Calvo Sotelo on 13 July, provoked the Nationalists' violent insurrection. The War and its aftermath can be understood as both an ideological battle between the broadly leftist Republicans and ultra-conservative Nationalists and, at the same time, a conflict between the feminist values that underpinned the Second Republic and the patriarchal, misogynistic ideation of the political right. Such a parallel, of course, suggests an organic symbiosis of leftist and feminist politics that, as we have seen, De la Torre problematises and interrogates in her works. Nevertheless, when confronted with the demise of her political project and, indeed, fearing for her life, De la Torre's priorities would focus on defending the Republic, like many Republican women whose contribution would prove critical to the war effort.[1]

As noted in the Introduction, De la Torre's political activism would, not unexpectedly, pique during the War. Likely spurred by the formation of Adolf Hitler's Nazi government in 1933, her criticism of war and fascism became public around this period. Her unapologetic contempt for Hitler is demonstrated in an article for *La Región*, printed in August 1934, in which she criticised the validity of a recent plebiscite, making parallels with the Primo de Rivera dictatorship, and referred to Hitler as 'el homosexual canciller'; a description that prompted legal action by the German state. Despite pressure from her own government, De la Torre refused to apologise.[2] Contemporary press sources identify her with the 'Contra la guerra y el fascismo' movement from 1934 (also see Checa Puerta 2009: 216),[3] and, in the same year, she would begin co-directing the Comité de Mujeres contra la Guerra y el Fascismo alongside Dolores Ibárruri, María Lejárraga and Isabel Oyarzábal (see García 2015). Having cultivated a reputation as one of the 'destacadas mujeres de los partidos extremistas' ('Un consejo de Guerra' 1935: 4) during her first spell in office, she would once again win the Oviedo seat for the PSOE in the February 1936 elections that would ultimately spark the flame of the rebels' coup d'état. Celebrated as a prominent figure in the Circulos Socialistas,[4] De la Torre would be appointed Ministro de Comercio Interior in September,[5] a role she held until 1937,[6] and would act as the Política Arancelaria under Largo Caballero's government (Rodrigo 1994: 301; Rubiales 2008).

The Civil War galvanised De la Torre's anti-fascist activism. Meeting with the Ministro de la Guerra on multiple occasions to declare her opposition to the rebels' revolt,[7] De la Torre would preside over the Asociación de Mujeres Antifascistas (la AMA) along with Dolores Ibárruri, Matilde Huici and Matilde Cantos (both socialists) from 1937 (Tavera 2005: 212; also see Zambrana Moral 2009). In the same year, she gave an anti-fascist speech[8] and attended the II Conferencia Nacional de Mujeres Antifascistas in Valencia (Martínez 2007: 69). As her cooperation with female colleagues evidences, women's experiences during the War was a particular concern for De la Torre. She was entrusted with the formation of the Secretariado Femenino, inaugurated at some point before 1938 (Capel Martínez 2008b: 121), and focused much of her anti-War activity on women's experiences of the conflict. Records indicate numerous speeches delivered celebrating the bravery of women who worked in arms factories (see Cabaleiro Manzanedo and Botinas i Montero 2003: 42) and, along with Ibárruri, she addressed thousands of women whose husbands were rebel miners, defeated, imprisoned and murdered by the Nationalists (Rodrigo 1994: 295: also see Rodrigo and Del Hoyo 2005: 302).

Public support for women producing ammunition is particularly intriguing, as it is in stark contrast to the criticisms of the protagonist of *Jardín de damas curiosas* (1917) that we saw in Chapter One. De la Torre's change of heart, it would seem, evidences both the self-conscious naivety of her protagonist in *Jardín* and, importantly for this chapter, how the Civil War caused her to re-evaluate her political positions. While she would, without question, be horrified by the brutality of the conflict, her commitment to the Second Republic and her socialist, anti-fascist convictions would mean that, for De la Torre, it was critical that the government be defended at all costs. For her efforts, De la Torre was classed 'one of the greatest social workers of Spain' in a 1939 article that commemorated the women of the Second Republic after the Nationalist victory, by which point she had sought exile in Mexico, along with Margarita Nelken and her other PSOE colleague Venerada García Manzano (Alted Vigil 2008: 70; Capdevila-Argüelles 2011: 15; Domínguez Prats 2012: 802).

After first seeking exile in France, De la Torre would then find refuge in Mexico, where her experiences of the War were published in *Mares en la sombra: Estampas de Asturias* (2007 [1940]; henceforth *Mares*), a testimony that is made up of articles written during the conflict. *Mares* provides an intimate account of the female experience of war[9] that denotes how violence, trauma and memory shape the author's political ideation. Drawing on theories of trauma and memory in contemporary Spain, this final chapter interrogates how the War informed De la Torre's politics and how the fall of the Republic impacted her views on liberal democracy. *Mares* is a series of snapshots that blend personal and collective memories in such a way as to reinforce a socialist ideation of collectivity that resists ideological erasure that, in Hunt's theorisation of memory, 'ensures continuity in a community', as the act of constructing collective memory reifies 'a sense of unity' (Hunt 2010: 105). While Bakhtinian theories of dialogism centre on the novel, the emphasis on dialogue in *Mares* allows for productive application in De la Torre's memoir. On the one hand, the historic link between dialogue and political liberty, given, as Ken Hirschkop notes, that dialogue is 'so powerful a value in a liberal democratic political culture' (1992: 102), encapsulates the ideological subtext of the text: to provide a voice for the silenced. At the same time, as we shall see, the rhetorical imperative of *Mares* strongly resonates with Bakhtin's focus on the interlocuter (or, in this case, reader).

Mares, in this sense, manifests the socialist voices erased by the conflict, while the act of narrating De la Torre's experiences facilitates a cathartic memorialisation that is inflected by her leftist and feminist politics. Having hypothesised a failed workers' uprising in *El banquete de Saturno* (1931), as discussed in the previous chapter, De la Torre parallels her reflections on the Nationalist uprising with memories of the Asturian revolution of 1934. Points of comparison between the October Revolution and Civil War have, of course, been noted by historians, not least of all because it was through the brutal repression of Asturian strikers that General Francisco Franco would rise to prominence in right-wing circles. While the previous chapters have presented numerous examples that evidence De la Torre's conscious manipulation of narrative as a means of both political propaganda and foreboding, it is in *Mares* that her desperation to record and publicise her thoughts is most tangible. The dialogic quality that characterises De la Torre's entire written output, thus, takes on an acutely ominous quality, as the compilation of her experiences connotes a desire to record details that would otherwise be forgotten and, more pertinently, work through the author's grief, anguish and trauma.

The nexus of creativity, political theory and commentary that, as we have seen, is central to De la Torre's output facilitates an examination of the relationship between literary strategy and political ideology that chronicles both her experiences of the conflict and escape into exile and her decision to weaponise narrative as a means of processing individual and collective trauma. *Mares* not only exemplifies the porous boundaries of fact and fiction, as De la Torre utilises artistic licence to make her account all the more affective, it is also the author's final publication. With this in mind, the frequent 'name dropping' of famous figures, with short biographies provided in the footnotes of Saiz Viadero's excellent edited edition (2007), suggest De la Torre's eagerness to underline her status; a somewhat tragic aim given her relative obscurity today. It is, moreover, revealing that all of the well-known figures she names are men, such as Javier Bueno Bueno, the director of the Asturian *Avance* newspaper (101), along with leading politicians in the Republican government, including Indalecio Prieto Tuero (178), who she describes as 'el líder socialista que mereció siempre la máxima devoción personal' (182), and Juan Negrín López (181).[10] Indicative of both the male-dominated world De la Torre operated in and her own prominence within socialist circles, these reflections on her male comrades, as the first section of this analysis will demonstrate, offer an intriguing insight into De la Torre's views on the politics of war and the Republican government's resistance.

'Nadie habla': The Political Voice and Republican History

The political capital of the vanquished voice and the collective memory it represents is central to histories of Francoist Spain. As evidenced throughout this book, De la Torre was acutely conscious of the relationship between power and language. Such symbiosis, as evidenced in my examination of *Jardín de damas curiosas*, is particularly pertinent in relation to the female voice, as it connotes both ideological agency and political parity. Indeed, a common trait of all of De la Torre's eclectic works is a metanarrative quality to the texts that delineates how she self-consciously textualises her political commentary. In *Mares*, she plays on time and perspective as a means of underscoring how the text manifests her memories and, critically, indexes the act of commemorating the Republican experience. In her prologue, De la Torre addresses the Mexicans who welcome the exiled Republicans, '[h]ermanos de América' (75), speaking, in her words, for 'el Espíritu de la Libertad' (79), a manifestation of the Republican spirit. Rather than present *Mares* as a simply a personal account, then, De la Torre utilises her memoir to give a voice to vanquished Republicanism; '[d]e la guerra de España os hablará' (79). In line with De la Torre's politics, she criticises the War as 'el gran crimen fascista' (109), describes her growing fear on hearing a radio broadcast about the ascent of Francoist forces (126) and condemns 'el esclavismo fascista' (77) implemented after the Nationalists' victory. At the same time, poignant reflections about her Republican allies, many of whom, De la Torre retrospectively explains to her reader, would subsequently be executed by the Nationalists, prompt intimate memories of her brother, Eduardo (103), who died in infancy.

   The way in which De la Torre conflates personal and political memories underscores how, to her mind, she embodies the Republican experience and connotes an organic symbiosis between the two. One consequence of this approach is that political commentary often seems to be prioritised over personal reflections in *Mares*; a style that mirrors the Civil War testimony of her friend and colleague María Lejárraga, whose memoir *Una mujer por caminos de España*, first published in 1950 during her exile in Argentina, constitutes, according to Concha Alborg, 'un texto autobiográfico [que] no es personal, sino histórico y político' (1996: 488; also see Mangini 1995: 63). Although it may be self-evident that *Mares* manifests De la Torre's political voice — a means of public expression she was acutely aware would soon be silenced in her homeland — it is, nevertheless, intriguing the way she conflates a collective Republican voice with her personal perspective. Shifting between the first-person plural ('nosotros') and singular 'yo' throughout the text, De la Torre utilises voice and expression as a means of conveying tensions between her internal sense of isolation and fear and the front of solidarity that she is determined to maintain. The choice of a singular or collective subject, moreover, reflects both De la Torre's geographical surroundings and her depleting optimism:

while the 'nosotros' voice is prioritised in her memories of Asturias, De la Torre switches to the first-person singular ('yo') after she is forced to flee to Madrid; a distinction that connotes a sense of dislocation and isolation, having abandoned her home and many of her comrades.

Though this literary strategy has been examined in other examples of De la Torre's writing, it is particularly telling in her personal testimony. Rather than simply a means of indexing ideological conviction and, indeed, doubts, the tensions between 'yo' and 'nosotros' in *Mares* also reflect the dynamics between personal and collective memories. A salient example to illustrate this point is found in a scene in which De la Torre describes political resilience, 'la lucha política' (104), as instinctive and innate: 'estaba latente en mi sangre y por ello, en la sangre de los míos' (104). The ambiguity of 'los míos', which Viadero takes as a reference to De la Torre's immediate family (104), but can, conceivably, also be read in relation to the author's political 'family', emblematises the nexus of personal and political that is bound up in De la Torre's narrative. There is, then, a concerted effort on De la Torre's part to not only cement a collective selfhood, in relation to her political allies, but also a discernible need to rationalise a personal identification with the self. As outlined in the previous chapter (in relation to the protagonist of *El banquete*), dialogue is critical to self-perception. Rather than the intratextual dialogue central to Bakhtinian criticism, De la Torre uses *Mares* as a means of dialoguing with her reader and, indeed, herself. The autobiographical component of the text is therefore key, as it reflects how the author aims to rationalise an individual experience that forms part of a collective social history. Textualising the inevitable solitude that war and exile engenders is a common leitmotif in Spanish women's exile writings. Alda Blanco, for example, observes how the 'una mujer' of Lejárraga's title (*Una mujer por caminos de España*) represents a means of disidentification with the autobiographical subject (2002: 182). In the memoir of another female Republican exile, María Teresa León, *Memoria de la melancolía* (written in Rome throughout the 1960s and published in Argentina in 1970), Ofelia Ferrán recognises a similar textual manifestation of disidentification: 'León's autobiographical voice', Ferrán explains, 'shifts throughout the text, alternating between first, second and third person narration', which results in an 'extreme division within the narrative voice' (2005: 62).

In *Mares*, there is only one scene that reflects disassociation to the same extent. Describing her stay in a bleak convent cell while in hiding in Oviedo, De la Torre depicts an unknown female figure:

> El tiroteo esmalta la noche cálida de agosto con restallidos de verbena. La muchacha de nuestro pueblo, pecho a tierra, ojo avizor, fusil a la mano, atisba... atisba... atisba... (105)

The ambiguous characterisation of a 'muchacha de nuestro pueblo' epitomises how De la Torre's autobiographical voice encapsulates both a personal and collective testimony. The *miliciana*, who attentively monitors the town ('atisba... atisba... atisba...'), can be seen to represent both De la Torre herself who, as this scene shows, casts a watchful eye (or 'ojo avizor') over the *pueblo*, and, at the same time, a personification of the Republican spirit for whom De la Torre speaks. The effect of this unknown figure being female is two-fold: firstly, it invites the reader to assume De la Torre is describing herself, given scant reference to other female Republicans in *Mares* (a point explored in detail later); and, in a symbolic sense, it evokes the personification of the Republic as a liberated woman. Blurring the boundaries between the self and political ideology in this way serves to articulate a sense of agency in both a political and personal sense, consolidating the two in such a way as to unify a collective political voice, echoing what Ferrán describes as 'an ongoing process of construction of the self' (2005: 65) in León's memoir. For De la Torre, this sense of self can be understood in relation to the individual and the political, with the inevitable tensions between the two indexed in the narrative through the shifts in narrative voice.

Comparing *Mares* with the testimonies of female counterparts raises two important points. Firstly, there is the question of authorial perspective: while Lejárraga and León both wrote their memoirs retrospectively during exile, *Mares* is predominantly made up of articles De la Torre wrote during the War. Not only is this distinction pertinent with regards to how collective memory is depicted, but so too does it impact the way in which political loyalties are portrayed. The fact that De la Torre shifts from 'yo' to 'nosotros', with this in mind, connotes a degree of solidarity that Lejárraga and Teresa León lack, as she is writing at a time when a Republican victory was still conceivable. Bearing in mind how narrative voice indexes political ideology, then, the second point is how (self-)representation links to the authors' intended readership. In *Mares*, the plurality and mutability of the narrative voice is also borne out in relation to De la Torre's envisaged interlocutor. Having examined the political undertones of De la Torre's intended readership in relation to *Jardín* in Chapter One, we may be inclined to focus on sex and/ or gender. De la Torre, however, switches between addressing readers identified with specific experiences of war and exile in her memoir, regardless of sex: the Mexicans welcoming the Spanish exiles; the fallen comrades she interacts with in the narrative; her homeland and the socialist politics it embodies; and the readers, De la Torre hopes, will keep her memory alive.

Through metanarrative asides in which the narrative voice directly addresses the reader, such as pre-empting questions ('ustedes preguntarán' [138]), elaborating on details ('[p]ues les diré' [138]) and self-consciously providing a mouthpiece for the citizens unable to recount their stories ('[n]o les oís; pero ellos os hablan' [160]), De la Torre presupposes a communicative channel with her readership. Engaging the reader in this way serve to underscore the importance of voice in *Mares*, as sound and silence function as a metaphor to convey both the ubiquity of danger and De la Torre's (well-founded) fear her account would be forgotten. The shift between addressing the readers as 'ustedes' (138) and 'vosotros' (159, 160, 206) indicates how De la Torre, on the one hand, envisages her readers to include personal and political allies, illustrated in her addresses '[a] vosotros, ciudadanos del mundo [...] A vosotros, compañeros en la lucha política por la Libertad del Hombre' (206). At the same time, the use of 'ustedes' implies a more general, and therefore politically ambiguous, readership that De la Torre also views as an important interlocutor. The mutability of De la Torre's envisaged readership is not only indicative of her authorial objectives — that is to say, her intention to publicise the Republican experience to readers of all political persuasions — but also evinces how, to De la Torre's mind, the text facilitates a dialogue with her leftist comrades and the Nationalist narrative of the War. (It is worth remembering here that, though many of the vignettes are reprints of press articles published during the conflict, *Mares* was revised and published during De la Torre's exile, after the Nationalist victory.)

The rhetorical imperative in *Mares*, then — what Bakhtin calls the 'orientation towards the listener and his [or her] answer' (1981: 280) — indexes the democratic politics that underpin the narrative; as noted above, dialogue constitutes 'the discursive form of democracy' (Womack 2011: 6) that presupposes equality between speaker/writer and addressee/reader. Through her direct communication with her reader, De la Torre invites questions about the War and her experiences in a way that highlights the pertinence of approaching history critically and presupposes the vitality of recorded memories. Even when reading De la Torre's account over eighty years after its first publication, her asides to the reader give the text a sense of presentism. The author's voice, in other words, is not resigned to the past, but, as De la Torre intended, lives on. For Bakhtin, this emphasis on the present is inherent to dialogic discourse, as a 'living mix of varied and opposing voices' (1981: 49) facilitates a process of 'interanimation' (1981: 47). In *Mares*, this 'interanimation' can be understood as an ongoing dialogue between her history and dominant discourses. Above all, the dialogism in *Mares* underscores how De la Torre utilises the narrative voice to self-consciously commemorate Republican history, (justifiably) fearing it would be erased from cultural and political memory. A similar strategy can be observed in León's memoir, as Ferrán notes what she describes as 'the desperate need for an addressee' (2005: 68), which reflects the 'responsibility of testimony' (2005: 68) and 'ethical imperative behind León's autobiography' (2005: 68); both characteristics that resonate with *Mares*. With this in mind, we are reminded of Shirley Mangini's definition of 'Spanish memory texts of war' (1995: 56) as 'women-woven texts, fused together to form a historical quilt' (1995: 56), as these female-authored war testimonies collectively historicise the Republican experience of the War.

The political imperative of remembering is underscored in *Mares* through self-reflexive remarks that, as we have seen, are common in De la Torre's writings. Not only does she provide intricate, affecting depictions of her experiences, even going so far as to ensure the reader in one scene that her recollections are accurate as the scene was 'inolvidable' (121), De la Torre also emphasises that she is recording collective memory. In her anguished reflections about the fate of her homeland, for instance, she acknowledges historical parallels with the October revolution, explored in more detail in the next section, and, accordingly, the perils of disregarding political history: 'Asturias... Asturias... ¿Cómo olvidar jamás tu gloriosa agonía?' (199). Moreover, it is De la Torre's dramatic account of finding governmental archives emptied — presumably destroyed by the Nationalists — that indicates her acute awareness of the need to conserve the Republican experience:

> Era el día 18 de octubre.
> No era un día diferente de los anteriores, porque no había días ni noches que se diferenciasen en la masa de dolor ambiente [...] Fue como un aviso de peligro mortal... De un brinco salí a los claustros... Escuché...
> *Nadie... Nada...*
> Entonces eché de ver que no había centinelas y que las puertas de los departamentos del Gobierno estaban abiertas... Corrí a los despachos ministeriales...
> *Nadie... Nada...* Es decir: sí; algo terrible: *Los archivos habían desaparecido.*
> Llamé a gritos, como niño miedoso...
> *Nadie... Nada...* (223–24; emphasis added)

The authorial decision to include the date serves both to imply a sense of veracity and accuracy to the scene and, crucially, self-consciously underlines how *Mares* substitutes a body of missing documents. Read retrospectively, De la Torre's concern for lost archives is tragically pertinent, given her own personal library in Santander was burnt down during the War (Lloréns and Aznar Sole 2006: 341), a possible reason that her works remain relatively unknown today. Through the repetition of 'Nadie... Nada...', De la Torre expresses her isolation, fear and terror, and, at the same time, foreshadows the imposed exile, and subsequent erasure, of Spanish Republicanism that, through *Mares*, she aims to document, transcribe and memorialise.

It is somewhat paradoxical, then, that silence is ubiquitous in the text. In the chapter entitled 'Silencio', De la Torre repeatedly underlines the (self-)imposed silence that was critical during battles. The word, 'silencio' (98; 99), is repeated in such a way as to emphasise the suffocating absence of sound, broken only by the 'grito del pájaro nocturno' (98). Not only does this scene effectively convey the tensions and anxieties of living under an ongoing conflict, it also metaphorically represents the voices and experiences that De la Torre aims to recount. Her evocative depiction of the '[s]ilencio campesino' (98) is as much a reflection of the landscape as it is an indicator of her concern for her Asturian comrades. Indeed, one of the most poignant moments in *Mares* is the scene in which De la Torre recalls fearing what would become of her *pueblo* should the Nationalists triumph:

> Es horrible pensar en la venganza fascista sobre el pueblo asturiano, que forzosamente va a quedar abandonando a su crueldad; pero es políticamente catastrófico ante el mundo entero el que los traidores triunfen tan absolutamente sobre la República. (217)

Although this reflection is, in part, indicative of the fact that *Mares* is made up of articles written during the War — that is, before the Nationalist victory had occurred — De la Torre's decision to not revise her temporal perspective not only makes her concerns all the more evocative, but also supposes authorial intent. Writing a war memoir, in other words, that orientates the reader within an ongoing conflict is both more affective and suggests that De la Torre capitalises on temporal paradigms so as to interrogate the conception, (re-)construction and disclosure of memory. The reader, furthermore, is invited to read such accounts both within the diegesis, a point underlined through the use of the present tense ('Es horrible'; 'va a quedar abandonando'; 'es políticamente catastrófico'), and retrospectively, juxtaposing two coexisting realities in order to index the act of commemorating political history.

In a development of an article published in the press in September 1936, two months after the outbreak of the conflict, the chapter 'La ciudad agonizante' recalls a bombing raid in rural Asturias. Darkness and silence connote the group's terror and vulnerability, as sounds of war indicate the violent destruction of the city:

> A momentos, se perciben pequeñas llamaradas de rojo intenso, semejantes a fogonazos de un cañón [...] De pronto, ya en el umbral de la noche, percibimos a nuestra espalda el zumbido del avión. (157)

An ambiguous sense of solidarity is suggested by the uncertainty surrounding the identities of the individuals grouped together for safety; the sense of security suggested by the group, which De la Torre implies through the first-person plural ('percibimos'), is not tangible to the reader who, at this point, has no indication of who the others may be. Such disorientation reinforces the group's anxieties, while the absence of any details about who accompanies De la Torre invites us to understand this plurality metonymically, as representative of the broader socialist collective. Indeed, the way in which De la Torre constructs unity by presenting the individuals as one homogenous mass is reminiscent of the chaotic scenes in *El banquete de Saturno*, in which Julio desperately searches for political allies. The terror is palpable, as the group is silenced by fear:

> Nadie habla. Escuchamos solamente.
> Escuchamos algo que no tiene expresión:
> el estertor de agonía de una gran ciudad [...]
> Nadie habla... Nadie habla...
> Nadie puede comentar lo que sucede entonces. (156–57)

Through the repetition of '[n]adie habla', De la Torre conveys both the dehumanising nature of war — as individuals are silenced so as to prioritise the needs of the masses — and evokes the silenced voices for whom her narrative voice speaks. The mass can therefore be understood to represent her fallen comrades and, ultimately, her failed political project. The speaking/listening dichotomy that De la Torre suggests here is also employed in another scene, in which the group band together, eagerly listening for signs of danger: 'No se oye una voz humana. Sólo aquel crepitar del rencor automático... Escuchamos...' (105). As well as alluding to a socialist collectivity represented by De la Torre, an act that emblematises her political career, this scene also reinforces the interconnectedness of capitalist politics and violent conflict; as noted earlier, De la Torre is quoted before the outbreak of the War as arguing, 'la guerra solo sirve para defender los intereses del capitalismo y destruir la Humanidad' ('Actos socialistas en Galicia', 1935: 8; 'Actuación de los partidos', 1935: 12).

A closer look at the juxtaposition of '[n]adie habla' and '[e]scuchamos' further implies a contrast between the collective experience and the singular voice. There is, thus, a metanarrative subtext as De la Torre appears conscious of the political undertones to this enforced silencing: 'Nadie puede comentar lo que sucede entonces' (157). Not only does this connote the political urgency that galvanised De la Torre to recount her memoirs, but it also delineates how the act of narration — oral or written — is in itself a political act that can reconcile trauma. In relation to collective memory, Nigel Hunt notes that 'being traumatised, being unable to form a narrative, reduces someone to less than a person because the traumatised person cannot tell the story of their experiences' (Hunt 2010: 198). Having established a link between trauma and voicelessness, De la Torre goes on to reclaim the collective voice as an act of empowerment:

> Hienden los aires con gritos de bronce... En la lejanía, este clamor adquiere tonos musicales monstruosos [...]
> Es el vocerío del pueblo. Grita la ciudad también;
> grita la gente en un alarido apocalíptico. (157–58)

Having illustrated in *Jardín de damas curiosas* that she was acutely conscious of the relationship between power and language, De la Torre can be seen here to reclaim a voice that has been silenced. The utilisation of voice in this scene foreshadows the ideological erasure of texts such as *Mares* in Nationalist Spain, a point that is underlined by comparing De la Torre's personification of the city and *pueblo* with Dulce Chacón's seminal *La voz dormida* (2002), a text that engages with the same questions of collective memory and repression as *Mares*. As Rachel Linville observes, the verbs 'gritar' and 'contar' are repeated in Chacón's work as a metafictional means of 'exteriorizing her recollections' (2014: 175), thus recuperating 'la voz dormida'; an argument that parallels with the textualisation of 'el vocerío del pueblo' (157–58) in *Mares*.

The sense of extra-textual solidarity that this implies is also tangible in the final chapter of *Mares*, when the ship De la Torre is aboard finally approaches land. Acutely aware of the passengers' vulnerability, De la Torre recounts repeated cries instructing those aboard to remain vigilant: 'No... ¡Dormir, no!...' (239); ¡No dormirse...! ¡No hay cuidado que nadie se duerma!' (241). Read retrospectively, these directions, much like De la Torre's reflection that '[l]a gente gritaba, gritaba, gritaba...' (138), both of which are meant literally, takes on an added meaning, with *Mares* manifesting the silenced voice of 'la gente' — or *el pueblo* — for whom the narrative speaks. There is, then, a tragic irony to De la Torre's rationalisation for the political imperative of remaining silent during the heat of battle, which is presented in poetic form:

> Si de alguno te quieres vengar,
> has de callar.
> Y nosotros quisiéramos vengarnos de aquella y de otras infamias. Por eso callamos. (163)

The duality of a narrative voice that is at once silenced and spoken encapsulates the paradoxical depictions of voice and power that permeate De la Torre's written output. Situating *Mares* within its cultural and critical contexts offers intriguing insight into embryonic forms of the textual manifestations of voice that would become central to post-War, and therefore post-memory,[11] writings and, as we shall see in the next section, allow for an alternative perspective on the construction of collective memory in war-torn Spain.

'Los de octubre': Collective Memory and Trauma

> Todos sabemos que caerá y que lo hará con arreglo
> a su clásico modo: heroica y gloriosamente. No le dedicamos
> un recuerdo a aquella brava tierra lejana porque
> ella vive permanentemente en nuestras almas.
> — MATILDE DE LA TORRE (quoted in Calderón 1984: 109)

De la Torre's ominous reflections on the valiant resistance displayed by the Republicans in Oviedo, where she was based at the beginning of the Civil War, is indicative of both her devotion to the region and its people and how the Nationalist uprising brought back memories of the Asturian revolt of 1934. The opening vignette of *Mares* draws the reader into a tense, vivid account of a meeting — a 'dramática conferencia' (80) — in which General Antonio Aranda is scrutinised about his loyalties, feigning ignorance of the uprising and his support for the Nationalist rebels: '¿Sublevaciones...? ¿Aquí... en Oviedo... en mi ciudad querida...? [...] ¿Ustedes "dudan de mi republicanismo"?' (80). De la Torre, like many of the (all male) group, sense his deception, criticising 'su angelical inocencia' (80), 'la suprema hipocresía' (80) and 'su mirada hipócrita' (81). De la Torre's account of the interrogation of Aranda whom she deems 'el demonio de la Traición' (81) — epitomises one core objective of this book: to further our understanding of seminal junctures in Spain's political history by examining an otherwise forgotten female voice. Perhaps unconsciously, De la Torre underscores how she is but one woman amongst men. While the politicians to whom she refers by name are all male, her reference to her fellow 'diputados' (81) is almost certainly an all-male group (De la Torre was the only female *diputada* in Asturias in 1936). The use of the collective 'nosotros', examined in the previous section, textualises how De la Torre was, in a pragmatic sense, a woman amongst men. At the same time, it also suggests an almost androgynous quality to the collective narrative voice, as, when describing the Republican experience, De la Torre identifies with her male comrades, with no suggestion that she feels othered because of her sex.

Although it is understandable that, in times of war, political loyalties may encourage bonds regardless of sex (a point explored in more detail later), it is, nevertheless, curious that De la Torre's references to other women suggest that she identifies *more* closely with her male allies. Two salient examples come to mind: in the first scene, De la Torre has a chance encounter with Javier Bueno Bueno, the editor of the *Avance* newspaper in which De la Torre published, who reveals that his mother and daughter have been captured by the Nationalists (101); and, in the second example, De la Torre makes brief reference to María Luisa, the wife of the syndicalist leader Graciano Antuña Álvarez. While, in the first example, De la Torre's concern is focused on Bueno's reaction (rather than considering the horrors that have likely befallen his mother and daughter), it is the somewhat reductionist description of María Luisa as simply the 'mujer de luchador socialista' (84) that evidences most clearly how De la Torre frames these episodes in relation to men. Foregrounding the activism and experiences of these women's male relatives, De la Torre only hints at the women's political involvement, an oversight that arguably reveals an understated commentary on women's political agency, intentional or not. The passivity that this implies is also tangible in a description of discussions amongst (male) republicans, which De la Torre witnesses, about the need to evacuate women and children (95) and a harrowing scene that details the bodies of women and children killed by aerial fire (101), as both present women as more vulnerable than men.

As we shall see later in the analysis, however, De la Torre *does* (as one would expect) emphasise women's critical, valiant contribution to defending the Republic. Thus, rather than read De la Torre's disconnection with her fellow Republican women as indicative of a lack of empathy or solidarity — a reading that would be incongruous with her political activism and literary outputs — I am inclined to understand De la Torre's lack of identification as indicative of her continued discomfort surrounding women's political agency; the core theme that links her politicised fiction. Intriguingly, androcentric War narratives are common amongst De la Torre's contemporaries. Lejárraga, for instance, fails to acknowledge the many women in attendance at the political meetings she details in *Una mujer por caminos de España* (see Cruz-Cámara 2009: 805), while Victoria Kent, a *diputada* for the Partido Republicano Radical Socialista, recounts her experience of exile in *Cuatro años en París (1940–1944)* (1997) through a male narrator, Plácido (see Twomey 2007: 77). In both instances, critics have convincingly argued that the erasure of women in these memoirs can be read as a commentary on women's political agency, a notion that will be explored in relation to *Mares* later in the chapter.

It is, however, necessary to briefly tackle the question of sex and agency here, as it is critical to how De la Torre conceives of collective memory. Indeed, as is the case with all of her works, it is important to bear in mind that *Mares* is, fundamentally, a *female*-voiced political commentary. There is, therefore, the omnipresent question of how being a woman shapes how De la Torre navigates socialist history. Intriguingly, memories are demarcated by sex, as key events focus almost exclusively either on men or women. In her reflections of the 1934 insurrection, De la Torre reveals how this shared trauma engendered bonding. Although her lived experience of the uprising centred mainly on the lives of women, it is the bravery of her male comrades during the uprising that she foregrounds in *Mares*. When referencing her fellow PSOE member Ramón González Peña, for instance, De la Torre describes him as a 'diputado socialista, líder máximo del Octubre' (82), the 'capitán del Octubre' (89, 91) and commends 'su papel del Octubre Glorioso' (86). There is, moreover, the sense that the Civil War will be 'como en Octubre' (88, 91) or (an) 'otro Octubre' (84), as the same leaders who defended the miners' strike — 'los de Octubre' (94), '[los] jefes de Octubre' (94), 'los mismos de Octubre' (95) and the 'capitanes de Octubre' (97) — would once more defend the *pueblo*, '[e]l pueblo mártir del Octubre Glorioso' (88).

The multiple quotations cited above illustrate the numerous references to Asturian revolution in a memoir that is, fundamentally, about the Civil War. The repetition of 'Octubre' connotes the style of political discourse, as these two historic events can be seen dialogue in such a way as to emphasise the significance of political legacy. Not only does this evince De la Torre's self-conscious objective to transcribe socialist history, of which the 1934 insurrection formed a core component, it also alludes to the political capital of collective memory. Though the Nationalist rebels are initially supressed by Republicans inspired by 'el fantasma del 34' (97), the eventual defeat and subsequent brutal repression dominate collective memory: 'estos hombres milagrosamente escapados del Octubre Glorioso sienten la trampa bajo sus pies' (82). The description of revolutionary spirit as 'el fantasma del 34' (97) is intriguing, as it evokes a bleaker, and arguably more accurate, mirror image of 'el Espíritu de la Libertad' (79) that encapsulates the Spanish Republicanism that De la Torre aims to commemorate. Haunted by memories of Asturias, then, these (male) Republicans are acutely conscious of the parallels between the failed revolution and the Civil War. There is, of course, an understated conflict between the androcentric collective memory that De la Torre recounts and her female narrative voice. By voicing these histories, De la Torre makes herself a critical component of this socialist past, identifying with the men she celebrates.

Another discernible tension relates to memory, as the metaphorical ghosts of the miners' strike illustrate the porous subjective and temporal boundaries in *Mares*. On the one hand, the way individual memories form part of a collective memory textualises the process by which political history is constructed, with the two interrelated and symbiotic. At the same time, juxtaposing the Asturian revolution with the Civil War presents these Republican histories as concurrent, illustrating how, for those who experienced the events of October, this experience was not resigned to the past. Such elasticity supposes trauma, which, as Susan Brison explains, engenders a 'severing of past from present' (1999: 39), as the coexistence of these collective socialist memories reflect both De la Torre's personal trauma and the shared trauma of the defeated revolutionaries. While Michael Richards rightly explains that it 'is essential to recount many individually traumatic experiences in order to make sense of and evaluate claims of collective trauma' (2013: 2), with specific reference to post-War Spain, what is interesting about *Mares* is how De la Torre consciously speaks on behalf of her Republican comrades. There is, therefore, a blurring between the individual and the collective that mirrors socialist ideation.

The physical and emotional toil of living through battle, for instance, is depicted as if the group were one collective entity, with De la Torre describing the sensations of '[n]uestros pies' (161) and, perhaps more tellingly, '[n]uestro cerebro' (161). Moreover, De la Torre recognises the authority this affords her, as illustrated in one aside to her reader when she reflects on how to recount a particular bombing raid using the first-person plural: 'Pues aquel día... ¿qué diremos?' (107). Both the use of the plural 'nosotros', mentioned above, which is to be understood both literally and metonymically, and the way the protagonists of the 1934 revolt shape De la Torre's reflections of the War, invite the reader to understand the text as a self-conscious manifestation of collective trauma. Metanarrative asides underline De la Torre's acute awareness of how memory functions, such as the scene in which she observes how her environment evokes former memories: 'aquel escenario patético había suscitado mis fantasmas' (104). *Mares*, in this sense, is at once an account of De la Torre's individual experiences that, like innumerable other accounts of the War, contributes towards a collective Republican history and, at the same time, a manifestation of collective memory in and of itself.

The Asturian strikers' defeat, of course, was a particular sore spot for De la Torre, as she devoted time, energy and resources to aiding the resistance. As contemporary press sources reveal, De la Torre worked closely with Dolores 'la Pasionaria' Ibárruri during the strike, collecting food and medical supplies and supporting the wives and families of striking and imprisoned workers (see Jackson 2010: 19).[12] After the uprising was crushed, she would continue to defend the strikers, as evidenced by her meeting with Niceto Alcalá-Zamora (president of the Second Republic) in October 1935, along with María Lejárraga, to speak in defence of an Asturian man sentenced to death.[13] With this in mind, it is curious that it is the lives of male Republicans that De la Torre foregrounds in *Mares*. On one level, De la Torre's ambiguous role on the periphery resonates strongly with her characterisation of María in *El banquete de Saturno*, as examined in the previous chapter. The dialogue in the diegesis of *Mares*, for instance, does not include De la Torre's own voice, as there is no indication in the narrative that De la Torre actively participated in the debates regarding strategy amongst the *diputados*. The lack of female agency that this suggests is exemplified in the tragic scene in which María Luisa, Antuña Álvarez's wife, powerlessly watches her husband detained by six guards; 'Jamás volverá a verlo. Fue fusilado' (85).[14] Much in the same way María Luisa is a passive bystander to her husband's arrest and execution, De la Torre presents herself — somewhat unjustly — as a spectator, observing and recording her male comrades' actions. There is, however, an authorial agency afforded to De la Torre, as it is she who acts as the spokes*woman* for her fallen allies. Utilising retrospective knowledge to frame her memoir, De la Torre juxtaposes various perspectives so as to underscore impending tragedy and, critically, highlight the political failings that impeded the Republican resistance.

In addition to the foreboding account of Antonio Aranda's deceit, another salient, ominous detail is the Republicans concern over the lack of arms: '¡¡No había armas...!! ¡¡No había armas...!!' (88). The government, which De la Torre denounces as 'un nido de caciques' (151), was ill-equipped for war, and the vulnerability of the Second Republic is criticised in forensic detail:

> ¡¡Todo está perdido!!
> *Ay, ¡cómo duelen ahora*, en el pensamiento, aquellas suicidas complacencias de la República rescatada a las derechas! *Ay, ¡cómo duelen*, con el dolor del trágico ridículo, aquellas negligencias, aquellas confianzas, aquellas estúpidas noblezas...! El renunciamiento al proceso de la Represión... Las cobardías del 16 de Abril... Y el desarme del pueblo... Aquel desarme criminal, de tipo alevoso, llevado a cabo por Gobiernos que jamás comprendieron la justicia ni siquiera gubernamental...

> Y ahora... *¡todo perdido!* El pueblo español sacrificado bárbaramente a una política idiota de borregos ante el carnicero...
>
> *¡Y pensar que* se pudieron tener armas... *¡Y pensar que* se tuvieron bajo el Gobierno de Gil Robles y no pudieron tenerse bajo los Gobiernos de febrero!
>
> *¡¡Armas...!!* Hace semanas que las pidieron los jefes obreros presintiendo la traición.
>
> *¡¡Armas...!!* El grito angustiado del pueblo en toda la historia del mundo... (89–90; emphasis added)

It is worth quoting this extended passage in its entirety as it exemplifies how De la Torre conveys a nexus of emotion and political commentary in such a way as to connote the confusion and panic of the War. Situating *Mares* within its broader cultural context, this depiction of disorientation and turbulence is typical of female-authored war narratives. In *Women and the War Story*, for example, Miriam Cooke writes that women's war stories 'allow for the narration of war's dynamism and incomprehensibility' (1996: 40); a characteristic Gina Herrmann (2003) observes in women's oral histories of the Spanish Civil War.

Not only does this scene narrate — and therefore publicise — (warranted) criticism of the Republic's failure to provide arms and the desperation and fear of De la Torre and her comrades, the use of repetition ('Ay, ¡cómo duelen [...]', '¡todo perdido!', '¡Y pensar que [...]' and '¡¡Armas...!!') also indicates trauma. Another revealing example of repetition is the (over-)use of 'cañón', which is used seventeen times in the short chapter of the same name (106–11). As Cathy Caruth explains, traumatic experiences cannot be assimilated, as they occur and, instead, return through repetitive flashbacks or nightmares; '[t]o be traumatized is precisely to be possessed by an image or event' (1995: 5). With this in mind, the repeated cries of fear and pain can be seen to textualise these cries as a means of replicating the sensation of being, to use Caruth's word, 'possessed' by the experience. At the same time, the repetition of critical, affective details is suggestive of political rhetoric, a characteristic Lesley Twomey observes in Kent's *Cuatro años en París (1940–1944)*, citing a passage that 'has many of the rhetorical qualities of a political speech, with its obsessive repetition of emotive phrases' (2007: 78). Rather than simply an indicator of their former political careers, this similarity also exemplifies how, for De la Torre and her contemporaries, such as Kent, their memoirs are as much a political commentary as a personal reflection of the War.

The way in which De la Torre re-organises time, recounting memories from September (107) and then August (114) in reverse order, for instance, delineates how *Mares* is not a chronological account of her experiences, but, perhaps more interestingly, a manifestation of her reaction and response to the War. De la Torre recognises the import of temporality in one poignant scene in which she parallels quintessential events during war, 'la guerra es así' (112), with the reality she witnessed, 'la guerra ésta "era así"' (112), a link that underscores both the commonality and singularity of her account. Through the use of quotation marks ('"era así"'), De la Torre emphasises how shifts in temporal perspective underpin her narrative. This authorial perspective is important as it demonstrates how the way De la Torre narrates her experiences is inflected by political ideation. The depiction of personal and collective memories, in other words, are constructed in such a way as to convey a political commentary. It is in the haunting recollection of visiting a site where her comrades had been imprisoned during the Asturian revolution (writing in 1936, she notes her memories are from two years prior) that De la Torre most closely engages with how collective memory functions. The act of visiting the burnt-out remains of a former convent that was used as a prison for socialist affiliates, a building that evokes '[u]na mezcla horrible de covento, cárcel y fortaleza' (120), recalls traumatic flashbacks for De la Torre:

> Yo conocí este lugar cuando aún era un edificio. Le visité mucho cuando en él se apretujaban millares de presos socialistas. Sé por ello de su fealdad externa y de su horror interno. Su mole me inspiraba ya repulsión hace dos años, porque allá dentro estaba el infierno de los míos... (120)

Claustrophobia, trauma and tragedy are depicted in such a way as to evoke pathos from the reader, suggesting an extratextual sense of solidarity that is indexed by the politically loaded use of 'los míos'. De la Torre, in this sense, identifies with her murdered comrades and, at the same time, implores her reader to do so too. While a reader sympathetic to De la Torre's politics would perhaps be more inclined to empathise, the harrowing image of thousands of imprisoned socialists also has the potential to resonate with political agnostics. At the very least, examples of mass violence such as this bring into question the Nationalists' humanity, providing a counternarrative to Francoist accounts of the War.

The contrast between the building's 'fealdad externa' and 'horror interno' functions as an apposite metaphor for the unspoken horrors that De la Torre aims to historicise in *Mares*, while the juxtaposition of contrasting times and places connotes how the narrative navigates between different historical pasts as a means of both reflecting and processing trauma. For Felman and Laub, writing such experiences consists 'of constructing a narrative, of reconstructing a history and essentially of *re-externalizing the event*' (1992: 69; original emphasis). De la Torre, in this sense, must communicate her experiences — this scene but one example in her memoir — in order to process past trauma. Dominick LaCapra terms this 'acting out' and 'working through', 'interrelated modes of responding to loss or trauma' (2001: 64). While acting out applies to a subject haunted by a past experience that dominates their thoughts, unable to distinguish past from present, working through occurs when 'the past becomes accessible to recall in memory, and [...] language functions to provide some measure of conscious control, critical distance and perspective' (2001: 90). Examining this scene in *Mares* not only indicates De la Torre's own personal trauma, which is amply evident in this emotive extract, but also supposes a collective trauma, shared by the author's fellow socialists. The use of the first-person singular ('yo') when describing the brutality experienced by the 'millares de presos socialistas' (120) connotes an ambiguous sense of solidarity, as time distances De la Torre from her comrades and, yet, the act of remembering these horrors facilitates a sense of collectivity and unity.

Critically, memory can be seen to function on multiple levels, as the narrative textualises both the act of visiting the site multiple times when it housed the socialist prisoners and, later, when it was reduced to burnt-out rubble. The way in which the act of (re-)visiting this place brings to mind former memories resonates with Maurice Halbwachs's work on collective memory. Remembering for the individual, Halbwachs explains, is facilitated by being within a social framework, considering that '[w]hile the collective memory endures and draws strength from its base in a coherent body of people, it is individuals as group members who remember' (1992: 48). De la Torre's socialist allies and their shared history, then, can be considered, to use Halbwachs' term, a 'social (and political) framework' that allows her to recall her experiences and, accordingly, contribute to a socialist collective memory. The self-conscious textualisation of formulating and recalling memories, underscored by De la Torre's observations as to how the site allows her to transcend temporal and geographical boundaries, not only reifies socialist history, but also speaks to Pierre Nora's theorisation of memory sites, *lieux de mémoire*, which he describes as 'the ultimate embodiments of a memorial consciousness' (1989: 12; 18–19). The former convent, utilising Nora's framework, can be understood as a 'material site', in the sense of a physical entity, and a 'symbolic site' of socialist history, while the text itself constitutes a 'functional' site (1989: 19) that facilitates the act of commemoration.

The way in which De la Torre depicts the political undertones of a location invested with Nationalist history evinces how, for the author, *Mares* encapsulates a Republican past that should not be forgotten. Describing a section of land that has become a make-shift graveyard for dead Nationalists, she recalls her reluctance to walk on 'este suelo maldito' (122); an ironic portrayal given it is within the convent grounds and, accordingly, believed to be consecrated. As well as reflecting De la Torre's contempt for her political enemies and understandable discomfort at walking on land that bears the scars of war, 'que rezuma sangre y podredumbre' (122), this also suggests a (well-founded) conflict between her Republicanism and religion, a point furthered by her criticism of the convent as 'un edificio feo de toda fealdad' (120). The graveyard can be seen to symbolise the National Catholicism that characterised Francoist Spain, while the juxtaposition of the recently planted crosses ('las cruces nuevas, de madera' [123]) and the aged land, disrupted by conflict, connotes how multiple political pasts coexist. The imagery of the crosses sprouting from the convent's soil, moreover, evokes the political evolution of Spanish Nationalism that, not without justification, emphasises the role played by the Church. With this in mind, what Nora calls the 'metamorphosis' (1989: 19) of memory sites, 'an endless recycling of their meaning and an unpredictable proliferation of their ramifications' (1989: 19), can be understood in *Mares* in relation to political ideation.

De la Torre's pointed refusal to interpret or record the '[n]ombres ilegibles' (123) on the graves, to which she refers as the '[n]ombres de equivocados' (123), forms part of this construction of political history, as, in a subversion of the Francoist erasure of the vanquished Republicans, De la Torre depicts Nationalist political history as forgotten and untraceable: 'Nunca se sabrá [...] El fuego lo borró todo' (123). While various scholars have observed that Spanish novels of the War and post-War era can be considered memory places (such as Moreno-Nuño 2006; Winter 2006), in line with Nora's work, an intriguing element of *Mares* is the way the text conflates history and memory. According to Nora, memory is in opposition to history, with memory inherently linked to the present: 'Memory is a perpetually actual phenomenon, a bond tying us to the eternal present; history is a representation of the past' (1989: 8). *Mares*, in this sense, can be seen to underline the porous boundaries between Nora's understanding of memory and history, as it is at once a manifestation of De la Torre's recollections and, at the same time, representative of the experiences of Republicans in war-ravaged Spain.

The benefit of examining *Mares* with a diachronic critical perspective in mind, then, is not just that it evidences how a binary understanding of memory and history is, as Jo Labanyi puts it, 'problematic' (2008: 121), but also that it sheds light on the ways De la Torre's politics shape her war narrative. Indeed, there is a fundamentally socialist subtext to the way in which De la Torre's memories form part of a broader collective memory, a symbiosis that is strongly implied through her shared experience with her political allies ('millares de presos socialistas' [120]). The dynamism of *Mares*, therefore, relates to the *effect* of these memories on the reader. In *Memories of Resistance: Women's Voices from the Spanish Civil War*, Shirley Mangini recognises the political capital of poignant scenes such as those found in *Mares*: 'The question of truth — that is to say, historical accuracy — therefore becomes irrelevant; what is important here is the "virtual reality", the emotive scenarios created by the women who have conjured up their lives from that stormy period' (1995: 57). As we shall see in the next section, the political capital of emotion, rather than historical 'truth', is central to the way in which De la Torre relates socialist collectivity to the female experience.

'[S]oy una mujer nada más': Gendering Political History

The androcentricity of war and conflict is reflected in its cultural and critical receptions. Female-narrated accounts (written or oral), Gina Herrmann observes in 'Voices of the vanquished: Leftist women and the Spanish Civil War', are 'often digressive and complicated, incomplete and fractured' (2003: 11), a characteristic that, for Herrmann, grants them a 'disruptive power' (2003: 11). As we have seen, the structure of *Mares*, a collection of vignettes, indexes a series of events in such a way as to reflect the fear and chaos experienced by De la Torre and her fellow Republicans. Although the author's socialist politics evidently shape her depiction of shared trauma and collective memory, her feminist ideation, at least ostensibly, is somewhat limited. Indeed, the focus on male comrades suggests an almost androgynous quality to the narrator at points, as there is little evidence of a sense of identification between De la Torre and her female counterparts. While, to some degree, this could be read in relation to De la Torre's use of a male narrator in *El banquete de Saturno*, which, as argued in the previous chapter, can be understood as a comment on female political agency, it is, of course, more telling in a first-person testimony of the Civil War. As De la Torre is telling her own story, that is to say, a reader may expect her account to be a more accurate reflection of her political career, which involved frequent collaboration with female colleagues.

Delineating an understated critique of gender and sexual politics through the narrative voice and perspective, however, is a common trait in female-authored war narratives, a point touched on earlier in the chapter. In relation to Kent's *Cuatro años en París (1940–1944)*, Lesley Twomey opines that Kent's choice of a male narrator, Plácido, suggests that 'she associates freedom with a masculine identity' (see Twomey 2007: 77). Similarly, Nuria Cruz-Cámara argues that the relative of absence of women in Lejárraga's *Una mujer por caminos de España* suggests that, rather than reflect reality, Lejárraga records an alternative truth, 'la verdad emocional' (2009: 806–07), which saw women's political emancipation obliterated by the dictatorship under which she wrote her memoir. The emphasis on emotion is central to women's testimonies. In relation to Lejárraga's memoir, Shirley Mangini (1995: 57) draws on Susanna Egan's concept of 'virtual events', distinguishable from actual events as they must 'convince' and 'contain an emotional factor' (1984: 14–15).

Somewhat paradoxically, then, the ubiquity of men in *Mares* draws key parallels with the memoirs of De la Torre's female comrades. Simultaneously a commentary on women's political agency and an affective reification of the sense of isolation or 'otherness' felt by the likes of De la Torre, Kent and Lejárraga, this literary technique indexes a core component of these women's political lives. Indeed, strategic depictions of the visibility of female figures is a common trope in De la Torre's work, as evidenced by the characterisation of María in *El banquete de Saturno*, a literary manifestation of sex-based exclusion or marginalisation within leftist political circles. The significance of what Mangini terms 'emotive scenarios' (1995: 57) is expressed in *Mares* in relation to gender. Despite foregrounding her relationships with male comrades, De la Torre is unapologetic about experiencing what she considers to be 'female' reactions. Confessing to crying on occasion, for instance, she insists she feels no shame as, to her mind, it is expected that women cry:

> Yo sí que a veces lloro, porque a mí me está permitido, que soy una mujer nada más y tengo el privilegio de no avergonzarme de llorar... (160)

She makes a similar observation in her reflections of the Cortes during the War, which have been published as part of María Francisca Vilches de Frutos's edited collection, *Matilde de la Torre: Las Cortes republicanas durante la Guerra Civil (Madrid 1936, Valencia 1937 y Barcelona 1938)* (2015). Writing in Madrid, De la Torre recounts being (gently) chastised by fellow Republican Pedro Martínez Cartón, a young communist *diputado*, for weeping in the Chamber:

> — No. Eso "no vale", Matilde... No es el momento.
>   Afortunadamente mi bien ganada fama de mujer tranquila en la guerra me salva de una mayor reprimenda. Reacciono como puedo:
> — Verdad. Pero es siempre terrible. Y yo... no soy más que una mujer.
> — Una mujer es Dolores. Mírela: serena. No llora. Aspira a vengarse. (Vilches de Frutos 2015: 89)

Intriguingly, it is De la Torre who expresses the more conservative take on gender politics here, using her sex to explain her reaction ('no soy más que una mujer'), while Martínez Cartón points to Dolores 'la Pasionaria' Ibárruri, a close companion of De la Torre, as a woman to emulate.[15]

The gendered subtext of crying in these two scenes is revealing, as it suggests a conflict between De la Torre's politics and her sex. The way in which she justifies her (perfectly legitimate) emotional reactions by describing women in reductionist terms — 'soy una mujer nada más' (160) and 'no soy más que una mujer' (Vilches de Frutos 2015: 89) — implies that, for De la Torre, she feels the trauma of the War more acutely because she is a woman, somewhat undermining her ample political credentials and resolute bravery in the face of the Nationalist rebels. The disconcerting implication here, of course, is that women's supposed vulnerability and sensitivity makes them weaker political candidates; a suggestion that De la Torre would dedicate her literary and political careers to disproving. Indeed, her description of Ibárruri in her reflections from the Cortes emphasises political excellence that is not mitigated by sex:

> De cualquier modo Pasionaria hace bien en mantenerse en el pedestal que su partido le ha levantado. Nadie lo tiene más ni mejor merecido. *Por méritos de antigüedad en la lucha, de valor personal, de disciplina en la política.*
>
> Y aun me permito para escarmiento de tímidos: *Pasionaria es infinitamente más sagaz y consecuente que muchos de estos señores políticos que hoy buscan su arrimo,* aceptando humillados, lo que discutirían libres (Vilches de Frutos 2015: 164; emphasis added)

De la Torre's references to her sex as if it were a defect, then, likely stem from her recognition of the societal paradigms under which she is judged. An example of the pervasiveness of patriarchal perspectives during De la Torre's career is evidenced by the apparent flattery with which a male journalist (writing in *La Libertad* in 1937) describes her as 'refinada en el corazón y cultísima en el intelecto; llena de suavidad como la miel y las rosas' (Mela 1937: 4); a 'compliment' that is imbued with understated misogyny. Rather than push back, in the examples cited above, De la Torre works within traditional gender norms. The way in which she does this, however, suggests a displacement of the masculine/political and feminine/domestic binary, as, while she does attribute her tears to her sex, she does not imply that this has any impact on her political efficacy.

With this in mind, framing her reflections in accordance with a traditional gender binary reflects both De la Torre's political reality and, in all likelihood, the sexist stereotypes that perturb her at her most vulnerable moments. That is to say, even a woman as remarkable as De la Torre is susceptible to assimilating patriarchal discourses; while displaying any form of emotion is, of course, not in and of itself a reflection of one's strength or intellect, the depiction of crying as a 'feminine' show of weakness is somewhat problematic. Fundamentally, it is the emphasis on hegemonic gender norms that allows De la Torre to narrate the emotional history of the conflict in a way that will resonate. On the one hand, this consideration for sentimentality humanises the War, focusing on the personal trauma of individuals; a micro-level perspective that is typical of female-authored war testimonies. Gendering war narratives in this way not only serves to foreground a female point of view, then, but also capitalises on gendered norms in order to present a *feminine* take that provides an alternative to androcentric discourses of war and politics.

As the focus on gender and emotion suggests, my reasoning here is informed by feminist approaches to affect theory. Elina Valovirta, for instance, observes the 'inextricable link between ethics and politics as imbued with affect' (2014: 6) and, accordingly, that 'affectivity is central to the meanings readers gain from textual encounters: the ways in which how we *feel* as readers impacts on the ethical and political choices we make, the way we *do* things' (Valovirta 2014: 5; original emphasis). De la Torre's evocative depictions of emotions — both sadness, expressed through her tears, and the fear and anxieties discussed earlier in the chapter — can therefore be understood not just in relation to the author and her companions, whose experiences are portrayed in *Mares*, but also the reader. It is through the emotive portrayal of political and personal tragedy, the two inherently interrelated, that De la Torre invites her reader to relate on both a human and an ideological level. To empathise in this way, therefore, is to identify with the author's politics. Read critically, the almost self-deprecating way in which De la Torre recounts weeping in *Mares*, an outburst she categorises as typical for women, could be taken as a strategic attempt to evoke empathy, particularly if De la Torre has a male reader in mind. Rather than reinforce sex stereotypes, however, outpourings of emotion are a means of displacing hegemonic gender norms, as men are also susceptible to expressions of grief during times of conflicts: 'trágicamente, que en las luchas políticas, los hombres lloran a veces, con más dolor que cuando entierran a su madre...' (180).

Comparing the War to a personal tragedy in this way blurs the boundaries between the personal and political self in such a way as to foreground the collective experience. As the above quotation illustrates, for De la Torre, political conflict is even more tragic than the death of a loved one (bearing in mind that the mother-child relationship is arguably the most primal and, therefore, the most painful loss). This sense of collectivity is tangible both in the bond it implies between those who, like the author, are devastated by the conflict and, critically, the readers who engage with the text. In *The Cultural Politics of Emotion*, Sara Ahmed perceptively notes that emotions are about 'attachments or about what connects us to this or that' (2004: 11); although emotional reactions have the effect of moving us, prompting a response, Ahmed explains, they also bond us. Accordingly, the connections cultivated by affect and emotion construct what Delgado, Fernández and Labanyi define as '"emotional communities" founded on common values and desires' (2016: 4). In *Mares*, these common values constitute leftist politics and a commitment to defending the Second Republic, regardless of sex. Nevertheless, De la Torre does allude to sex being critical to the way histories of the War are commemorated. Reflecting on a village devastated by Francoist forces, for instance, she draws attention to the significance of emotional reactions, observing how '[c]on mujeres que no lloran ni se enlutan es difícil calcular los estragos de la invasión' (203). Women and, henceforth, traditionally feminine emotions, function as a barometer for the trauma of the collective, with public expression a fundamental component of historicising violence and pain.

At the same time, De la Torre's willingness to publicly acknowledge her tears — despite the shame they seem to cause her — can be understood in relation to what Javier Krauel terms the 'emotional self-control with a markedly masculinist sense of pride' (2016: 153) promulgated during the Second Republic by Josep Maria de Sagarra, Manuel Chaves Nogales and Francisco Ayala. These (male) journalists, Krauel explains, 'used the periodical press to strengthen the regime's legitimacy by advocating emotional self-control' (2016: 146). If we re-read Martínez Cartón's admonishment of De la Torre for crying in the Cortes, cited above, in relation to this politically charged conception of emotions, an ideological subtext is discernible. Ibárruri's stoicism and ability to suppress her emotions, Martínez Cartón suggests, is a critical political asset. De la Torre's inverse depiction of this paradigm — that is, a Republican woman openly crying, as opposed to a female politician reflecting masculinist self-control — suggests a link between 'feminine' emotions and political liberty. At the very least, there is an understated criticism of this intersection of gender, politics and emotion that De la Torre can be seen to challenge directly in *Mares*, as she observes how the 'hombres valerosos' (160) who accompany her 'no logran disimular su emoción tremenda' (160). To resist the politically charged projection of 'masculine' behaviours is not just indicative of individual liberty, but also a means of withstanding ideological homogenisation. Her self-identification as 'una mujer nada más' (160) therefore takes on an understated sense of liberation from masculinist — and therefore oppressive — behaviours.

Conceiving of a more democratic, humanitarian political structure that benefits from female — and, accordingly, feminine — input is, as we have seen, tangible throughout De la Torre's writings. In *Jardín*, for example, the protagonist argues for legal structures 'al modo mujeril' (215), while *El banquete* dialogues with Flora Tristan's feminist approach to socialism. This interface of masculine politics and feminine qualities is tangible in two scenes in *Mares*. In the first, De la Torre observes flowers, which are traditionally associated with women and femininity, growing amongst bombed-out rubble. The implicit contrast of masculine violence and feminine pacifism takes on a political subtext, as amongst 'las Valientes flores' (111) she recognises roses and carnations, both of which are identified with leftist politics.[16] In another scene, De la Torre is invited to play a piano and performs the revolutionary anthems 'la Internacional', 'el Himno de Riego' and 'el Gernikako Arboa' (104), underscoring the political capital of music, which, like horticulture, is associated with femininity. In both instances, the blurring of gendered spheres connotes a sense of symbiosis and hints at the commonality of femininity in political discourses. Utilising gendered metaphors therefore facilitates an affective impact on the reader that goes beyond narrating personal or collective memories. De la Torre's depiction of extreme cold and rampant hunger, for instance, is given more resonance by the image of starving women who, nevertheless, maintain beauty standards: 'En las colas, las muchachas se pintaban los labios hambrientos y era milagro que no se comieran la barrita de carmín...' (201).

The emphatically gendered nature of experiences of war is expressed most clearly in the forms of violence specifically designated for women. Of the brutal scenes in *Mares*, the description of Republican women forced to ingest copious amounts of castor oil are amongst the most shocking. This form of torture, De la Torre writes, was known to be an abuse favoured by the Nationalists 'principalmente contra nuestras mujeres...' (215), an observation confirmed by historians (see Graham 2005: 135; Preston 2012). These 'ritual shamings had an undoubtedly gendered form' (Flesler and Pérez Melgosa 2020: 262), with castor oil considered a means of violently cleansing the victim of her Republican ideals. The quantity of liquid forced on these women, De la Torre explicates in *Mares*, is related to their relative status: 'medio litro a las hijas e esposas de los menos significados como jefes y un litro a los familiares de los principales responsables...' (215). The majority of the women died within hours, brutally succumbing to 'vómitos fecales y vómitos de sangre' (215), while the few survivors were left with permanent damage. The prevalence of this tactic, for De la Torre, exemplifies 'la miseria moral de nuestros enemigos' (215).

Juxtaposing the use of the possessive in De la Torre's descriptions of 'nuestros enemigos' (215) with 'nuestras mujeres...' (215)[17] illustrates the ambiguous sense of identification she feels with these women; while they are, evidently, her political allies, she speaks of Republican women as 'ours' rather than 'us'. In part, this is probably due to the fact that her experience of the War bore more similarities to that of her male political allies. When confronted with Nationalist violence, however, the abused women are united with De la Torre and her male comrades against 'nuestros enemigos' (215). To some degree, this alludes to the agency De la Torre's personal and professional life afford her; not only did her career open doors closed to most women, but the fact she was unmarried and had no children made her something of an anomaly. Mangini observes, for instance, that the War testimonies of Ibárruri and Constancia de la Mora are shaped by their experiences as wives and mothers (1995: 60–61). For De la Torre, on the other hand, the critical distance caused by her lack of common ground with other women allows for a more objective commentary that, as we shall see in the next section, facilitates a more theoretical perspective.

'Mocinas de Asturias': Female Solidarity

It is in the vignette 'Mocinas de Asturias', a reprint of an article published in *El Socialista* in 1937, that De la Torre focuses on women's quotidian reality during the War. The implicit solidarity that permeates *Mares* is reflected in the title, 'Mocinas de Asturias', as De la Torre uses local dialect and direct reference to her political homeland to connote a sense of community and collectivity amongst the working women. Centring on her visits to an ammunition factory, the political undertones of this chapter evidence how the War has galvanised De la Torre to revise her politics and ethics. As we have seen, De la Torre's feminist politics exemplify the porous boundaries of difference and equality feminism in contemporary Spain: while, in line with difference feminists, she celebrates many stereotypically feminine qualities, her political aspirations and unwavering support for female suffrage positions her firmly within the equality category. Chapter One's analysis of how De la Torre navigates between oppositional theorisations of feminism in *Jardín* allows us to examine this melding of (supposedly) contrary takes diachronically. On one level, the plurality of De la Torre's feminist thought indexes the inevitable tensions that arise growing up in a liberal, intellectual family in a conservative Catholic country. The conflict between these environments reflects the oppositional discourses that shaped De la Torre's ideation, and would mean that, for the young De la Torre, the domestic sphere constituted liberty, while the public realm represented oppression. Nevertheless, the reality of being a woman within leftist political circles would mean that she was often isolated, excluded or 'othered'; an injustice that is personified by the character of María in *El banquete de Saturno*.

The ambiguity that characterises De la Torre's sense of belonging to a broader female collective is tangible in her description of the female factory workers and reflects how she negotiates between antagonistic discourses in order to present women as amply capable of this work and, at the same time, deserving of sympathy, respect and recognition for their critical role in the war effort. The colleagues with whom De la Torre tours the factory ('mis acompañantes' [143]), are presumably all men, as is the case throughout *Mares*, which puts De la Torre in the unusual position of observing the female experience as an outsider. A group of women, De la Torre observes, '[t]odas jóvenes, todas bellas' (143), work tirelessly, preparing dangerous explosives that, to De la Torre's mind, could detonate at any moment. Ever-present danger and shared politics therefore bonds 'todas estas muchachas' (143) with the mixed-sex group for whom De la Torre speaks (using the 'nosotros' voice [143]), as De la Torre and her companions observe the women working:

> Ninguna alza la cabeza para mirarnos. Están trabajando. Trabajan en el manejo de la muerte. Y no de una muerte lenta, oscura, de absorción de gases tóxicos o polvillo de algodón en rama. No, no. Estas muchachas trabajan en el manejo de una sustancia estruendosamente mortífera. (142–43)

Accidents, she explains, are common. Women are scalded, blinded and lose their hair, their gums bleed and lungs are burnt, as the workers risk their lives and sacrifice their youth: 'La obrera se juega la vida y lo que vale más que la vida: la juventud' (143). The monotony and brutality of how the work is depicted has a distinctly Marxist quality, as De la Torre recounts the female workers' physical and economic vulnerability:

> Las muchachas saben todo lo horrible de lo que hacen. Pero hay que ganar el jornal, y en las regiones industriales el jornal es así: la vida puesta al albur de una carta cuya jugada dura ocho horas diarias. Y cada mañana, cuando el sol amanece, estas muchachas vienen aquí y se ponen esos delantalotes negros y esas botas forradas y se cubren las manos de trapo, y empuñan esos cucharones de palo... Y se arriman a los bordes de la paila mortífera... (143)

Rather than show fear, however, the 'dulces muchachas' (143) and '[m]ujeres graciosas' (145) handle the materials effortlessly, 'con delicadeza instintiva' (143), and maintain their enthusiasm, refusing to be brutalised by their violent work: 'El carbón no tiñó los pensamientos ni la herrumbre endureció los corazones' (145). War-time work, then, can be seen to simultaneously subvert hegemonic norms of gendered behaviour — as women join the workforce to carry out manual labour —

and, at the same time, reinforce traditional notions of femininity, as, despite these circumstances, women maintain their 'natural' delicacy and sensitivity.

The most salient change from De la Torre's earlier writings is the broadly positive depiction of women's role in arms' production. In *Mares*, the female factory workers are presented as heroic, a drastic shift from the emphatically pacifist position defended by her protagonist in *Jardín*. Rather than defend a fundamentally female-centric pacifist stance, a notion which is also tangible in *El banquete*, De la Torre focuses on how the female factory workers' femininity is utilised in their contributions to the war effort in *Mares*. On the one hand, her ideological shift is not unexpected given her dogged commitment to defending the Second Republic, as the role of working- and middle-class women would prove critical to the war effort (see Graham 1996: 10). A more nuanced approached to the question of women and pacifism is also evident in 'Feminismo y pacifismo', a speech she presented at the 'I Jornadas Eugénicas Españolas: Genética, eugenesia y pedagogía sexual' in 1933. Unequivocal in her rejection of the assumed pacifist nature of all women, as noted in the previous chapter, De la Torre argues: 'Las mujeres no somos pacifistas por doctrina y ni aun por sentimiento. Es más: las hembras en general no son pacifistas: son hembras nada más' (1934: 57–58). In the same speech, she explains that women's *potential* for motherhood, nevertheless, makes them acutely aware of the needs of the species and therefore more inclined to be opposed to war and violence. It is for this reason, she argues, that 'maternidad consciente', facilitated by effective birth control, is preferable to high birth rates in the current social and political circumstances.

In addition to offering some clues as to why De la Torre may have not borne children,[18] the arguments she puts forth in 'Feminismo y pacifismo' offer intriguing insight into how biological determinism shapes her gender politics. As Marie-Aline Barrachina explains, De la Torre 'reivindica una identidad femenina basada en la condición de hembra de la especie que posee naturalmente el instinto de lo que en un momento dado necesita dicha especie' (2004: 1020). In her defence of feminism, for instance, she presents women's social and economic rights as integral to humanity:

> Y con el Feminismo se plantea la cuestión primordial de la Humanidad: Su propagación y defensa. Aquel concepto ardiente del Amor primitivo, tan intenso como era necesario que lo fuera para defender la Especie, estaba principalmente fundamentado en la misión de la hembra, guardiana de la raza y su garantía única en muchos casos. (De la Torre 1934: 42)

Reflecting how De la Torre works within hegemonic norms in order to theorise feminist arguments, a notion that is discernible throughout her works and career, this passage also alludes to women's inherent superiority in defending the human race. At the very least, it presupposes that women have unique skills that men lack. In *Mares*, this manifests in relation to the female factory workers' deft skill and ample bravery, as noted above, and the way in which the realities of war are demarcated by sex. The male fighters, whom De la Torre calls '[l]os guajes' (202) so as to reflect her geographical and political loyalties, go into battle, while women, specifically a mother in De la Torre's description, act as guardians. The mother ('[l] a madre' [202]), she writes, stays at home, cultivating a refuge for the soldiers:

> Tiene a sus hombres en la batalla. A veces, en un remanso del fuego suelen llegarse hasta aquí; comen; duermen un par de horas mientras se enfría el fusil... Ellos descansan al amparo de la hembra que vigila todos los ruidos y conoce todas las señales del peligro... (202)

The focus on the female's perspective and the implication that she is an authority figure, textualised by '[t]iene a *sus hombres*' (202; emphasis added), repackages a stereotypically feminine role to underline her dependability. In this instance, of course, such responsibility and loyalty can be understood in a political sense, as this woman plays a critical role in the Republican resistance. The mother figure can be read liberally, a point that is perhaps underlined through the description of 'hombres' rather than 'hijos', as 'madre' and 'hembra' are used interchangeably to allude to woman's primal role as the protector of humanity.

In times of conflict, of course, the concept of women's inherently protective, caring nature takes on an important political component. There is an almost primitive subtext to the way the 'mother' keeps a vigil over the soldiers, as she 'conoce cada creciente y cada menguante de aquel estrépito de la guerra' (202) and keeps guard with heightened senses: 'Los ojos grises de la campesina escrutan todas las sombras; los oídos afinados por el instinto interpretan todos los murmullos del ambiente' (202). As well as reinforcing the rationalisation of feminism De la Torre advocates in 'Feminismo y pacifismo', the depiction of women as 'natural' guardians has distinctly socialist undertones. As touched on in the previous chapter, motherhood and birth — literal and metaphorical — are critical to Marxist cultural and political consciousness. Primal instinct, nevertheless, can clash with collectivity, particularly in times of war. In *Mares*, De la Torre interrogates this conflict directly, concerned as to what extent solidarity is innate (213) and somewhat soothed by a (male) companion who assures her that humane treatment of men, women and children is inspired by the 'fuerza de disciplina socialista' (213).

It is the tensions between 'el hombre' (213), which is at once a generic reference to the human race and an emphatically sexed allusion to individualism, and 'la Naturaleza madrastra' (213) that reflects the way gendered metaphors inform De la Torre's conceptualisation of collectivity. Women's instinctive inclination towards nurture and protection manifests as an organic form of socialism, as the group of female workers connotes a sense of gynocentric solidarity from which De la Torre, like her male companions, is excluded. This is illustrated in part through the shifts in narrative perspective, as De la Torre expresses her trepidation on entering the factory using the singular 'yo' (141) before reorienting to the 'nosotros' voice so as to include her male companions' experience, which contrasts with that of the women, 'ellas', that she is describing. Juxtaposing 'Mocinas de Asturias' with the following chapter, 'El "Sin Fusil"' (149), which centres on an unidentified, injured male combatant, further adds to the implicit unity and conformity of the women. Whereas the unknown male figure in 'El "Sin Fusil"' is isolated, the female factory workers are depicted as a homogenous group. A sense of sex-based solidarity amongst the women is connoted by this cohesion, as it is '[m]ujeres, siempre mujeres' (144), the '[m]ujeres de Asturias' (144), that carry out these dangerous tasks.

Much in the same way that the mother figure discussed above utilises feminine behaviours so as to support the war effort, so the factory workers support their sons, husbands and partners in the fight against Francoist troops. Waiting anxiously to see who safely returns from battle, the women prepare food for the men, maintaining gender norms against the backdrop of canon fire and the resounding thunder of the factory machines (146). These women routinely and unquestionably provide backup and respite, bravely attending the front lines without complaint or hesitation:

> Y *las muchachas aquellas llegan a las trincheras de primera línea.* Y, sin alharacas, ni fotografías, ni pintura en los labios, ni monos lindos, reparten la comida, y... Y, *mientras los hombres comen, ellas cogen los fusiles y se sientan en el escaño de tierra, ante las ametralladoras, como si se sentaran ante la máquina de coser...*
> Disparan...
> Disparan a manta; serenamente, continuamente... (147; emphasis added)

In a fundamentally feminist reappropriation of stereotypically female behaviour, De la Torre underscores how the women employ female skills in defence of the Second Republic. Rather than display 'female' outpourings of emotion, they work serenely, projecting a stoicism that evokes admirable strength. The political relevance of De la Torre's depictions of these women functions on multiple levels. Theoretically, the productive contribution of both the women and the femininity they embody presupposes a feminist socialism, one in which women are recognised as equals to men, with their 'female' skills celebrated. The factory workers therefore embody the same nexus of a feminine and feminist socialism as the characterisation of María in *El banquete* and, indeed, De la Torre herself. Lejárraga's description of De la Torre in *Una mujer por caminos de España* illustrates this point, reflecting the synthesis of femininity and strength that underpins De la Torre's depiction of politically-active women: 'No he conocido nunca espíritu más indomable unido a la más atrayente suavidad femenina, mayor eficacia con más dulzura' (1989: 220–21). Lejárraga's glowing endorsement would suggest that, during her political tenure, De la Torre was effective in emulating her conception of politically emancipated women.

Unbeknown to De la Torre, remembering that she first reported this scene in *El Socialista* in 1937, her portrayal of Asturian women fighting on the front would likely be one of the last times women would partake in active battle, with most women recalled by July 1937 (Herrmann 2003: 14).[19] *Mares* therefore acquires a critical and political relevance that De la Torre may not have envisaged. Not only would the *milicianas* be 'effectively erased from history because they dared to enter the supposedly male arena of frontline warfare' (Lines 2012: 3), making De la Torre's account an important contribution to Republican history, but, perhaps more pertinently, the *milicianas* would also be betrayed and disrespected by their male comrades. Lisa Margaret Lines notes that, although it may be impossible to confirm specific details regarding dates and policy,[20] what is clear is that 'while the male leaders of the Republic all agreed with this move, the women themselves saw it in a very different light' (2012: 16). The ingrained sexism with leftist and republican circles, then, which is central to De la Torre's tense relationship with socialism, would severely disable the Republican defence. De la Torre's decision to celebrate the contribution of these women on the front can therefore be understood as a fundamentally feminist act. To do so in an article for *El Socialista*, moreover, underscores how De la Torre, albeit subtly in this instance, publicises her (female) experience of the War in such a way as to highlight her male comrades blindspots and oversights.

With this in mind, and despite De la Torre's numerous references to the male revolutionaries of October 1934, it is arguably the histories of the forgotten Republican women that make *Mares* such an intriguing historical artefact or, to use Nora's terminology, a 'functional' memory site. In stark contrast to the affective scenes that recount collective trauma, the depictions centring on the Asturian women are somewhat detached, as there is little in the way of hyperbole or evocative adjectives. Rather than read this in a negative light over, the matter-of-fact tone of these observations only serves to reinforce the loyalty and dependability of the *milicianas*, as the women routinely and effectively respond to danger:

> Y si por acaso (ya sucedió más de una vez) se produce un ataque enemigo, nada se altera. Ellas arrecian en el fuego y dan tiempo a que aquellos beban el último sorbo y se limpien la boca con la manga y, desentumeciendo sus piernas, *se acerquen a recoger aquel fusil caliente de la vida femenina*, y se sienten ante la ametralladora que, generalmente, ya ha rectificado bien su radio de fuego... (148; emphasis added)

Their sacrifice and commitment is made clear, as De la Torre explains there is no laughter, nor personal exchanges, '[e]llas no se están divirtiendo' (148); '[e]stán cumpliendo el deber de aparar la vida de sus compañeras' (148). The absence of public expressions of emotion resonates strongly with the link between stoicism and ideological integrity; a Republican ideal personified by these women. By foregrounding their femininity without revealing any signs of weakness or vulnerability, De la Torre presents sexual difference as a strength rather than a hinderance. It is the particular focus on the women's lives — 'la vida femenina' (148) — and their dedication to defending one another that connotes the women's sex-based solidarity, bonded as they are by their double-militancy. De la Torre pointedly underlines how these women, and others like them, are forgotten martyrs for the Republic, 'las heroínas cotidianas' (148); '[n]o por marimachos ni por heroínas de drama truculento, sino porque están habituadas al ambiente' (148).

Through *Mares*, then, De la Torre simultaneously refutes the common belief amongst Republican men that warfare would brutalise or 'masculinise' women (they are not, she clarifies, 'marimachos' [148]) and records the collective history of these *milicianas*. It is somewhat ironic, then, that it is the anonymity of the Asturian women (none are named and no personal details provided) that most effectively epitomises De la Torre's conceptualisation of how feminist and socialist politics intersect. On the one hand, it reflects the dehumanising nature of war, as the brutality of the conflict strips them of individuality and personal aspiration; both of which are fundamental to De la Torre's critique of socialist doctrine. Conversely, the lack of individualism can also be seen to further underline the allegorical subtext of the scene: as readers, we are invited to interpret these women as a reification of a female-led socialism, as they work collaboratively, prioritising the good of the many over the needs of the few. The traditionally female behaviours and feminine qualities so typically derided and undermined by male leftists only serve to enhance their input. The inevitable tensions between De la Torre's political idealism and reality, however, are borne out in her commemoration to these heroic women. Although she recognises the ideological blindspots and practical shortcomings of discounting these 'heroínas cotidianas' (148), her lived reality as a female politician in a theoretically and literally androcentric space, nevertheless, distanced her from the women she sought to represent. De la Torre's seeming inability to connect with her fellow *mocinas* as she does her male comrades, in this sense, provides an apt analogy for the ultimate question of her career: how to coalesce her socialist and feminist principles.

Notes to Chapter 4

1. See, for instance: Ackelsberg 1991; Di Febo 1979; Herrmann 2003; Nash 1995; Preston 2002; Richmond 2003; Rodrigo 2002.
2. Legal proceedings sourced in 'recurso' n° 13/1935, Archivo Histórico Nacional, Madrid.
3. 'Noticias de toda España' 1934: 8
4. 'Figuras y figurones de las nuevas cortes' 1936: 16
5. 'El consejo de ministros de ayer' 1936: 4; 'El subsecretario de Industria y la directora de Comercio, en Valencia' 1936: 2; 'La sesión del Parlamento' 1936: 4; also see Pérez-Bustamante Mourier 2009: 25.
6. 'La *Gaceta de la República*' 1937: 4
7. 'La mañana del jefe del gobierno' 1936: 2; 'Habla Matilde de la Torre' 1936: 2
8. 'Importante acto antifascista en Orihuela' 1937: 2
9. As Maryellen Bieder and Roberta Johnson observe in their introduction to *Spanish Women Writer's and Spain's Civil War*, men's experiences and male-authored testimony dominate criticism of the Civil War (2017: 4–5).
10. Hereafter all in-text references to *Mares en la sombra: Estampas de Asturias* will be to the 2007 edition.
11. As Marianne Hirsch explains, a 'past-memory' is a memory inherited from the previous generation; 'the experience of those who grow up dominated by narratives that preceded their birth, whose own belated stories are evacuated by the stories of the previous generation, shaped by traumatic events that can be neither fully understood nor re-created' (1996: 659).
12. De la Torre was particularly involved with supporting the children of miners, providing financial support for the *Infancia Obrera* ('Anales de una convulsión' 1935: 7) and working with orphans after the conflict ('Anales de una convulsión' 1935: 7; 'Subscripción a favor de los niños huerfanos de Asturias' 1935: 1; *La Libertad* 1935: 3).
13. 'Peticiones de indulto: Por un trabajador asturiano condenado a muerte' 1935: 4; 'Una petición de indulto: Voces de clemencia ante el presidente de la República' 1935: 6.
14. As Saiz Viadero explains (2007: 85), Antuña Álvarez had fled into exile to avoid retribution for his role in the Asturian revolution, before returning to Oviedo after his electoral victory in February 1936. In accordance with De la Torre's account, he was arrested on 20 July in Oviedo and executed by firing squad in Luarca in 1937.
15. The imposing presence of Ibárruri is also recognised by De la Torre in another extract in *Las Cortes republicanas*, as she describes 'la formidable figura física de Pasionaria' (Vilches de Frutos 2015: 162) and celebrates her political prowess: 'la recia figura de Pasionaria le añade a su estatura corporal una estatura política parlamentaria muy respetable' (Vilches de Frutos 2015: 162–63).

16. It is worth noting that *Mares* was published after the notorious execution of 'las Trece Rosas' on 5 August 1939, the thirteen female members of the Juventudes Socialistas Unificadas (JSU) who have become synonymous with Francoist repression of Republican women. The groups' epithet encapsulates the same nexus of femininity and leftist politics that De la Torre's reference to roses and carnations evokes.

17. The possessive ('nuestras mujeres'), in this case, can be read in reference to both northern Spaniards, as De la Torre is specifically focusing on '[l]a horrible experiencia del resto del Norte' (215), and Republicans in general; two communities that De la Torre likely conflates given the Asturian revolution.

18. Although it is not clear whether not having children was a conscious decision on De la Torre's part, her arguments here may suggest that this was the case.

19. It is, perhaps, worth clarifying that De la Torre explains that these events took place eight months prior to writing her account (148), before women began retreating from the front.

20. Lines observes the lack of consensus amongst historians as to when women would be officially removed from the front, with Nash arguing that a sanction was passed by the socialist Prime Minister Largo Caballero in August 1936 (1995: 110) and others, such as Fraser (1979: 287) and Coleman (1999: 50), proposing that the decision was not made until March 1937.

CONCLUSION

❖

Throughout her diverse, eclectic career, De la Torre utilised written output as a means of working through and testing out her political ideals. A negotiation of her socialist, feminist and democratic convictions underpins all of De la Torre's politically motivated texts, as writing allowed her a means of interrogating tensions between these oft-antagonistic ideals. In her efforts to consolidate her conflicting political objectives into one coherent revolutionary project, De la Torre capitalised on the elasticity and mutability of literary texts in order to scrutinise both her politics and those of the movements with which she identified. Recognised as an 'oratoria serena y convincente' (Samblancat Miranda 2006: 10), De la Torre manifests her political voice in her writings, conscious of how 'el ideario socialista' that permeates her output (Núñez 1998: 404) is inflected by her lived experience as a left-wing woman. Though the works selected for analysis in this study all focalise seemingly unrelated topics and follow different generic conventions, there are ample points of aesthetic and ideological overlap. The present enquiry has focused on the politics of De la Torre's oeuvre, arguing that the ubiquity of dialogue and discourse in the works reflects her fundamental endeavour to conceptualise a feminist-socialist reformative model. Whether focusing on feminist discourses, Spain's undemocratic political history, authoritarian socialism or the fall of the Second Republic, her feminist, leftist and democratic principles — all of which, to De la Torre's mind, are dependent on a republican regime — are inflected in her argumentation and aesthetics. Rather than conceive of a fixed, dogmatic philosophy, which would be incongruent with her staunchly held belief in political liberty, De la Torre applies democratic liberalism to theories of feminism and socialism in order to foreground a revolutionary system that prioritises individual agency.

The most salient feature of De la Torre's output is how she reifies, subverts and mimics political discourses in order to scrutinise the hypocrisies and blind spots of doctrine and policy. Her particular focus on dialogue is underscored from her first publication, *Jardín de damas curiosas* (1917), given the epistolary paradigm foregrounds voice, and is utilised throughout her oeuvre: in *Don Quijote, rey de España* (1928), *El ágora* (1930) and *Mares en la sombra* (1940) De la Torre engages with androcentric historical and political discourses; whilst, in *El banquete de Saturno* (1931), the ubiquity of (fictional) male voices underscores the implicit patriarchy that underpins socialist debates, in theory and in practice. Theories of heteroglossia and feminist dialogics have illuminated how De la Torre's texts dialogue with contemporaneous debates in such a way as to foreground her own voice. The plurality of thought that the multiple voices in De la Torre's works connotes, which is indexed through direct and oblique echoes of political discourses, signifies a literary reification of democratic debate and the heterogeneity of feminist ideations. Thus, not only is De la Torre's oeuvre a means through which she can construct and promulgate her own political voice, it also opens a space for dialogue between author and reader that invites ideological introspection on an individual and collective level.

Critics of feminist dialogics, a field that would boom in the wake of second-wave feminism, have noted how polyvalent texts index and facilitate an alternative to hegemonic patriarchal ideation. By re-examining the 'very basis of narrative itself' (1994: 152), Suzanne Rosenthal Shumway writes, feminist literary criticism benefitted from the Bakhtinian method of disrupting the 'masculine (or phallocentric) discourse [that] is seen as a representation of the unified symbolic order' (1994: 154). The politically motivated texts examined in this study illustrate how De la Torre mimics and critiques androcentric debates in order to present a female-voiced alternative: in *Jardín de damas curiosas*, this is reflected through the dominant (and somewhat domineering) female protagonist; left-wing women's lack of ideological agency is indexed through the silenced María in *El banquete de Saturno*; and in *Don Quijote*, *El ágora* and *Mares en la sombra*, De la Torre's own voice takes centre stage. As well as functioning at a textual level, this multitude of female and feminist voices would also be realised in De la Torre's political career through her collaboration with left-wing (though not necessarily Socialist) female colleagues and concerted efforts to empower and support working-class women. Spanish women's political emancipation, which was enabled by the feminist reforms of the Second Republic, therefore allowed De la Torre to effectuate the female-centric political debate that she had theorised in her first text, published over a decade earlier.

To some degree, the pervasiveness of speech and political theory is conceivably one reason that De la Torre's written output has received less critical attention than that of her contemporaries as, unlike Burgos's melodrama and Montseny's politicised love stories, her texts eschew generic categorisation. Whilst it has been argued throughout this study that this is congruent with both De la Torre's maverick critical approach and her strategy of linking the aesthetic and ideological, this style does, nevertheless, make her work less accessible — and, arguably, less appealing — to a wide readership. On one level, De la Torre's evident reluctance to commit to a specific genre reflects her strategy of implementing literary traits and generic paradigms that reinforce her political arguments. The interface of genre and ideology that characterises her work not only indicates her vast critical awareness, but also denotes how, for De la Torre, the political supersedes the art form. Indeed, while *El banquete de Saturno*, for instance, likely reached a smaller readership than the work of her left-wing contemporaries, the ideological and literary richness of the novel is unprecedented.

Another intriguing reason for De la Torre's disinclination to mass-produce popular fiction is her own insecurity as an author. Writing to Miguel Artigas, then director of the Biblioteca Menéndez Pelayo (Santander), in a letter dated 14 January 1926, De la Torre reveals her self-doubt and reluctance to continue as a writer:

> Yo siempre tuve amor a la literatura y aún hace bastantes años escribí un librito,
> un epistolario. El libro fue muy malo; yo misma lo reconocí y me abstuve de
> nuevas aventuras literarias. (quoted in Madariaga de la Campa 1983: 43–44)

The dates and reference to the epistolary genre suggest that the text in question was De la Torre's first work, *Jardín de damas curiosas*, and offers some explanation for the eleven-year gap between the publications of *Jardín* and *Don Quijote*. Whilst literary merit is inherently subjective, the positive write-up published in *La Atalaya* in 1918 and the echoes of *Jardín* in *Eva curiosa: Libro para mujeres* (1930),[1] written by María Lejárraga and published under her husband's name, indicate that De la Torre's first work was well-received by some, despite the author's own misgivings. At the very least, the nuanced, expansive political introspection and acerbic wit that permeates the novel makes for an entertaining, informative read. Comparing *Jardín* with *Eva curiosa* also points to a thorny, somewhat contentious, reason that could explain De la Torre's limited output and insecurities as a writer: unlike many of her left-wing contemporaries, such as Lejárraga (whose husband, Gregorio, published many of her works) and María Teresa León (the wife of Rafael Alberti), De la Torre did not have a husband who supported or enabled her career. It is, moreover, worth underscoring that, regardless of how one judges the quality or marketability of De la Torre's written output, her oeuvre provides unparalleled insight into the ideological stances and development of one of Spain's leading feminist republicans, effectively fulfilling what was almost certainly her core objective as a writer.

The extent to which De la Torre's arguments influenced her peers and her readership is as nebulous as it is critical to this study. On the one hand, the echoes of De la Torre's first foray into politicised fiction (*Jardín de damas curiosas*) in Lejárraga's oeuvre (*Eva curiosa: Libro para mujeres*) indicate that De la Torre's lifelong friend and political ally engaged with her written work in addition to collaborating with her on social projects, which connote the symbiosis of ideological and literary production that characterises De la Torre's output. Beyond her inner circle, however, there is little evidence that De la Torre's political texts shaped the views of a wide readership. Part of the reason for this is that her work was typically aimed at those who would be unwilling to engage with the material: it is improbable, for example, that the masculinist establishment that she critiques in *El ágora* would be swayed by a socialist, republican feminist. The analyses elaborated in this study, moreover, have demonstrated the complexity and density of De la Torre's texts that make her work oblique and, therefore, alienating for a broader audience. Instead, De la Torre was writing for those who, like Lejárraga, broadly share her political objectives and, crucially, her social background, as the high-brow references that pervade her oeuvre (particularly in *El banquete de Saturno*) are unlikely to resonate with the working-classes that she defends, given it reveals a bourgeois, academically inclined education. Thus, rather than utilise her writing as a form of literary propaganda intended to convert ideologically opposed readers, De la Torre's texts can be understood as an intimate reflection of how her ideas dialogue with the political landscape. Whilst readers who share the author's leftist, democratic and feminist convictions will no doubt identify with many of her ideas, the core takeaway from

De la Torre's output is the critical and political capital of ideological meditation and scrutiny. Rather than interpret the prioritisation of introspection over didacticism as a shortcoming, this approach could be understood as an indication of De la Torre's faith in both her politics and her readership. To De la Torre's mind, that is to say, not only is her readership capable of nuanced ideological inquiry, but so too are her leftist, feminist and democratic ideals sufficiently robust to withstand scrutiny.

A common trope of De la Torre's political texts is how sex and gender are inflected in her argumentation of socialist and democratic principles. On one level, De la Torre's experiences as a left-wing woman and how this impacts her material reality are tangible in her texts. Whilst her efforts to theorise a coherent feminist script in *Jardín* connote De la Torre's own frustrations and anxieties with antagonistic discourses and objectives, the characterisation of María in *El banquete de Saturno* delineates the author's own exclusion from socialist debates (remembering the text was published before she was elected to office). In both novels, there is a discernible tension between De la Torre's authorial voice and those of her characters, with speech signifying political agency. The latent conflict between author and protagonist that permeates *Jardín* and *El banquete de Saturno* is also present in De la Torre's political commentaries that, although non-fiction, are still imbued with literary and aesthetic character. In *Don Quijote* and *El ágora*, this plays out in relation to De la Torre's engagement with the masculinist political and historical discourses that she mimics and critiques, dialoguing with hegemonic paradigms in order to interrogate debates from a female republican's perspective. It is the voices of her fallen socialist and republican comrades that De la Torre focalises in *Mares en la sombra*, including the female factory workers whose experiences of the conflict exemplify how gender and leftist ideation intersect in this context. Throughout the political texts examined in this study, there is a concerted effort to acknowledge women's subordination and otherness without being overly damning of the men that enforce or overlook this asymmetric power imbalance. Whether it is through her delineation of her relationship and dialogue with male socialists, both real (evidenced throughout *Mares*) and fictional (the protagonist Julio in *El banquete*), or the dialectic between Pulquería in *Jardín* and her nephew, the value — and, indeed, necessity — of collaborating with men is a persistent theme. The implicit need for collaboration is made manifest in her texts through the omnipresent motif of the oft-silenced female voice that, if afforded the opportunity, could proffer productive alternatives to male-centric revolutionary discourses, which would benefit from female input.

Examining her oeuvre as a whole raises two intriguing points about how De la Torre's sex and lived experience as a socialist woman shape her politics. It is worth remembering here that despite the feminist legal and political reforms that enabled De la Torre's political career, politically emancipated women like De la Torre and the militancy that they espoused were still 'una rareza en el panorama político de la década de 1930' (Trueba Mira 2002: 182–83). Accordingly, her emphasis on open dialogue with men, noted above, reflects both a political pragmatism and a recognition of the male-dominated political landscape in which she operated.

Julián Zugazagoitia, who was De la Torre's PSOE colleague and an accomplished journalist, alludes to this when recalling her political activities in the summer of 1936 (during the outbreak of the Civil War), recalling that De la Torre 'puso en el de sus deberes ciudadanos una emoción cumplimiento y republicanos y un escrúpulo que hubiese ido bien a infinidad de varones' (1977: 51–52, 101; also see Tavera 2005: 215). Such a favourable comparison with men offers some insight into how De la Torre was viewed by her male comrades: a woman both willing and able to doggedly support the cause, with no suggestion that her sex impedes her political initiatives.

The evolution of De la Torre's politically motivated writings further evince how she resisted reductive assessments of her political enterprises or texts based on sex. On the one hand, De la Torre's narrative voice shifts as her writing career develops, progressing from an empathically female-voiced protagonist in *Jardín*, who personifies a matriarchal, traditionalist feminist thought in dialogue with hegemonic patriarchy and a revolutionary, egalitarian feminism, to the author's own voice which speaks on behalf of her fallen socialist comrades (both female and male) in *Mares*. In *El banquete*, the conflict between female author and male protagonist delineates both a scathing critical commentary of androcentric socialist doctrine and a pragmatic realisation that most readers would, like the narrator, be male socialists. Similarly, the subject matter and intended audience of *Don Quijote* and *El ágora* mean that De la Torre subverts masculinist paradigms from within, with her own (female) voice and the hegemonic debates with which she engages in a constant dialogue. Rather than consider De la Torre's shift from a female- and feminist-centric text (*Jardín*) to male-voiced narratives as her career progressed as indicative of a betrayal of her feminist convictions, a more plausible explanation is that she became increasingly focused on amalgamating her core belief systems. Though her texts can be understood as focalised analyses of distinct political philosophies, specifically feminism (*Jardín*), democracy (*Don Quijote* and *El ágora*) and socialism (*El banquete*), these strands coalesce in her final political text, *Mares*. It stands to reason, with this in mind, that De la Torre's self-deprecating review of *Jardín* signals her reluctance to demarcate herself as a female or feminist writer, preferring to utilise her female perspective to critique a mixed-sex political culture.

Sex also takes on a metaphorical function in De la Torre's works, as she examines Spanish political history through a gendered lens. As examined in Chapters Two and Four in particular, she utilises sexed imagery and symbolism to critique Spain's androcentric political history and to identify the Spanish nation with the feminine. Through this parallel, De la Torre plays on the dichotomy of a female, natural world and the masculine political sphere, coding the androcentric fields of culture and politics male in such a way as to highlight the phallocentricity of Spain's political structures. In *Don Quijote* and *El ágora*, maternity functions as a symbolic depiction of the regeneration and genesis that characterises De la Torre's political objectives. Similarly, the evocation of motherhood is utilised in both *Jardín* and *El banquete de Saturno* to connote the birth of a revolutionary project: in *Jardín*, it is the matriarchal protagonist who negotiates ideological extremes to conceive of an inclusive feminism; while, in *El banquete*, we learn that it was the protagonist's mother who nurtured his socialist beliefs. The primal strength and resilience of the land — 'la Madre Tierra' — is explored in *Don Quijote*, with colonisation and conquest delineated through the sexed metaphor of a penetrative invasion that is somewhat resisted by the inherently female natural order. It is in *Mares* that De la Torre develops these strands further, presenting qualities such as protection and caregiving as critical to socialist ideation, a notion that is also hinted at in her elusive references to the unrealised, pacifist revolutionary model presupposed by the insightful, yet overlooked, character of María in *El banquete*.

Throughout her writing career, therefore, De la Torre capitalises on the symbolic significance of maternity and femininity as a means of theorising and delineating her political ideals. Whilst this is not uncommon for revolutionary women, it is somewhat unexpected as De la Torre never had children. She did, however, conceive of political models and social projects that benefitted from traditional understandings of maternal instinct and behaviour. To some degree, this is in consonance with her character: though De la Torre never became a mother, she did spend much of her life caring for her disabled brother and so, in essence, fulfilled a maternal role. Indeed, and as Marie-Aline Barrachina writes in her analysis of De la Torre's 1934 speech 'Feminismo y pacifismo', De la Torre was of the view that even the potential for childbearing gave women an in-depth insight into society's needs; 'es porque son *madres potenciales* por lo que las mujeres siempre han tenido el sentido de las necesidades de la especie, según los tiempos y según las circunstancias' (2004: 1020; emphasis added). Women's disposition for nurturing children, she therefore reasoned, can conceivably be understood in relation to political projects, particularly given the historic need to have multiple children had become anachronistic. As Barrachina explains:

> De la misma manera que el nacimiento del sentimiento amoroso respondería a una necesidad coyuntural de la especie que, en algún momento, necesitaría proceder a alguna forma de selección, la maternidad prolífica también resultaría de una necesidad de la especie en un primer tiempo, de las naciones en un segundo momento, y de una necesidad industrial, para terminar. (2004: 1020)

Conceptualising the nation as a sexed construct insinuates that citizens' relationships with the state are shaped by their sex and, by extension, that gender inflects how political structures are understood. Motherhood, in this sense, is conceived of as an organic extension of womanhood, with the positive attributes that it evokes essential for a virtuous revolutionary model.

On one level, this could be interpreted in broadly feminist terms. In *La mujer española ante la República* (Martínez Sierra 1931), Lejárraga proposes that 'para los hombres [la Patria] es *la madre*, para las mujeres es *el hijo*' (Martínez Sierra 1931: 9; original emphasis). Accordingly, she continues:

> Los hombres aman a su madre con exaltación; las mujeres aman a sus hijos con preocupación. Un hombre bien nacido está dispuesto a dar gallardamente la vida por su madre. Todavía mujer quiere, implacablemente, que su hijo viva. (Martínez Sierra 1931: 9)

Not only does Lejárraga presuppose a sense of caution and protectiveness that is congruent with De la Torre's depiction of motherhood, she does so in such a way as to present men as impulsive and potentially reckless, subverting the gendered stereotype of women as hysterical and irrational. For both De la Torre and Lejárraga, the inherently female fortitude of maternity is invested with political potential, which speaks to the personification of a Republic as an empowered woman. The abstract, symbolic significance of the nation as mother is all the more compelling given neither woman had children. Thus, rather than evoke the traditionalist strand of difference feminism, or, indeed, patriarchal discourses, that construe women's role as mothers as a method of shaping public life and nurturing the nation (in line with Francoist views of womanhood), the politicisation of maternity functions as a reification of feminist values that resonates across the political spectrum.

That is not to suggest, however, that De la Torre's political opponents were receptive to her logic. In response to an all-woman manifesto dated 17 November 1938, which demanded an end to the Nationalist assault and was signed by De la Torre (along with Ibárruri and Nelken, amongst others), the right-wing press were indignant that the signatories made use of maternal symbolism, describing themselves as 'madres españolas' wanting to protect '[n]uestros niños' from the brutality of war. In both *El Progreso* ('Las hermanas pasionarias' 1938: 4) and *El Día de Palencia* ('Ni madres, ni españolas' 1938: 3), the signatories are castigated as '[n]i madres ni españolas', with De la Torre specifically condemned as 'inepta estéticamente para la concepción' in *El Progreso* and 'estéticamente contraria al matrimonio' in *El Día de Palencia*. Enraged by what they consider to be a form of political extortion ('chantage' [*sic*]), the (almost certainly male) journalist(s) deride the women as 'anti-España' and, as expressed in *El Progreso*, insist that motherhood serves a sacred function: ¿No lo habéis advertido? La fisiología más avezada no podría ni sabría crear una función espiritual'. The vitriol aimed at the women who endorsed the manifesto, which is particularly personal given the direct speech ('¿No lo habéis advertido?') and derogatory (and flagrantly untrue) insults about De la Torre's appearance, speaks to the misogyny that drives this abuse and illustrates how motherhood is coveted by antagonistic ideologies. The multiple ways that De la Torre relates the Spanish nation and socialist ideation to maternal imagery, in this sense, can be considered a fundamentally feminist reclaiming of a paradigm that is inherently linked to women.

A final ideological thread discernible throughout De la Torre's work is her fundamentally pessimistic outlook. Her first work, *Jardín*, centres on the con-flicts within first-wave Spanish feminisms and, from there, her focus becomes increasingly bleak: *Don Quijote* and *El ágora* examine the corruption and failings of Spain's political structure; *El banquete* laments the improbability of an egalitarian socialist revolution; and, in *Mares*, the narrative details the tragic fall of the Second Republic and, with it, De la Torre's political dream. Though allusions to positive, promising alternatives yet to be realised can be gleaned throughout her work, there is, nevertheless, a focus on pragmatic failings, ideological blind spots and unrealised aspirations. Not only can such despondency be read in relation to De la

Torre's biting cynicism, it also characterises a Republican government that became increasingly vulnerable to infighting and the emergence of a unified, combative political right. Despite the reforms that made De la Torre's political career possible, there were ample reasons for her pessimism, from the difficulties she faced as a woman in socialist circles to the 1933 electoral victory of the right-wing CEDA coalition and the capitulation of the 1934 Asturian revolution. De la Torre's cautious approach is also indicative of another quality that characterises her written output: foresight. Indeed, her disapproving critique of a fractured women's movement (*Jardín*), distaste for Spain's undemocratic political structures (*Don Quijote* and *El ágora*), ominous foreshadowing of an authoritarian socialist regime (*El banquete*) and the tragic fall of the Second Republic (*Mares*) illustrate that her caution was not unwarranted. With this in mind, her cynicism could be understood in relation to her political shrewdness, as, regrettably, her trepidation regarding Spain's receptiveness to revolutionary politics would prove tragically prophetic.

De la Torre's political opponents recognised the somewhat defeatist undertones of her work and were brutal in their criticism: in *El Progreso* in April 1938, one anonymous critic (who was presumably male and right-wing) published a short piece entitled 'Nuevos pesimismos de Matilde de la Torre', which constituted a character assassination seemingly written with the intention of eliciting a response from De la Torre. (In today's parlance, this snippet could be considered an example of 'trolling'.) She is, apparently, 'una escritora derrotista' (1931: 1) who exhibits 'un pesimismo fundamental' (1931: 1) and, so, the newspaper's editorial team are perplexed as to why the left have not abandoned her: 'No sabemos cómo los rojos no la han pasado todavía por las armas' (1931: 1). Whilst this irascible review was no doubt published in order to publicly humiliate De la Torre, it also implies that her career and writings greatly aggravated the political right; a reaction that the author would have most certainly intended and, likely, relished. The impact of De la Torre's writing on Spain's collective political consciousness can therefore be measured with some degree of success, as she became both a well-respected figure within leftist circles and a target for her right-wing adversaries. In an ironic twist that De la Torre herself would no doubt appreciate, her critic quotes her verbatim in order to highlight, and therefore ridicule, her concerns for the Spanish economy should the Second Republic fall. In doing so, the journalist promulgates De la Torre's political argumentation in such a way as to foreground her voice; effectively, and unwittingly, realising her core objective as a writer.

Given De la Torre's relatively cynical, pessimistic approach, it is unexpected that she was amongst the most avowed defenders of the crumbling Second Republic. Even when the outcome looked dire, De la Torre (at least publicly) maintained the faith and, characteristically, capitalised on the political capital of speech and dialogue, both written and spoken, to reflect and inspire. In one of her final letters to Juan Negrín, written in 1945 and published posthumously in *El Socialista*, De la Torre optimistically hopes that the Second Republic will be restored: 'Brota hoy un rayo de sol de libertad que promete restituirnos a nuestra patria con nuestras instituciones republicanas puras y esenciales' (quoted in Domínguez Prats 1998:

1247). Hope and faith that the Republic will withstand the Nationalists' revolt is the central message of one of De la Torre's final public political addresses, which was published in *Justicia Social* on 11 January 1939, just three months before the Nationalists declared victory. Poignantly entitled 'Un emocionado saludo de Matilde de la Torre a sus camaradas de Menorca', the speech was written, rather than delivered, due to De la Torre's rapidly declining health. Addressing a broadly left-wing audience, she commends the people of Menorca (the last of the Balearic Islands to fall) for their mettle and valour:

> Vosotros, camaradas de Menorca; republicanos y socialistas; campesinos, industriales y letrados; acaso no os dais cuenta completa de vuestro papel en el mundo actual. Pero es la verdad que sois como un faro en medio de la mar y como un rayo de sol entre la tormenta. Muchas veces se ha hecho el símil de vuestra hermosa isla como de un barco en el océano. ('Un emocionado saludo' 1939: 1)

Describing Menorca as an isolated ship, echoing the symbolism in 'La ciudad nueva' and *Mares en la sombra*, De la Torre expounds how 'el alma de la Libertad de España' ('Un emocionado saludo' 1939: 1) is aboard, with the island amongst the last refuges where 'ondea la bandera del Pueblo Republicano español' ('Un emocionado saludo' 1939: 1). In an impassioned rallying cry that connotes De la Torre's aim to galvanise the people and, at the same time, suggests a degree of desperation, she declares that the heroism of the Menorcan people is world-renowned:

> El Mundo entero sabe de vosotros; sabe de esa isla perdida en la inmensidad de los mares. *Cuando se habla de vosotros, se os compara a los héroes de leyenda.* Sin más coraza que la lealtad diamantina de vuestras almas; sin más fuerza que la vosotros forjáis cada día en el fondo inagotable de vuestra voluntad de vencer, habéis permanecido más de dos años y medio bloqueados por la cobardía del Mundo y por la osadía de dos pueblos esclavistas. *A muchos otros pueblos les han puesto el yugo esos dos Estados esclavistas. Pero a vosotros, no.* Porque vosotros, al menor asomo de agresión cobarde, les habéis hecho saber que sabíais *defender el tesoro de vuestra libertad y la independencia* de ese trozo del solar patrio, y que primero haríais de vuestra hermosa isla una gigantesca sepultura, que vivir encade nados al enemigo sobre esa corteza heroica, pedazo del corazón de España. ('Un emocionado saludo' 1939: 1; emphasis added)

Commending the 'obra magnífica de la defensa de Menorca' ('Un emocionado saludo' 1939: 1), she commends the Republican forces for refusing to capitulate to 'la esclavitud fascista' (1939: 1) and the *pueblo* in their struggle to 'librarse del veneno fascista' ('Un emocionado saludo' 1939: 1).

De la Torre's affecting communication to one of the last strongholds of the Second Republic offers a fruitful means of concluding this study, as it encapsulates many of the core themes that pervade her oeuvre and the synergy of political agency and dialogue that characterises her texts. While her work typically focalises critique and ideological introspection, De la Torre's aim here is to defend and bolster the republican regime that defined and revolutionised her life and career. In a reflection that is particularly poignant when read retrospectively, she maintains that the Second Republic will prevail:

> Esto lo sabemos y lo sentimos cada español de la martirizada Metrópoli. Con
> avanzadas como la vuestra, las líneas de combate de la República están seguras.
> ('Un emocionado saludo' 1939: 1)

Through the use of the first-person plural ('lo sabemos y lo sentimos'), De la
Torre speaks on behalf of the Spanish people, intimating a degree of solidarity and
unification amongst a population that was, in reality, internecine and fractured.
Reinforcing her belief (or, perhaps, hope) that the Nationalists will be defeated, she
declares that 1939 will see victory for the Second Republic:

> En este año de victoria os deseo, camaradas todos, la alegría de saber libre a la
> Madre común; la Metrópoli española. ('Un emocionado saludo' 1939: 1)

In reality, Menorca would be taken by the rebels after a two-day assault that
would conclude on 9 February, less than a month after De la Torre's address.
Republican Spain, which she depicts as 'la Madre común' in accordance with her
conceptualisation of maternity as reformative and revolutionary, would be usurped
by patriarchal Francoism and, with it, the socialist, democratic and feminist values
that facilitated and shaped De la Torre's career. As her obstinate conviction that the
Second Republic would triumph is incongruent with much of her written output,
which is distinctly cautious and critical given De la Torre's political acumen, the
optimism that characterises her address suggests a utopian turn in her political
ideation. When confronted with the impending destruction of her political ideals,
her core objective was maintaining the faith, in spite of the unpropitious circumstances, and, for De la Torre, this would be exteriorised through dialogue with her
Republican comrades.

Notes to the Conclusion

1. As well as the intertextual linkage of the titles and echoes of the Garden of Eden narrative in
   both *Jardín de damas curiosas* and *Eva curiosa: Libro para mujeres*, there are also overlaps in the texts.
   A salient example is the short play entitled 'La madre y el filósofo en el jardín' in *Eva curiosa*
   (Martínez Sierra 1930: 129–37) that narrates a conversation between 'La Madre' and 'El Filósofo',
   which echoes the dialogue between De la Torre's matriarchal protagonist, *tía* Pulquería, and the
   androcentric philosophical debates that she critiques.

BIBLIOGRAPHY

❖

Matilde de la Torre

TORRE, MATILDE DE LA. 1917. *Jardín de damas curiosas* (Madrid: Imprenta de Juan Pueyo)
—— 1930. *El ágora* (Santander: Aldus)
—— 1931. *El banquete de Saturno: Novela social* (Barcelona: Ediciones Mentora)
—— 1934. 'Feminismo y pacifismo', in *Genética, eugenesia y pedagogía sexual: Libro de las primeras jornadas eugénicas españolas*, ed. by Enrique Noguera and Luis Huerta (Madrid: Morata), pp. 33–59
—— 1948. *Soles y brumas de España: Pequeña antología de canciones y romances del folklore español* (Mexico City: [Unknown])
—— 1979. *La montaña en Inglaterra*, ed. by J. R. Saiz Viadero (Santander: Puntal)
—— 2000. *Don Quijote, rey de España* (1928), ed. by Antonio Martínez Cerezo (Santander: Servicio de Publicaciones, University of Cantabria)
—— 2007. 'El sin fusil' (1937), in *Crónica general de la Guerra Civil*, ed. by María Teresa León (Seville: Editorial Renacimiento), pp. 61–65
—— 2007 [1940]. *Mares en la sombra: estampas de Asturias*, ed. by José Rámon Sáiz Viadero ([Unknown]: Ediciós do Castro)

References

ACKELSBERG, MARTHA A. 1991. *Free Women of Spain: Anarchism and the Struggle for the Emancipation of Women* (Bloomington: Indiana University Press)
'Actos socialistas en Galicia'. 1935. *La Libertad*, 27 August, p. 8
'Actuación de los partidos'. 1935. *El Heraldo de Madrid*, 27 August, pp. 12–13
AGUADO, ANA. 2005. 'Entre lo público y lo privado: Sufragio y divorcio en la Segunda República', *Ayer*, 60: 105–34
AGUILAR, MARIO. 1931. *El proceso Dreyfus* (Barcelona: Ediciones Mentora)
AGUADO, ANA. 2005. 'Entre lo público y lo privado: Sufragio y divorcio en la Segunda República', *Ayer*, 60: 105–34
AHMED, SARA. 2004. *The Cultural Politics of Emotion* (New York: Routledge)
'Al ministro de Instrucción Pública'. 1931. *Crisol*, 15 December, p. 10
ALBA, VÍCTOR. 1983. *The Communist Party in* Spain, trans. by Vincent G. Smith (New Brunswick, NJ: Transaction Books)
ALBA, VÍCTOR, and STEPHEN SCHWARTZ. 1988. *Spanish Marxism Versus Soviet Communism: A History of the P.O.U.M.* (New Brunswick, NJ: Transaction Book)
ALBORG, CONCHA. 1996. '*Una mujer por caminos de España*: La seudoautobiografía de María Martínez Sierra (1874–1974)', *Revista de Estudios Hispánicos*, 30: 485–95
ALCALDE, CARMEN. 1983. *Federica Montseny: Palabra en rojo y negro* (Barcelona: Argos Vergara)
ALDARACA, BRIDGET. 1991. *El ángel del hogar: Galdós and the Ideology of Domesticity in Spain* (Chapel Hill: University of North Carolina Press)
ALFORD, VIOLET. 1934. 'Cantabrian Calendar Customs and Music', *Musical Quarterly*, 20: 435–51

ALEXANDER, GERARD. 1999. 'Women and Men in the Ballot Box: Voting in Spain's Two Democracies', in *Constructing Spanish Womanhood: Female Identity in Modern Spain*, ed. by Victoria Lorée Enders and Pamela Beth Radcliff (Albany, NY: SUNY Press), pp. 349–73

ALPERT, MICHAEL. 2007. *The Republican Army in the Spanish Civil War* (Cambridge: Cambridge University Press)

ALTED VIGIL, ALICIA. 2008. 'Mujeres españolas emigradas y exiliadas: Siglos XIX y XX', *Anales de Historia Contemporánea*, 24: 59–75

ÁLVAREZ-URÍA, F. 2013. 'Mujeres y política: Las políticas de las mujeres en la España de la Segunda República y la Guerra Civil', *Revista de Sociología*, 98: 629–46

AMORÓS, CELIA. 2007. 'Thinking Patriarchy', in *Feminist Philosophy in Latin America and Spain*, ed. by María Luisa Femenías and Amy A. Oliver, trans. by Celieta Marques Amorós (Amsterdam; New York: Rodopi), pp. 109–2

'Anales de una convulsión'. 1935. *La Libertad*, 14 March, p. 7

ANDERSON, WILLIAM. 1982. *Essays on Roman Satire* (Princeton: Princeton University Press)

ARENAL, CONCEPCIÓN. 2009. *La mujer del porvenir: La educación en la mujer* (Barcelona: elitterae)

ARKINSTALL, CHRISTINE. 2009. *Histories, Cultures, and National Identities: Women Writing Spain, 1877–1984* (Lewisburg, PA: Bucknell University Press)

ÁVILA, DEBBIE. 2005. 'The Romance Novel of the 1930s and 40s in Spain and Portugal: The Cases of Carmen de Icaza and Alice Ogando' (Unpublished Doctoral Thesis: University of California)

BAKHTIN, MIKHAIL. 1981. *The Dialogic Imagination: Four Essays*, ed. by Michael Holquist, trans. by Caryl Emerson and Michael Holquist (Austin: University of Texas Press)

BALFOUR, SEBASTIAN. 1995. 'Riot, Regeneration and Reaction: Spain in the Aftermath of the 1898 Disaster', *The Historical Journal*, 38(2): 405–23

BALFOUR, SEBASTIAN. 1997. *The End of the Spanish Empire, 1898–1923* (Oxford: Clarendon Press)

BALLESTEROS, ISOLINA. 1994. *Escritura femenina y discurso autobiográfico en la nueva novela española* (New York: Peter Lang)

BARÓ LLAMBIAS, MÒNICA. 2006. 'Les edicions infantils i juvenils de l'Editorial Joventut', (Unpublished PhD Thesis: University of Barcelona)

BARRACHINA, MARIE-ALINE. 2004. 'Maternidad, feminidad, sexualidad: Algunos aspectos de las *primeras jornadas eugénicas españolas* (Madrid, 1928–Madrid, 1933)', *Hispania*, 64(218): 1003–26

BARRETT, MICHÈLE. 1988. *Women's Impression Today: The Marxist/Feminist Encounter* (London: Verso)

BARTLEY, PAULA. 2002. *Emmeline Pankhurst* (London: Routledge)

BAUER, DALE M. 1988. *Feminist Dialogics: A Theory of Failed Community* (Albany: State University of New York Press)

BAUER, DALE M., and SUSAN JARET MCKINSTRY. (eds). 1991. *Feminism, Bakhtin, and the Dialogic* (Albany: State University of New York Press)

BELLVER, CATHERINE. 2001. *Absence and Presence: Spanish Women Poets of the 20s and 30s* (Lewisburg, PA: Bucknell University Press)

BENDER, REBECCA. 2016. 'Theorizing a Hybrid Feminism: Motherhood in Margarita Nelken's *En torno a nosotras* (1927)', *Bulletin of Hispanic Studies*, 93(2): 131–48

BERENS, E. M. 2007. *Myths and Legends of Ancient Greece and Rome* (New York: Maynard, Merrill & Co.)

BERGÉS, CONSUELO. 1935. *Explicación de octubre: Historia comprimida de cuatro años de República en España* (Madrid: Garcigoy)

BERGMANN, EMILIE L., and RICHARD HERR, EDS. 2007. *Mirrors and Echoes: Women's Writing in Twentieth-Century Spain* (Berkeley: University of California Press)

BIEDER, MARYELLEN. 2018 'First-Wave Feminisms, 1800–1919', in *A New History of Iberian Feminisms*, ed. by Silvia Bermúdez and Roberta Johnson (Toronto: University of Toronto Press), pp. 158–81

BIEDER, MARYELLEN, and ROBERTA JOHNSON. (eds). 2017. *Spanish Women Writer's and Spain's Civil War* (London: Routledge)

BLANCO, ALDA. 1998. '*A las mujeres de España*: The Feminist Essays of María Martínez Sierra', in *Spanish Women Writers and the Essay: Gender, Politics and the Self*, ed. by Kathleen M. Glenn and Mercedes Mazquiarán de Rodríguez (Columbia: University of Missouri Press), pp. 75–99

—— 2002. '*Una mujer por caminos de España*: María Martínez Sierra y la política', in *María Martínez Sierra y la República: Ilusión y compromiso*, coord. by Juan Aguilera Sastre (Logroño: Instituto de Estudios Riojanos), pp. 173–88

—— 2007. 'Desde la pared de vidrio hasta la otra orilla: El exilio de María Martínez Sierra', in *Mirrors and Echoes: Women's Writing in Twentieth-Century Spain*, ed. by Emilie Bergmann and Richard Herr (Berkeley: University of California Press), pp. 78–92

BOCK, GISELA, and SUSAN JAMES. 1992. 'Introduction: Contextualizing Equality and Difference', in *Beyond Equality and Difference: Citizenship, Feminist Politics and Female Subjectivity*, ed. by Gisela Bock and Susan James (London: Routledge), pp. 1–13

BOHNERT, CHRISTIANE. 1995. 'Early Modern Complex Satire and the Satiric Novel: Genre and Cultural Transposition', in *Theorizing Satire: Essays in Literary Criticism*, ed. by Brian A. Connery and Kirk Combe (New York: St Martin's Press), pp. 151–72

BOLUFFER PERUGA, MÓNICA. 2018. 'New Inflections of a Long Polemic: The Debate between the Sexes in Enlightenment Spain', in *A New History of Iberian Feminisms*, ed. by Silvia Bermúdez and Roberta Johnson, trans. by Elizabeth Franklin Lewis (Toronto: University of Toronto Press), pp. 38–49

BOOTH, WAYNE. 1982. 'Freedom of Interpretation: Bakhtin and the Challenge of Feminist Criticism', *Critical Inquiry*, 9: 45–76

BRANCIFORTE, LAURA. 2009–2010. 'Legitimando la solidaridad femenina internacional: El Socorro Rojo', *Arenal*, 16: 27–52

BRISON, SUSAN. 1999. 'Trauma Narratives and the Remaking of the Self', in *Acts of Memory: Cultural Recall in the Present*, ed. by Mieke Bal, Jonathan Crewe and Leo Spitzer (Hanover: University Press of New England), pp. 39–54

BRITT-ARREDONDO, CHRISTOPHER. 2005. *Quixotism: The Imaginative Denial of Spain's Loss of Empire* (New York: State University of New York Press)

BROOKSBANK JONES, ANNY. 1997. *Women in Contemporary Spain* (Manchester: Manchester University Press)

BROWN, JOAN L. (ed.). 1991. *Women Writers of Contemporary Spain: Exiles in the Homeland* (Newark: University of Delaware Press)

BURGOS, CARMEN DE. 1906. *La mujer en España* (Valencia: Sempre y Compañía)

—— 1921. *El artículo 438* (Madrid: Publicaciones Prensa Gráfica)

—— 2007. *La mujer moderna y sus derechos* (1927) (Madrid: Biblioteca Nueva)

CABALEIRO MANZANEDO, JULIA, and ELENA BOTINAS I MONTERO. 2003. *L'activitat femenina a Molins de Rei: Les dones durant la Guerra Civil* (Barcelona: Publicacions de l'Abadia de Montserrat)

CALDERÓN GUTIÉRREZ, MARÍA CARMEN. 1984. *Matilde de la Torre y su época* (Santander: Ediciones Tantin)

CAPDEVILA-ARGÜELLES, NURIA. 2011. 'Autobiografía y autoría de mujer en el exilio', *Journal of Iberian and Latin American Research*, 17: 5–16

CAPEL MARTÍNEZ, ROSA MARÍA. 2007. 'De protagonistas a represaliadas: La experiencia de las mujeres republicanas', *Cuadernos de Historia Contemporánea*, 11–12: 35–46

—— 2008A. 'Clara Campoamor, la urna como instrumento de lucha', in *Dones contra l'estat*, ed. by Juncal Caballero y Sonia Reverter (Castelló de la Plana: Seminari d'Investigació Feminista. Universitat Jaume I), pp. 21–49

—— 2008B. 'Mujer y socialismo (1848–1939)', *Pasado y Memoria: Revista de Historia Contemporánea*, 7: 101–22

—— 2012. 'Una mujer y su tiempo: María de la O Lejárraga de Martínez Sierra', *Revista arenal*, 19: 5–46

CARUTH, CATHY. (ed.). 1995. *Trauma: Explorations in Memory* (Baltimore: John Hopkins University Press)

CASTAÑADA, PALOMA. 1994. *Carmen de Burgos, Colombine* (Madrid: Horas y Horas)

CHACÓN, DULCE. 2002. *La voz dormida* (Barcelona: Penguin)

CHECA PUERTA, JULIO E. 2009. 'María Martínez Sierra, una escritora en el exilio', *Foro hispánico*, 34: 207–28

CIBREIRO, ESTRELLA, and FRANCISCA LÓPEZ. 2013. *Global Issues in Contemporary Hispanic Women's Writing: Shaping Gender, the Environment, and Politics* (New York: Routledge)

CIPLIJAUSKAITÉ, BIRUTE. 1988. *La novela femenina contemporánea (1970–1985): Hacia una tipología de la narración en primera persona* (Madrid: Anthropos)

CIXOUS, HÉLÈNE. 1976 [1975]. 'The Laugh of the Medusa', trans. by Keith Cohen and Paula Cohen, *Signs*, 1(4): 875–93

CLARK, KATERINA. 1981. 'Socialist Realism *with* Shores: The Conventions for the Positive Hero', in *Socialist Realism Without Shores*, ed. by Thomas Lahusen and Evgeny Dobrenko (Durham, NC: Duke University Press), pp. 27–50

—— 1997. *The Soviet Novel: History as Ritual* (Bloomington: Indiana University Press)

'Código Penal de 8 de Septiembre de 1928'. 1929. *Codigo Penal de 8 de septiembre de 1928: Con las correcciones y aclaraciones oficiales y algunas notas y referencias* (Madrid: Gongora)

COLE, GREGORY. 2000. *Spanish Women Poets of the Generation of 1927* (Lewiston, PA: Mellen)

'Código civil'. 1889. <https://www.boe.es/buscar/doc.php?id=BOE-A-1889-4763> [accessed 30 April 2021]

'Código penal reformado'. 1870. <http://sirio.ua.es/libros/BDerecho/codigo_penal/index.htm> [accessed 30 April 2021]

COFFEY, MICHAEL. 1976. *Roman Satire* (London: Methuen and Co Ltd; Barnes & Noble)

COLLINS, MARIE, and SYLVIE WEIL-SAYRE. 1973. 'Flora Tristan: Forgotten Feminist and Socialist', *Nineteenth-Century French Studies*, 1(4): 229–34

COLEMAN, CATHERINE. 1999. 'Women in the Spanish Civil War', in *Heart of Spain: Robert Capa's Photographs of the Spanish Civil War*, ed. by Juan P. Fusi Aizpurau and Richard Whelan et al. (New York: Aperture), pp. 43–51

CONDE, CARMEN. 1954. *Poesía femenina española viviente: Antología* (Madrid: Castilla)

—— 1967. *Poesía femenina española (1939–1950)* (Barcelona: Bruguera)

—— 1971. *Poesía femenina española (1950–1960)* (Barcelona: Bruguera)

'Constitución de la República Española'. 1931. <https://bit.ly/3urnSzy> [accessed 7 May 2021]

COOKE, MIRIAM. 1996. *Women and the War Story* (Berkeley: University of California Press)

CRUZ-CÁMARA, NURIA. 2009. 'La doctrina socialista y el público en *Una mujer por caminos de España* de María Martínez Sierra', *Bulletin of Spanish Studies*, 86(6): 793–807

—— 2015. *La mujer moderna en los escritos de Federica Montseny* (Tamesis Books)

ČAVOŠKI, KOSTA. 1986. *The Enemies of the People* (London: Centre for Research into Communist Economies)

DAVIES, CATHERINE. 1994. *Contemporary Feminist Fiction in Spain: The Work of Montserrat Roig and Rosa Montero* (Oxford: Berg)

—— 1998. *Spanish Women's Writing 1849–1996* (London: Athlone Press)

DELGADO, IRENE, and MIGUEL JEREZ. 2008. 'Mujer y política en España: Un análisis comparado de la presencia femenina en las asambleas legislativas (1977–2008)', *Revista española de ciencia política*, 19: 41–78

DELGADO, LUISA ELENA, PURA FERNÁNDEZ and JO LABANYI. (eds). 2016. *Engaging the Emotions in Spanish Culture and History* (Nashville, TN: Vanderbilt University Press)

DELGADO CRUZ, SEVERIANO. 2008. 'Mujeres republicanas en las Cortes y en el Gobierno: Su memoria en Internet', in *Curso Mujeres republicanas en la memoria*, ed. by Josefina Cuesta Bustillo and Rosa María Merino Hernández (Salamanca: Universidad de Salamanca), unnumbered

DI FEBO, GIULIANA. 1979. *Resistencia y movimiento de mujeres en España, 1936–1976* (Barcelona: Icaria)

DÍAZ FERNÁNDEZ, PALOMA. 2005. 'La dictadura de Primo de Rivera: Una oportunidad para la mujer', *Espacio, Tiempo y Forma, Serie V, Historia Contemporánea*, 17: 175–90

DOBRENKO, EVGENY. 2011. 'The Epic Retreat: Political Culture and Cultural Policy in 1930s Stalinist Russia', in *Red Cavalry: Creation and Power in Soviet Russia between 1917 and 1945*, ed. by Rosa Ferré (Madrid: La Casa Encendida), pp. 372–415

DOBSON, ANDREW. 1989. *An Introduction to the Politics and Philosophy of José Ortega y Gasset* (Cambridge: Cambridge University Press)

DOMINGO, JOSÉ. 1973. *La novela española del siglo XX. 1, De la generación del 98 a la guerra civil* (Barcelona: Editorial Labor)

DOMINGO, CARMEN. 2004. *Con voz y voto: Las mujeres y la política en España (1931–1945)* (Barcelona: Lumen)

DOMÍNGUEZ PRATS, PILAR. 1998. 'Intelectuales españolas en el exilio de México: Margarita Nelken y Matilde de la Torre', Paper Presented at the *XIII Coloquio de historia canario-americano*, Las Palmas de Gran Canaria, pp. 1237–50

—— 2009. 'La actividad política de las mujeres republicanas en México', *ARBOR Ciencia, Pensamiento y Cultura*, 735: 75–85

—— 2012. 'Silvia Mistral, Constancia de la Mora y Dolores Martí: Relatos y memorias del exilio de 1939', *Revista de Indias*, 72: 799–824

EGAN, SUSANNA. 1984. *Patterns of Experience in Autobiography* (Chapel Hill: University of North Carolina Press)

'El consejo de ministros de ayer'. 1936. *El Sol*, 20 September, p. 4

'El subsecretario de Industria y la directora de Comercio, en Valencia'. 1936. *La Voz*, 29 September, p. 2

'El parlamento: Ayer continuó la aprobación de actas'. 1933. *La Libertad*, 14 December, p. 8

'El programa parlamentario para mañana'. 1935. *La Voz*, 25 March, p. 9

ELLIOT, ROBERT. 1971. 'The Satirist and Society', in *Satire: Modern Essays in Criticism*, ed. by Ronald Paulson (Englewood Cliffs, NJ: Prentice-Hall), pp. 205–16

'En Madrid y provincias: Varios actos de propaganda política y social'. 1932. *El Sol*, 24 May, p. 4

'En Madrid y provincias: Varios actos de propaganda política'. 1932. *La Libertad*, 24 May, p. 6

ENDERS, VICTORIA LORÉE. 1999. 'Problematic Portraits: The Ambiguous Historical Role of the *Sección Femenina* of the Falange', in *Constructing Spanish Womanhood: Female Identity in Modern Spain*, ed. by Victoria Lorée Enders and Pamela Beth Radcliff (Albany: University of New York Press), pp. 375–97

ENGELS, FRIEDRICH. 1968A. 'The Origin of the Family, Private Property and the State' (1884), in *Karl Marx and Frederick Engels: Selected Works in One Volume* (London: Lawrence and Wishart), pp. 461–583

—— 1968B. 'Engels to Franz Mehring' (1893), in *Marx and Engels Correspondence*, trans. by Donna Torr (New York: International Publishers)

—— 1971A. 'Principles of Communism' (1847), in *Birth of the Communist Manifesto*, ed. by Dirk J. Struik (New York: International Publishers), pp.169–89

—— 1971B. 'Draft of the Communist Confession of Faith' (1847), in *Birth of the Communist Manifesto*, ed. by Dirk J. Struik (New York: International Publishers), pp.163–69

ESTEBAN, JORGE DE., and LUIS LÓPEZ GUERRA. 1982. *Los partidos políticos en la España actual* (Barcelona: Planeta)

FAGOAGA, CONCHA. 1985. *La voz y el voto de las mujeres: El sufragio en España 1877–1931* (Barcelona: Icaria)

FALCÓN, LÍDIA. 1981. *La razón feminista: La mujer como clase social y económica. El modo de producción doméstico* (Barcelona: Fontanella)

FEINBERG, LEONARD. 2008. *Introduction to Satire* (Santa Fe, NM: Pilgrims Process, Inc)

FELMAN, SHOSHANA, and DORI LAUB (eds). 1992. *Testimony: Crises of Witnessing in Literature, Psychoanalysis, and History* (New York: Routledge)

FERNÁNDEZ SEGURA, LUCÍA. 2012. 'Estudio Preliminar', in *Cuentos de la prensa santanderina*, ed. by Fernando Segura Hoyos and Lucía Fernández Segura (Santander: University of Cantabria Press), pp. 11–68

FERRÁN, OFELIA. 2005. '*Memoria de la melancolía* by María Teresa León: The Performativity and Disidentification of Exilic Memories', *Journal of Spanish Cultural Studies*, 6(1): 59–78

FERRÁN, OFELIA. and KATHLEEN GLENN. (eds). 2002. *Women's Narrative and Film in Twentieth-Century Spain: A World of Difference(s)* (New York: Routledge)

FERRÉ, ROSA. (ed.) 2011. *Red Cavalry: Creation and Power in Soviet Russia between 1917 and 1945* (Madrid: La Casa Encendida)

'Figuras y figurones de las nuevas cortes'. 1936. *El Heraldo de Madrid*, 24 March, p. 16

FLESLER, DANIELA, and ADRIÁN PÉREZ MELGOSA. 2020. *The Memory Work of Jewish Spain* (Bloomington: Indiana University Press)

FOX-LOCKERT, LUCIA. 1979. *Women Novelists in Spain and Spanish America* (Metuchen, NJ: Scarecrow Press)

FRANCO RUBIO, GLORIA ANGELES. 1982. 'La contribución de la mujer española a la política española contemporánea: De la Restauración a la guerra civil (1876–1939)', in *Mujer y Sociedad en España 1700–1975*, ed. by Rosa María Capel Martínez (Madrid: Ministerio de Cultura), pp. 241–66

FRANKOVÁ, MILADA. 2013. 'Dystopian Transformations: Post-Cold War Dystopian Writing by Women', *Brno Studies in English*, 39(1): 211–26

FRASER, RONALD. 1979. *Blood of Spain: The Experience of the Civil War, 1936–1939* (London: Allen Lane)

FUCILLA, JOSEPH C. 1932. '*El banquete de Saturno* by Matilde de la Torre', *Books Abroad*, 6(2): 210

FUENTES, VÍCTOR. 1980. *La marcha al pueblo en las letras, 1917–1936* (Madrid: Ediciones de la Torre)

FUENTES PERIS, TERESA. 2003. *Visions of Filth: Deviancy and Social Control in the Novels of Galdós* (Liverpool: Liverpool University Press)

GAJIC, TATJANA. 2000. 'Reason, Practice and the Promise of a New Spain: Ortega's 'Vieja y nueva política' and *Meditaciones del "Quijote"* ', *Bulletin of Hispanic Studies*, 77(3): 193–215

GALERSTEIN, CAROLYN (ed.). 1986. *Women Writers of Spain: An Annotated Bio-Bibliographical Guide* (New York: Greenwood Press)

GALVARRIATO, J.V. 1929. ' "Don Quijote, Rey de España" ', *Nuevo Mundo*, 5 April, p. 3

GARCÍA, HUGO. 2015. 'La República de las pequeñas diferencias. Cultura(s) de izquierda y antifascimo(s) en España, 1931–1939', in *Del franquismo a la democracia: 1936–2013*, coord. by Manuel Pérez Ledesma and Ismael Saz, pp. 207–37

GARCÍA COLMENARES, CARMEN. 2010. 'Psicólogas republicanas en el exilio: Las excusas maltrechas de la memoria', in *El exilio científico republicano*, ed. by Josep L. Barona (Valencia: University of Valencia), pp. 53–65

GARCÍA MÉNDEZ, ESPERANZA. 1979. *La actuación de la mujer en las Cortes de la II República*, 2nd edn (Madrid: Ministerio de Cultura

GARCÍA SANTOS, JUAN FELIPE. 1980. *Léxico y política de la Segunda República* (Salamanca: Ediciones Universidad de Salamanca)

GIJÓN, VICTOR. 1984. 'La vida de Matilde de la Torre, evocada en el centenario del nacimiento de la escritora', *El País*, 3 April, unnumbered

GIMENO DE FLAQUER, CONCEPCIÓN. 1900. *Evangelios de la mujer*, 2nd edn (Madrid: Fernando Fe)

GLEN, KATHLEEN M. and KATHLEEN McNERNEY (eds). 2008. *Visions and Revisions: Women's Narrative in Twentieth-Century Spain* (Amsterdam: Rodopi)

GOLDSMITH, ELIZABETH C. 1989. 'Introduction', in *Writing the Female Voice: Essays on Epistolary Literature*, ed. by Elizabeth C. Goldsmith (Boston: Northeastern University Press)

GÓMEZ, MAYTE. 2002. 'Bringing Home the Truth about the Revolution: Spanish Travellers to the Soviet Union in the 1930s', in *Cultural Encounters: European Travel Writing in the 1930s*, ed. by Charles Burdett and Derek Duncan (New York: Berghahn Books), pp. 65–83

GONZÁLEZ, MARÍA JESÚS. 2002. '"Neither God nor Monster": Antonio Maura and the Failure of Conservative Reformism in Restoration Spain (1893–1923)', *European History Quarterly*, 32(3): 307–34

GONZÁLEZ HOYOS, JAVIER. 2014. 'La evolución del juego simbólico del Bolo Palma a través de los cambios sociales, demográficos y reglamentarios desde el siglo XIX a la actualidad' (Unpublished Bachelors Dissertation: University of León)

GRAHAM, JOHN T. 1994. *A Pragmatist Philosophy of Life in Ortega y Gasset* (Columbia: University of Missouri Press)

GRAHAM, HELEN. 1996. 'Women and Social Change', in *Spanish Cultural Studies: An Introduction. The Struggle for Modernity*, ed. by Helen Graham and Jo Labanyi (Oxford: Oxford University Press), pp. 99–115

—— 2005. *The Spanish Civil War: A Very Short Introduction* (Oxford: Oxford University Press)

GRAHAM, JOHN T. 2001. *The Social Thought of Ortega y Gasset: A Systematic Synthesis in Postmodernism and Interdiscplinarity* (Columbia: University of Missouri Press)

GRAUPERA, ÁNGELA. 1918A. 'Desde Grecia: Los dramas del espionaje', *Las Noticias*, 2 June, p. 3

—— 1918B'. 'Desde Grecia: Atropellos en Turquía — prisoneros bulgaros — los santos lugares', *Las Noticias*, 21 January, p. 3

—— 1935. *El gran crimen: Lo que he visto yo en la guerra* (Barcelona: Publicaciones de La Revista Blanca)

GRIFFIN, DUSTIN. 1994. *Satire: A Critical Reintroduction* (Lexington, KY: University Press of Kentucky)

GUALLART, ARTURO. 2011. *Carmen de Burgos, la Colombine: Libre y luchadora* (Málaga: C&T)

GUETTEL, CHARNIE. 1974. *Marxism and Feminism* (Toronto: Canadian Women's Educational Press)

GUTIÉRREZ BRINGAS, MIGUEL ÁNGEL. 1989. 'La prensa diaria de Santander en octubre de 1934: aproximación a un estudio metodológico', *Altamira: Revista del Centro de Estudios Montañeses*, 48: 319–39

GUNTHER, RICHARD, JOSÉ RAMÓN MONTERO and JOAN BOTELLA. 2004. *Democracy in Modern Spain* (New Haven: Yale University Press)

'Habla Matilde de la Torre'. 1936. *La Voz*, 7 August, p. 2

HALBWACHS, MAURICE. 1992. *On Collective Memory*, ed. and trans. by Lewis A. Coser (Chicago: Chicago University Press)

HARO HONRUBIA, ALEJANDRO DE. 2018. 'La teoría del amor en el pensamiento de Ortega a la altura de 1914: Clave ético-filosóficas y antropológicas de *Meditaciones del Quijote*', 35(1): 175–204

HART, STEPHEN. 1993. *White Ink: Essays on Twentieth Century Feminine Fiction in Spain and Latin America* (London: Tamesis)

HARTMANN, HEIDI. 1981. 'The Unhappy Marriage of Marxism and Feminism: Towards a More Progressive Union', in *Women and Revolution: A Discussion of the Unhappy Marriage of Marxism and Feminism*, ed. by Lydia Sargent (Quebec: Black Rose Books), pp. 1–42

HAUG, FRIGGA. 2015A. 'The Marx within Feminism', in *Marxism and Feminism*, ed. by Shahrzad Mojab (London: Zed Books), pp. 76–101

—— 2015B. 'Gender Relations', in *Marxism and Feminism*, edited by Shahrzad Mojab (London: Zed Books), pp. 33–75

HEIKINEN, DENISE. 1994. 'Is Bakhtin a Feminist of Just Another Dead White Male?', in *Dialogue of Voices: Feminist Literary Theory and Bakhtin*, ed. by Karen Hohne and Helen Wussow (Minneapolis: University of Minnesota Press), pp. 114–27

HERNÁNDEZ ALFONSO, LUIS. 1931. 'Comentarios. "El ágora"', *La Libertad*, 10 March, p. 1

HERNDL, DIANE PRICE. 1991. 'The Dilemmas of a Feminist Dialogic', in *Feminism, Bakhtin, and the Dialogic*, ed. by Dale M. Bauer and Susan Jaret McKinstry (Albany: State University of New York Press), pp. 7–24

HERRMANN, ANNE. 1989. *The Dialogic and Difference: "An/other Woman" in Virginia Woolf and Christa Wolf* (New York: Columbia University Press)

HERRMANN, GINA. 2003. 'Voices of the Vanquished: Leftist Women and the Spanish Civil War', *Journal of Spanish Cultural Studies*, 4(1): 11–29

—— 2005. 'Teresa Pámies and the Spanish Communist Memoir: Between Devotion and Disillusion', *Revista Canadiense de Estudios Hispánicos*, 30(1): 89–108

HIBBS-LISSORGUES, SOLANGE. 2008. 'Escritoras españolas entre el deber y el deseo: Faustina Sáez de Melgar (1834–1895), Pilar Sinués de Marco (1835–1893) y Antonia Rodríguez de Utrera', in *La mujer de letras o la letra herida: Textos y representaciones sobre la mujer escritora en el siglo XIX*, ed. by Pura Fernández and Marie-Linda Ortega (Madrid: Consejo Superior de Investigaciones Científicas), pp. 325–43

HILLEGAS, MARK. 1967. *The Future as Nightmare: H. G. Wells and the Anti-Utopians* (Carbondale: Southern Illinois University Press)

HIRSCH, MARIANNE. 1996. 'Past Lives: Postmemories in Exile', *Poetics Today*, 17: 659–86

HIRSCHKOP, KEN. 1992. 'Is Dialogism for Real?', *Social Text*, 30: 102–13

HOHNE, KAREN, and HELEN WUSSOW. (eds). 1994. *Dialogue of Voices: Feminist Literary Theory and Bakhtin* (Minneapolis: University of Minnesota Press)

HOZ REGULES, JERÓNIMO DE LA. 2012. 'La eclosión de las vanguardias en una capital de provincia: Política y cultura en el Ateneo de Santander de los años veinte. Entre la tradición y la modernidad', *Espacio, Tiempo y Forma*, 25: 223–44

HUNT, NIGEL. 2010. *Memory, War and Trauma* (Cambridge: Cambridge University Press)

IBÁRRURI, DOLORES. 1979. *El único camino* (Barcelona: Bruguera)

'Importante acto antifascista en Orihuela'. 1937. *La Libertad*, 31 March, p. 2

'Información general de España'. 1931. *Voz española*, 12 September, pp. 3, 5–9, 12

'Información política'. 1934. *El Sol*, 9 August, p. 2

JACKSON, GABRIEL. 2010. *Juan Negrín: Physiologist, Socialist and Spanish Republican War Leader* (Eastbourne: Sussex Academic Press)

JOHNSON, ROBERTA, 1993. *Crossfire: Philosophy and the Novel in Spain, 1900–1934* (Lexington: University of Kentucky Press)

—— 2002. 'Women Novelists of the Vanguard Era (1923–1952)', in *Women's Narrative and Film in Twentieth-Century Spain: A World of Difference(s)*, ed. by Ofelia Ferrán and Kathleen M. Glenn (New York: Routledge), pp. 40–55

—— 2003. *Gender and Nation in the Spanish Modernist Novel* (Tennessee: Vanderbilt University Press)

—— 2019. *Major Concepts in Spanish Feminist Theory* (Albany: State University of New York)

JOHNSON, ROBERTA and OLGA CASTRO. 2018. 'Historical Background in Spain', in *A New History of Iberian Feminisms*, ed. by Silvia Bermúdez and Roberta Johnson (Toronto: University of Toronto Press), pp. 213–20

JUANA, JOSÉ MARÍA DE. 2019. *El largo y duro camino recorrido por la mujer en España (1868–1940)... y murieron en el exilio* (Madrid: éride)

KAPLAN, TEMMA. 1977A. 'Women and Spanish Anarchism', in *Becoming Visible: Women in European History*, ed. by Renate Bridenthal and Claudia Koonz, 1st edn. (Boston: Houghton Mifflin)

—— 1977B. *Orígenes sociales del anarquismo en Andalucía: Capitalismo agrario y lucha de clases en la provincia de Cádiz, 1868–1903*, trans. by Joaquim Sempere (Barcelona Crítica)

KERN, ROBERT. 1978. *Red Years, Black Years: A Political History of Spanish Anarchism, 1911–1937* (Philadelphia: Institute for the Study of Human Issues)

KIRKPATRICK, SUSAN. 2003. *Mujer, modernismo y vanguardia en España (1898–1931)* (Madrid: Ediciones Cátedra)

KNOCHE, ULRICH. 1975. *Roman Satire*, trans. by Edwin S. Ramage (Bloomington: Indiana University Press)

KRAUEL, JAVIER. 2016. 'The Battle for Emotional Hegemony in Republican Spain (1931–1936)', in *Engaging the Emotions in Spanish Culture and History* (Nashville, TN: Vanderbilt University Press), pp. 141–58

KUMAR, KRISHAN. 1987. *Utopia and Anti-utopia in Modern Times* (Oxford: Basil Blackwell)

KOONZ, CLAUDIA. 1998. 'The "Woman Question" in Authoritarian Regimes', in *Becoming Visible: Women in European History*, ed. by Renate Bridenthal and Claudia Koonz, 3rd edn. (Boston: Houghton Mifflin)

'La *Gaceta de la República*'. 1937. *La Libertad*, 9 March, p. 4

'La inauguración de Cortes y el momento político español'. 1933. *Nuevo mundo*, 15 December, p. 9

La Libertad. 1935. 13 April, p. 3

'La mañana del jefe del gobierno'. 1936. *El Sol*, 8 August, p. 2

'La sesión del Parlamento'. 1936. *La Libertad*, 2 October, pp. 3–4

La Unión ilustrada. 1930. 20 July, p. 36

'La vida musical: El coro *Voces Cántabras* en el T.L.N.'. 1932. *El Sol*, 2 December, p. 2

LABANYI, JO. 2002. 'Resemanticizing Feminine Surrender: Cross-Gender Identifications in the Writings of Spanish Female Fascist Activists', in *Women's Narrative and Film in Twentieth-Century Spain: A World of Difference(s)*, ed. by Ofelia Ferrán and Kathleen M. Glenn (New York: Routledge), pp. 75–92

—— 2008. 'The Politics of Memory in Contemporary Spain', *Journal of Spanish Cultural Studies*, 9(2): 119–25

LACAPRA, DOMINIC. 2001. *Writing History, Writing Trauma* (Baltimore: Johns Hopkins University Press)

LAFUENTE, ISAÍAS. 2012. *Agrupémonos todas: La lucha de las españolas por la igualdad* (eBook: Aguilar)

'Las hermanas pasionarias'. 1938. *El Progreso*, 29 November, p. 4

'Las mujeres de la democracia: Matilde de la Torre'. 1931. *La Calle*, no. 24 (July), p. 11

'Las primeras cortes ordinarias de la República'. 1933. *Luz*, 9 December, p. 1

LANNON, FRANCIS. 1991. 'Women and Images of Women in the Spanish Civil War', *Transactions of the Royal Historical Society*, 1: 213–28

—— 2011. 'Gender and Change: Identity and Reform in the Second Republic', in *A Companion to Spanish Women's Studies*, ed. by Xon de Ros and Geraldine Hazbun (Woodbridge: Tamesis), pp. 273–86

LAYNA RANZ, FRANCISCO. 2019. 'Don Quijote y el error americano: Matilde de la Torre revisa la historia y la política españolas en los preliminares de la guerra civil', in *Cervantes transatlántico*, ed. by Francisco Ramírez Santacruz and Pedro Ángel Palou (New York: Peter Lang), pp. 15–32

LEGATES, MARLENE. 2001. *In Their Time: A History of Feminism in Western Society* (New York: Routledge)

LEGGOTT, SARAH. 2008A. 'The Female Intellectual in 1920s Madrid: Writing the Lyceum Club', in *Journal of the Australasian Universities Language and Literature Association*, 110: 95–112

—— 2008B. *The Workings of Memory: Life-Writing by Women in Early Twentieth-Century Spain* (Lewisburg: Buckell University Press)

LEÓN, MARÍA TERESA. 1979. *Una estrella roja* (Madrid: Espasa Calde)

'Libros'. 1931. *El Sol*, 11 September, p. 2

LLORÉNS, VICENTE, and MANUEL AZNAR SOLER. 2006. *Estudios y ensayos sobre el exilio republicano de 1939* (Seville: Renacimiento)

L'HOIR, FRANCESCA. 1990. 'Heroic Epithets and Recurrent Themes in *Ab Urbe Condita*', *Transactions of the American Philological Association (1974–)*, 120: 221–24

LINES, LISA MARGARET. 2012. *Milicianas: Women in Combat in the Spanish Civil War* (Plymouth: Lexington Books)

LINVILLE, RACHEL. 2014. 'Tomasa's Traumatic Memories in *La voz dormida*', *Hispanic Research Journal*, 15(2): 167–80

LODDER, CHRISTINA. 2011. 'The Experiments at the Vkhutemas School', in *Red Cavalry. Creation and Power in Soviet Russia between 1917 and 1945*, ed. by Rosa Ferré (Madrid: La Casa Encendida), pp. 104–23

LÓPEZ SOBRADO, ESTHER. 2012. 'Pintura Cántabra en París (1900–1936). Entre la tradición y la vanguardia' (Unpublished PhD Thesis: University of Valladolid)

LORENZO, FÉLIX. 1932A. 'Charlas al sol', *Luz*, 12 December, p. 3

LORENZO, FÉLIX. 1932B. 'Charlas al sol', *Luz*, 17 December, p. 3

'Los partidos proletarios'. 1935. *La Libertad*, 19 November, p. 6

LOUIS, ANJA. 2005. *Women and the Law: Carmen de Burgos, an Early Feminist* (Woodbridge: Tamesis)

LUQUE MUÑOZ, MARÍA ISABEL, and ROSA MARÍA SOLANO FERNÁNDEZ. 2008. 'El papel de la mujer durante la guerra civil', *Cuadernos de pedagogía*, 375: 34–37

MADARIAGA DE LA CAMPA, BENITO. 1983. *Santander y la Universidad Internacional de verano* (Santander: Ayuntamiento y Universidad Internacional 'Menéndez Pelayo')

MADDEN, DEBORAH. 2021. 'Marx's Minerva: Sex, Socialism and Soviet Russia in Matilde de la Torre's *El banquete de Saturno* (1931)', *Journal of Spanish Cultural Studies*, 22(1): 39–57

MAIER, CAROL. 1994. 'Translator's Afterword', in *Memoirs of Leticia Valle*, ed. by Carol Maier (Lincoln: University of Nebraska Press)

MANGINI, SHIRLEY. 1987. 'Women and Spanish Modernism: The Case of Rosa Chacel', *Anales de la literatura española contemporánea*, 12(1/2): 17–28

—— 1995. *Memories of Resistance: Women's Voices from the Spanish Civil War* (New Haven: Yale University Press)

—— 2001. *Las modernas de Madrid: las grandes intelectuales españolas de la vanguardia* (Barcelona: Ediciones Península)

——— 2006. 'El Lyceum Club de Madrid: un refugio feminista en una capital hostil', *Asparkía: Investigació Feminista*, 17: 125–40

——— 2009. 'El papel de la mujer intelectual según Margarita Nelken y Rosa Chacel', in *Roles de género y cambio social en la literatura española del siglo XX*, ed. Pilar Nieva-de la Paz (Amsterdam: Rodopi), pp. 171–86

MARRAST, ROBERT. 1984. *Rafael Alberti en México* (1935) (Santander: Sur)

MARTÍNEZ, JOSEBE. 2007. *Exiliadas: escritoras, guerra civil y memoria* (Madrid: Intervención Cultural)

MARTÍNEZ CEREZO, ANTONIO. 2000A. 'Estudio Preliminar', *Don Quijote, rey de España*, by Matilde de la Torre (Santander: Servicio de Publicaciones, University of Cantabria), pp. 11–48

——— 2000B. '*La ciudad nueva* de Matilde de la Torre', *Altamira: Revista del Centro de Estudios Montañeses*, 56: 37–52

MARTÍNEZ SIERRA, GREGORIO. 1930. *Eva curiosa: Libro para mujeres* (Madrid: Renacimiento)

MARTÍNEZ SIERRA, MARÍA. 1931. *La mujer española ante la República* (Madrid: Esfinge)

——— 1989. *Una mujer por caminos de España*, ed. by Alda Blanco (Madrid: Castalia, Instituto de la Mujer)

MATEOS, MARÍA ANTONIA. 2007. *¡Salud, compañeras! Mujeres socialistas en Asturias (1900–1937)* (Oviedo: Trabe)

MARX, KARL. 1957. 'Revelation of the Mystery of the Emancipation of Women, or Louise Morel' (1845), in *The Holy Family or Critique of Critical* Critique, by Karl Marx and Friedrich Engels, trans. by R. Dixon (Moscow: Foreign Languages Publishing House), pp. 258–60

——— 1970. 'A Contribution to the Critique of Hegel's "Philosophy of Right"' (1844), in *Critique of Hegel's 'Philosophy of Right'*, ed. by Joseph O'Malley, trans. by Annette Jolin and Joseph O'Malley (Cambridge: Cambridge University Press), pp. 129–42

——— 1971. *A Contribution to the Critique of Political Economy* (London: Lawrence & Wishart)

——— 1972. *The Revolutions of 1848–49* (1848), ed. by Frank Eyck (Edinburgh: Oliver and Boyd)

——— 1976. *Capital: A Critique of Political Economy* (1867), trans. by Ben Fowkes (London: New Left Review)

MARX, KARL, and FRIEDRICH ENGELS. 2009. *The Communist Manifesto* (1848), intro. by Robert Conquest, trans. by Samuel Moore (Washington, DC: Regnery Publishing)

MEIEROVICH, CLARA. 1989. 'Revaloración y tribute a veinte años de la ausencia de Virginia Rodríguez Rivera', *Anales*, 60: 170–201

MELA. 1937. 'Episodios de la epopeya española', *La Libertad*, 6 June, p. 4

MEYER, A. 1977. 'Marxism and the Women's Movement', in *Women in Russia*, ed. by Dorothy Atkinson, Alexander Dallin and Gail Warshofsky Lapidus (Stanford, CA: Stanford University Press), pp. 85–112

MILL, JOHN STUART. 1861. *Considerations on Representative Government* (London: Parker)

——— 1869. *The Subjugation of Women* (London: Longmans, Green, Reader and Dyer)

——— 1993. *On Liberty & Utilitarianism*, ed. by Alan M. Dershowitz (New York: Bantam)

MILLER, DALE E. 2000. 'John Stuart Mill's Civic Liberalism', *History of Political Thought*, 21(1): 88–113

MONTERDE GARCÍA, JUAN CARLOS. 2010. 'Algunos aspectos sobre el voto femenino en la II República Española: Debates parlamentarios', *Anuario de la Facultad de Derecho*, 28: 261–77

MONTSENY, FEDERICA. 1923. 'El movimiento femenino internacional', *La Revista Blanca*, 15 August: 3–5

——— 1924. 'Feminismo y humanismo', *La Revista Blanca*, 1 October, pp. 12–14

——— 2003. *Heroínas* (1935/36), in *Novela corta española, II: Las novelas de tesis*, ed. by Jesús Felipe Martínez (Barcelona: Debate), pp. 169–238

MORENO-NUÑO, CARMEN. 2006. *Huellas de la guerra civil: Mito y trauma en la narrativa de la España democrática* (Madrid: Libertarias)

Mundo gráfico. 1918. 13 May, p. 13

NASH, MARY. 1975. 'Dos intelectuales anarquistas frente al problema de la mujer: Federica Montseny y Lucía Sánchez Saornil', *Convivium: Revista de filosofía*, 44–45: 72–99

—— 1988. 'Género, cambio social y la problemática del aborto', *Historia Social*, 2: 19–35

—— 1995. *Defying Male Civilization: Women in the Spanish Civil War* (Denver, CO: Arden Press)

- 1998. '"Ideals of Redemption" Socialism and Women on the Left in Spain', in *Women and Socialism, Socialism and Women: Europe between the Two Wars*, ed. by Helmut Gruber and Pamela Graves (Oxford: Berghahn Books), pp. 348–80

—— 1999. 'Un/Contested Identities: Motherhood, Sex Reform and the Modernization of Gender Identity in Early Twentieth-Century Spain', in *Constructing Spanish Womanhood: Female Identity in Modern Spain*, ed. by Victoria Lorée Enders and Pamela Beth Radcliff (Albany: University of New York Press), pp. 25–49

—— 2003. 'Women's Role in the Spanish Civil War', in *Political and Historical Encyclopedia of Women*, ed. by Christine Fauré (New York: Routledge), pp. 533–48

—— 2004. 'The Rise of the Women's Movement in Nineteenth-Century Spain', in *Women's Emancipation Movements in the Nineteenth Century: A European Perspective*, ed. by Sylvia Paletschek and Bianka Pietrow-Ennker (Stanford, CA: Stanford University Press), pp. 243–62

NAVAJAS, GONZALO. 1991. 'La novela rosa en el paradigma literario: *Inmaculada* de Rafael Pérez y Pérez', *Monographic Review/Revista Monográfica*, 7: 364–81

NAVAS OCAÑA, ISABEL. 2018. 'Leyendo a Ortega como una mujer', *Studia Neophilologica*, 90(1): 126–40

NELKEN, MARGARITA. 1922. *La condición social de la mujer en España: Su estado actual* (Madrid: CVS Ediciones)

—— 1927. *En torno a nosotras* (Madrid: Editorial Páez)

—— 1930A. *Las escritoras españolas* (Barcelona: Editorial Labor)

—— (ed.). 1930b. *La novela femenina* (Barcelona: Publicaciones Mundial)

—— 1931. *La mujer ante las cortes constituyentes* (Madrid: Editorial Castro)

—— 1975. *La condición social de la mujer en España* (Madrid: CVS Ediciones)

'Ni madres, ni españolas. El más reciente chantage de la anti-España'. 1938. *El Día de Palencia*, 22 December, p. 3

'Noticias de toda España'. 1934. *El Heraldo de Madrid*, 3 September, p. 8

'Noticias teatrales'. 1932. *Luz*, 29 November, p. 7

NORA, PIERRE. 1989. 'Between Memory and History: Les Lieux de mémoire', trans. by Marc Roudebush, *Representations*, 26: 7–25

'Nuevos pesimismos de Matilde de la Torre', *El Progreso*, 7 April, p. 1

NÚÑEZ, MARÍA GLORIA. 1998. 'Políticas de igualdad entre varones y mujeres en la segunda república española', *Espacio, Tiempo y Forma*, 11: 393–445

O'BYRNE, PATRICIA. 2014. *Post-War Spanish Women Novelists and the Recuperation of Historical Memory* (Woodbridge: Tamesis)

OFER, INBAL. 2009. *Señoritas in Blue: The Making of a Female Political Elite in Franco's Spain* (Sussex Academic Press)

OFFEN, KAREN. 2000. *European Feminisms, 1700–1950: A Political History* (Stanford, CA: Stanford University Press)

OLARTE MARTÍNEZ, MATILDE MARÍA. 2010. 'Las anotaciones de campo de Kurt Schindler durante sus grabaciones en España', *Etnofolk Revista de Etnomusicología*, 16–17: 1–24

OOSTERVELD, WILLEM THEO. 2015. *The Law of Nations in Early American Foreign Policy: Theory and Practice from the Revolution to the Monroe Doctrine* (Leiden: Brill)

'Otro periodo histórico. Ayer inició sus tareas el segundo parlamento de la República y nombro presidente a don Santiago Alba'. 1933. *La Libertad*, 9 December, p. 3

ORTEGA Y GASSET, JOSÉ. 1924. 'Epílogo', in *De Francesca a Beatrice* a través de la Divina Comedia, by Victoria Ocampo (Madrid: Editorial Revista de Occidente)

ORWELL, GEORGE. 1951 [1945]. *Animal Farm: A Fairy Story* (Harmondsworth: Penguin)

PARDO BAZÁN, EMILIA. 1889. 'The Women of Spain', *The Fortnightly Review*, 65: 879–904

—— 1907. 'La Revolución y la novela en Rusia', vol. 33 of *Obras completas*. 4th ed. (Madrid: Administración Calle San Bernardo)

—— 1972. *La vida contemporánea, 1896–1915* (Madrid: Editorial Magisterio Español)

—— 1976. *La mujer española y otros artículos feministas* (1890), ed. by Leda Schiavo (Madrid: Editora Nacional)

—— 1981 [1893]. 'Concepción Arenal y sus ideas acerca de la mujer', *Nuevo Teatro Crítico*, 3(26): 269–304

PAVIS, PATRICE. 1998. *Dictionary of the Theatre: Terms, Concepts, and Analysis*, trans. by Christine Shantz (Toronto: University of Toronto Press)

PAYNE, STANLEY G. 1993. *Spain's First Democracy: The Second Republic, 1931–1936* (Madison, WI: The University of Wisconsin Press)

PAZ, PILAR DE LA. 1993. *Autoras dramáticas españolas entre 1918 y 1936: Texto y representación* (Madrid: Consejo Superior de Investigaciones Científicas)

PÉREZ, JANET. 1988. *Contemporary Women Writers of Spain* (Boston: Twayne Publishers)

PÉREZ-BUSTAMENTE MOURIER, ANA SOFÍA. 2009. 'Historia supersónica de la poesía española escrita por mujeres', in *Desde contextos espaciales y temporales dispares. Una visión interdisciplinar sobre el género y la condición femenina*, ed. by Laura Triviño Cabrera (Cádiz: Servicio de Publicaciones de la Diputación Provincial de Cádiz), pp. 4–49

PERIS SUAY, ÁNGEL. 2014. 'El socialismo en el pensamiento político de Ortega y Gasset', *Revista Internacional de Filosofía*, 19(1): 47–64

PESTAÑA, ÁNGEL. 1925. *Setenta días en Rusia: Lo que yo vi* (Barcelona: Tipografía Cosmos)

'Peticiones de indulto: Por un trabajador asturiano condenado a muerte'. 1935. *La Libertad*, 25 October, p. 4

POZZI, GABRIELA. 2000. 'Carmen de Burgos and the War in Morocco', *MLN*, 115(2): 188–204

PRAT, JOSÉ. 1994. 'Introduction', *María Lejárraga una mujer en la sombra*, ed. by Antonina Rodrigo (Barcelona: Círculo de Lectores), pp. 11–13

PRESTON, PAUL, 1986. *The Triumph of Democracy in Spain* (London: Methuen)

—— 2002. *Doves of War: Four Women of the Spanish Civil War* (London: HarperCollins)

—— 2012. *The Spanish Holocaust: Inquisition and Extermination in Twentieth-Century Spain* (New York: W. W. Norton & Co.)

'Propaganda republicana feminina en Ávila'. 1932. *Luz*, 23 May, p. 4

PURKEY, LYNN. 2013. *Spanish Reception of Russian Narratives, 1905–1939* (Rochester, NY: Tamesis)

PURVIS-SMITH, VIRGINIA. 1994. 'ideological becoming: mikhail bakhtin, feminine *écriture*, and julia kristeva', in *Dialogue of Voices: Feminist Literary Theory and Bakhtin*, ed. by Karen Hohne and Helen Wussow (Minneapolis: University of Minnesota Press), pp. 42–58

QUAGGIO, GIULIA. 2017. 'La cuestión femenina en el PSOE de la Transición: De la marginación a las cuotas', *ARENAL*, 24(1): 219–53

REDONDO GOICOECHEA, ALICIA. 2001. 'Introducción literaria: Teoría y crítica feministas', in *Feminismo y misoginia en la literatura española: Fuentes literarias para la historia de las mujeres*, ed. by Cristina Segura Graíño (Madrid: Narcea), pp. 19–46

RIAL, JAMES H. 1986. *Revolution from Above: The Primo de Rivera Dictatorship in Spain, 1923–1930* (London: Associated University Press)

RICHARDS, MICHAEL. 2013. *After the Civil War: Making Memory and Re-Making Spain Since 1936* (Cambridge: Cambridge University Press)

RICHMOND, KATHLEEN. 2003. *Women and Spanish Fascism: The Women's Section of the Falange, 1934–1959* (London: Routledge)

ROA-DE-LA-CARRERA, CRISTIÁN. 2005. *Histories of Infamy: Francisco López de Gómara and the Ethics of Spanish Imperialism*, trans. by Scott Sessions (Boulder: University Press of Colorado)

RODRIGO, ANTONINA. 1994. *María Lejárraga: Una mujer en la sombra* (Barcelona: Círculo de Lectores)

—— 2002. *Mujeres para la historia: La España silenciada del XX* (Barcelona: Carena)

RODRIGO, ANTONIA, and ARTURO DEL HOYO. 2005. *María Lejárraga: Una mujer en la sombra*, 3rd edn (Madrid: Algaba Ediciones)

ROIG. MONSERRAT. 1981. *Mujeres en busca de un nuevo humanismo* (Barcelona: Aula Abierta Salvat)

ROIG I BERENGUER, ROSA MARI. 2006. 'Las mujeres candidatas al Congreso de los Diputados en España (1979–2000)', *Cuadernos Constitucionales de la Cátedra Fadrique Furió Ceriol*, 57: 163–72

ROMERO SALVADÓ, F. J. 2012. 'Antonio Maura: From Messiah to "Firefighter"', in *Right Wing Nationalism in the Civil War Era*, ed. by A. Quiroga, and M. Ángel Arco (London: Continuum), pp. 1–22

ROSENTHAL SHUMWAY, SUZANNE. 1994. 'The Chronotope of the Asylum: *Jane Eyre*, Feminism, and Bakhtinian Theory', in *Dialogue of Voices: Feminist Literary Theory and Bakhtin*, ed. by Karen Hohne and Helen Wussow (Minneapolis: University of Minnesota Press), pp. 152–70

RUBIALES, A. 2008. *Una mujer de mujeres* (eBook: Aguilar)

RUDD, NIALL. 1986. *Themes in Roman Satire* (London: Duckworth)

SAINZ CIDONCHA, CARLOS. 1976. *Historia de la ciencia ficción en España* (Madrid: Organización Sala Editorial)

SAIZ VIADERO, JOSÉ RAMÓN. 2006. 'Mujer, guerra civil y represión franquista en cantabria', conference paper given at the *La Guerra Civil Española, 1936–1939* conference, Madrid, pp. 1–22

—— 2007 'Introducción' in *Mares en la sombra: Estampas de Asturias*, by Matilde de la Torre ([Unknown]: Ediciós do Castro), pp. 9–62

—— 2010. 'Zenobia Camprubí y las mujeres republicanas en el exilio', in *Zenobia Camprubí y la Edad de Plata de la cultura española*, ed. by Emilia Cortés Ibáñez (Andalucía: International University of Andalucía), pp. 307–28

SALSINI, LAURA A. 2010. *Addressing the Letter: Italian Women Writers' Epistolary Fiction* (Toronto: University of Toronto Press)

SAMBLANCAT MIRANDA, NEUS. 2006. 'Los derechos de la mujer moderna', *Cuadernos hispanoamericos*, 671: 7–19

SÁNCHEZ BLANCO, LAURA. 2013. 'Una historia diferente, 80 años después de que las mujeres votasen por primera vez: Mujeres conservadoras, católicas y radicales', *Aportes: Revista de Historia Contemporánea*, 28: 101–23

SÁNCHEZ MEDERO, GEMA. 2008. 'El papel de las mujeres en la política española: El caso del PSOE', *Revista Estudos Feministas*, 16(2): 433–62

SCANLON, GERALDINE. 1986. *La polemica feminista en la España contemporánea 1868–1974* (Madrid: Ediciones Akal)

SCHROEDER, SUSAN. 2010. 'The History of Chimalpahin's "Conquista" Manuscript', in *Chimalpahin's Conquest: A Nahua Historian's Rewriting of Francisco López de Gómara's 'La conquista de México'*, ed. and trans. by Susan Schroder, Anne J. Cruz, Cristián Roa-de-la-Carrera and David E. Távarez (Stanford, CA: Stanford University Press), pp. 3–16

SCOTT, CATHERINE V. 1995. *Gender and Development: Rethinking Modernization and Dependency Theory* (Boulder, CO: Lynn Riener)

SERVÉN DÍEZ, CARMEN. 2013. 'El "feminismo moderado" de Concepción Gimeno de Flaquer en su contexto histórico', *Revista de Estudios Hispánicos*, 47(3): 397–415

SICKER, MARTIN. 2002. *The Geopolitics of Security in the Americas: Hemispheric Denial from Monroe to Clinton* (Westport, CT: Praeger)

SIERRA ÁLVAREZ, JOSÉ. 2004. 'Paisaje y patrimonio mineros en Urdías, Cantabria', *Ería*, 63: 59–71

SMITH, ANGEL. 2016. 'The Rise and Fall of "Respectable" Spanish Liberalism, 1808–1923: An Explanatory Framework', *Journal of Iberian and Latin American Studies*, 22(1): 55–73

SMITH, THERESA ANN. 2016. *The Emerging Female Citizen: Gender and Enlightenment in Spain* (Berkley: University of California Press)

SMITH, W. 1881. *A Classical Dictionary of Biography, Mythology, and Geography*, 17th ed. (London: John Murray)

'Sobremesa'. 1933. *La Voz*, 16 December, p. 3

SOPER, KATE. 2000. 'Naturalized Woman and Feminized Nature', in *The Green Studies Reader: From Romanticism to Ecocriticism*, ed. by Laurence Coupe (London: Routledge), pp. 139–43

STITES, RICHARD. 1989. *Revolutionary Dreams: Utopian Vision and Experimental Life in the Russian Revolution* (New York: Oxford University Press)

STUCKI, ANDREAS. 2019. *Violence and Gender in Africa's Iberian Colonies: Feminizing the Portuguese and Spanish Empire, 1950s–1970s* (London: Palgrave Macmillan)

SUÁREZ, FEDERICO. 2002. *Intelectuales antifascistas* (Madrid: Ediciones Rialp)

'Subscripción a favor de los niños huerfanos de Asturias'. 1935. *La Libertad*, 9 April, p. 1

SUVIN, DARKO. 2016. *Metamorphoses of Science Fiction: On the Poetics and History of a Literary Genre*, ed. by Gerry Canavan (Oxford: Peter Lang)

TAILLOT, ALLISON. 2009. 'De la crónica a la alegoría: Evolución de las representaciones de la violencia de la Guerra Civil en los escritos de las intelectuales antifascistas', in *Sucesos, guerras, atentados: La escritura de la violencia y sus representaciones*, coord. by Marie-Claude Chaput and Manuelle Peloille ([Unknown]: PILAR), pp. 83–98

TAVERA, SUSANA. 2005. 'La memoria de las vencidas: Política, género y exilio en la experiencia republicana', *Ayer* 60: 197–224

TEST, GEORGE AUSTIN. 1991. *Satire: Spirit and Art* (Tampa: University of South Florida Press)

THOMAS, BRONWEN. 2012. *Fictional Dialogue: Speech and Conversation in the Modern and Postmodern Novel* (Lincoln: University of Nebraska Press)

THOMAS, PAUL. 2008. *Marxism and Scientific Socialism: From Engels to Althusser* (London: Routledge)

THOMPSON, DENNIS. 1976. *John Stuart Mill and Representative Government* (Princeton, NJ: Princeton University Press)

TOLLIVER, JOYCE. 2011. 'Politics and the Feminist Essay in Spain', in *A Companion to Spanish Women's Studies*, ed. by Xon de Ros and Geraldine Hazbun (Woodbridge: Tamesis), pp. 243–56

TORRE, GIUSEPPE. 1931. *El fascismo al desnudo* (Barcelona: Ediciones Mentora)

TORRE, MATILDE DE LA. 'El absentismo español'. 1928. *Vida económica*, 28 September, pp. 383–84

TRALLERO CORDERO, MARÍA DEL MAR. 2004. 'La huella de la amistad en los exilios de Concha Méndez' (Unpublished Masters Dissertation: University of Texas)

TRINCADO, ESTRELLA, and JOSÉ-LUIS RAMOS. 2011. 'John Stuart Mill and Twentieth-Century Spain', *Journal of the History of Economic Thought*, 33(4): 507–26

TRISTAN, FLORA. 1843. *L'union ouvrière* (Paris: Edition Populaire)

TRUEBA MIRA, VIRGINIA. 2002. 'La autobiografía femenina: La mujer como escritura (sobre felicidad blanc)', *Hesperia. Anuario de Fiología Hispánica*, 5: 175–94

TWOMEY, LESLEY. 2007. 'Four Years in Paris: Victoria Kent, a Spanish Politician in Exile', in *Women in Europe between the Wars: Politics, Culture and Society*, ed. by Angela Kershaw and Angela Kimyongür (Aldershot-Burlington: Ashgate), pp. 73–91

'Un consejo de Guerra condena a una mujer de cinco años a reclusión'. 1935. *La Época*, 24 May, p. 4

'Un emocionado saludo de Matilde de la Torre a sus camaradas de Menorca'. 1939. *Justicia Social*, 11 January, p. 1

'Una escritora montañesa: *Jardín de damas curiosas*'. 1918. *La Atalaya*, 1 March, p. 1

'Una petición de indulto: Voces de clemencia ante el presidente de la República'. 1935. *La Libertad*, 26 October, p. 6

URRUELA, MARÍA CRISTINA. 2005. 'El "ángel del hogar": María Pilar Sinués y la cuestión de la mujer', in *Literatura y feminismo en España (s. XV–XXI)*, ed. by Lisa Vollendorf (Barcelona: Icaria Editorial), pp. 155–69

VAN ROOY, CHARLES A. 1966. *Studies in Classical Satire and Related Literary Theory* (Leiden: E. J. Brill)

VALOVIRTA, ELINA. 2014. *Sexual Feelings: Reading Anglophone Caribbean Women's Writing Through Affect* (Amsterdam: Rodopi)

VÁZQUEZ RAMIL, RAQUEL. 2012. *Mujeres y educación en la España contemporánea: La institución libre de enseñanza y su estela. La residencia de señoritas de Madrid* (Madrid: Ediciones Akal)

VILCHES DE FRUTOS, MARÍA FRANCISCA. 1982. 'El compromiso en la literatura: La narrativa de los escritores de la generación del nuevo romanticismo (1926–1936)', *Anales de la Literatura Española Contemporánea*, 7: 31–58

—— (ed.). 2015. *Matilde de la Torre: Las Cortes republicanas durante la Guerra Civil (Madrid 1936, Valencia 1937 y Barcelona 1938)*

VILLALAÍN-GARCÍA, PABLO. 2012. 'El voto de la mujer, ¿Debate historiográfico y/o político? El caso de España en 1933', *Contribuciones a las ciencias políticas*, unnumbered

WINTER, ULRICH. 2006. (ed.). *Lugares de memoria de la guerra civil y el franquismo: representaciones literarias y visuales* (Madrid: Iberoamericana)

WOMACK, PETER. 2011. *Dialogue* (London: Routledge)

YAEGER, PATRICIA. 1991. 'Afterword', in *Feminism, Bakhtin, and the Dialogic*, ed. Dale M. Bauer and Susan Jaret McKinstry (Albany: State University of New York Press), pp. 239–46

ZAMBRANA MORAL, PATRICIA. 2009. 'El feminismo y el elemento femenino en el pensamiento del jurista Ángel Ossorio y Gallardo (1873–1946)', *Contribuciones a las Ciencias Sociales*, unnumbered

ZINOV'EVICH BESEDOVSKII, GRIGORII. 1931. *Memorias por un diplomático soviético* (Barcelona: Ediciones Mentora)

ZUGAZAGOITIA, JULIÁN. 1977. *Guerra y vicisitudes de los españoles* (1940) (Barcelona: Crítica)

INDEX

❖

www.ingramcontent.com/pod-product-compliance
Lightning Source LLC
Chambersburg PA
CBHW050658110426

42739CB00035B/3447